CW01666888

A Theology of Dalitism

A Theology of Dalitism

Rev. Dr. Jacob Devadason

PUNTHI PUSTAK
KOLKATA : 2021

Published by :

Sirshendu Bhattacharya
PUNTHI PUSTAK
Publisher, Bookseller & Exporter
136/4B, Bidhan Sarani,
Kolkata - 700 004
Phone : 033-2555 5573, 9831318787
E-mail : punthipustak@hotmail.com

1st Edition : 2021
copyright Reserved by the Author

ISBN : 978-93-81209-46-2

Price : 1180/-
USD : 30/-
GBP : 20/-
EURO : 35/-

Type Setting:

The Hallmark
68/1B, Sikdar Bagan Street
Kolkata - 700 004

Printed at :
Kolkata

Table of Contents

Acknowledgements

I am grateful to Rev. Dr. John Parry, former professor of World Mission, Northern College, Luther King House, Manchester, who is the supervisor of this research, without whom this thesis would not have been a reality. I am very grateful for his encouragement, support, kindness and patience while guiding through this research.

I express my deep gratitude to the former professor of Manchester Metropolitan University Prof. Margaret Beetham, Veronica Singh and Stephanie & Bill Holford for being so kind enough to read and correct the manuscripts. Their encouragement and help have been so helpful to complete this work. Words are not enough to express my gratitude for their support.

I am very grateful to Revd. Sheila Maxey former Moderator of the United Reformed Church and the Council for World Mission for helping me with the scholarship.

I am very grateful to Rev. Dr. Terry Biddington for his friendship, collegiality, scholarly support and encouragement during this research.

I would like to thank my good friend Mr. Yuin Mo for helping me with editing and formatting to make the manuscript complete and ready for submission,printingand publication.

I would also like to thank Mrs. Jenny Arnold, my former Church member (Christ Church, Croydon) for the cover design illustrated by her art work.

My deep gratitude to my wife Rev. Dr. Jasmine Devadason, who supported me and took all the care of my well-being and the family during the research, and my sons Jachin and Jonathan for their patience and forbearance.

Above all, I thank God for giving me His grace and opportunity to do this research.

Foreword

All theological enterprises are ensconced within larger cultural frameworks and contexts that help to give shape to any specific or generic attempt to speak of the divine. Despite the alleged attempts to do objective, universal forms of theological scholarship, all theological endeavours are contextual. I recall listening to my all time scholarly hero, James H. Cone, the founding patriarch of academic Black Theology, who once opined that theology was a human enterprise as it was 'human speech about God....God Doesn't do theology, we do'. Cone's dictum is timely and apt for it is a critical reminder of the human endeavour to speak of God in ways that are intelligible to us as individuals and communities within specific times and spaces in which our human consciousness is located. There is no doubting the truth that the very best of our human endeavours to do theology can and often do transcend the immediacy of the context that first gave rise to them, but it is equally true, that all theology emerges from specific contexts.

The rise in prominence of Contextual theologies has reminded us also of the ideological basis of much that can be construed as theology. Any casual observance of the role that Christianity played in the construction of the British Empire cannot but help notice the ways in which Eurocentric, Christian theology provided the buttressing for the ideological claims to subjugate and occupy lands and people's minds. In the now famous dictum of Stanley Livingstone the British Empire was founded on the triumvirate of 'Christianity, Commerce, and Civilisation.'

I offer these introductory remarks in order to place the richness of this text into a wider scholarly context. Dr. Jacob Devadasan has provided us with a deeply insightful and engaging text that provides a compelling and exhaustive analysis of the nature of Dalit identities and its concomitant cultural hinterland. As he is at pains to delineate, this work is not concern with 'Dalit Theology' in the more narrow sense of seeking to articulate a systematic approach to understanding the Christian faith from the perspective of Dalit themes and concerns. Not that the author is wishing to undermine the importance of such work. Rather, Dr. Devadason's fine work is concerned with providing a theological underscoring for the whole nature and contextual understanding for what it means to be a Dalit in and of itself. His theology of Dalitness provides a theological interpretation of the broader contours that permeate the very existential realities that ground the being and nature of what it is to be a Dalit and the ways in which God is revealed within this milieu.

This is a ground breaking piece of work that challenges not only the theological production of Indian Christian theology and the mission of the church in that locale, it also provides a compelling case for how predominantly White scholars in the west contextualise or not, as the case may be, their theologies. In so much of the theological work that is produced in the west, I see precious little scholarship that foregrounds questions of power, agency and subjectivity. Many White male theologians write as if their embodied realities and the concomitant privileges that emerge from their embodiment are of no significance to the words they write on page and screen. And yet, as Dr. Devadason has demonstrated in this compelling text, the visceral nature in which power, privilege and visibility, or the lack thereof, shapes the whole world view of millions of people. The lack of agency for most if not all Dalits, within church and the wider society is testament to the fact that what happens in front of the page has a bearing on what transpires within it. The dearth of Dalit or Black people within University theology and religious studies departments in Britain (and as a corollary, the surfeit of White privileged men resplendent in their posts) is testament to the fact that an honest appreciation of the methodology and the theological outcomes of contextualisation is a prerequisite for any notion of justice and equity in the world.

In this excellent text, my friend, Dr. Devadason has crafted a passionate and engaged scholarly piece of work that asks critical questions for all forms of theological inquiry. Namely, to what extent is our theological construction mindful of the wider hinterland of experience and context that influences how we talk about God? Or are we operating in forms of self-delusional obfuscation as we seek to repeat the mantra of 'rhubarb, rhubarb, rhubarb' with our hands over our fears, seeking to drown out the messiness and rawness of the contexts in which we are emerged, while it attempts to penetrate our carefully, crafted systems of abstract, analytical thought?

Towards A Theology of Dalitness is an essential text that will help us all in our attempts to write truthful and engaged theology that speaks to the realities of the places and the spaces in which the divine has placed us.

Dr. Anthony G. Reddie

Editor: 'Black Theology : An International Journal' & Author of SCM Core Text: Black Theology

FOREWORD

Towards a Theology of Dalitism

'Dalitism' is broadly known as an 'Ideology of inclusivism' emerged to counter 'Brahmanism' and its offshoots 'Casteism and Untouchability' to ensure dignity, equality, freedom, justice and peace, not only for 260 million Dalits world-wide but also to free all non-Dalits who are mentally oppressed to perpetuate casteism and caste-based violence. 'Dalit Theology' that emerged in 1980s as 'Liberational and Contextual Theology' was critical of the Brahmanical 'thought forms' of Indian Christian Theology propounded by Non-Dalit Theologians, but anchored its base on the caste-inflicted pathetic life experience of Dalits who are socially stigmatized, economically exploited, culturally sidelined and politically powerless. Dalit Theologians argued that the liberational insights of Dalit Theology have enormous potential to motivate Dalits to involve in struggles to challenge caste practices and get freed from caste-oppression to lead a life with dignity.

Having realized the increasingstagnated status of Dalit Theologyand itshelplessness to broad base its progressive insights for the emancipation of Dalits, Rev Dr. Jacob Devadason - my longtime friend and a fellow-campaigner for Dalit Rights, who himself had undergone umpteen number of caste based discriminations and violence at various stages of his life- undertookthis timely and significant research on the 'Method and Scope of Dalit Theology'which ponders the liberation and empowerment of Dalits. His Thesis, 'Towards a Theology of Dalitism', a new visionary search,extensively deals with (i) the conceptsand insights of 'Transformative Ideologies' that aimtoinspire the bonded and also (ii) the lacuna that existsamong such ideologies in bringing desired results. Equally, his thesis elaborately agues (i) the origin, development, viability and capabilityof Dalit Theology, but very essentially (ii) the methodological gap thatdeters doing theology among Dalits.

This research helped Dr. Devadason to envisiona new 'methodological framework'and he suggests 'Theology of Dalitism' as an alternate to the present 'Dalit Theology'. In concrete terms, he suggests for linking both 'Ideology and Theology'together and frames 'Ideology of Life and Theology of Resistance'. This new concept, according to him, would help in a couple of ways- (i) to understand and analyze the current life experience of Dalits in one hand and on the other (ii) to resist the oppressive forces with a Christian Theological insight – the Nazareth vision and the prophetic tradition.In addition, he envisages that this concept would help all marginalized communities in the world beyond Dalits for their liberation and empowerment.

This observation and finding of Dr. Devadason, I am sure, will certainly attract not only Dalit Theologians but also Dalit and other Movement leaders of the marginalized communitiesacross the globe for a closer look, deeper reflection and to engage with. As a Dalit Practical Theologian and Dalit Human Rights defender, I am delighted to enforce this 'methodological frame work' to ensure its capability to empower the inner person of Dalits to inspire them to strive for empowerment at all levels to regain the human dignity and life that was destroyed by Casteism.

I congratulate, appreciate and thank -Dr. Devadason for this contextual research- a scholarly piece!

Rev Dr. Vincent Manoharan

PhD., Dalit Theologian – Lawyer,
Convenor – National Dalit Christian Watch,
New Delhi - India

Introduction

Wherever God 'keeps company with the companionless among the poorest, the lowliest, and the lost'[1] isthe new *locus theologicus*.These words from Tagore provide the basis for the need of a contextual theology on Indian soil because it explains the contextual reality of the oppressed and socially excluded. In every local theology, the regional conditions or contexts are included. Theology in India has always attempted to relate itself to the conditions of India.But there is a change in the situation in India and this is because of people's awareness of their identity and consciousness of their place and role in their society; that is, the changed present day Indian context poses a serious challenge to theology. Unless the changed Indian context is much more seriously taken into account, theology cannot and will not serve any useful purpose. The emergence of the Dalit theology has to do with the challenge that is posed by the Indian context.

In the classical way of doing theology, the theologians in the relative calm and seclusion of the seminary or university or monastery, detached from the world of their surroundings, reflect on the texts of the past as their basic resources and produce large and scholarly forms of Systematic Theology; that is, theology, in the classical way, is understood as an academic discipline, a methodological quest, and therefore as an individual's intellectual pursuit after truth. This point is clearly brought out by Western Churches in their discussion with the Christian Conference of Asia in 1976. The position paper from the Western Churches read as follows:

> Theology is understood as an academic discipline which feels entitled, because of its declared commitments to the principles of a methodological quest for truth, to a definite place in the modern university. Its specific subject is the testimony of faith as contained in the scriptures and interpreted in the traditions of Christianity. The hoped for results of this process are twofold: firstly, the believer is to be enabled to believe with intellectual honesty. Secondly, theology is to contribute to a proclamation of faith which is understandable to modern man in as much as his self-perception and general world view are shaped by science and philosophy. As far as the Church is concerned, theology is an ongoing process of criticism of Christian practice by the standards of an intellectual honest, intelligible faith.[2]

However, theology will fulfil its task only if it is for people - for people who strive for social justice and humanity. That is, the prime mission of theology is to give human life a certain direction and purpose because the subject of doing theology is human life. Only then can theology be a living option. In the Indian context, in which Christianity finds itself as a minority religion, it is necessary that theology strives to aid all people who struggle for justice, dignity of life and humanity. Very little attempt has been made in the past to understand the world views of marginalised people. In the past, rejection of Dalit religion was accompanied by the rejection of Dalit culture, and it is so even now. This approach to Dalit religion and culture cannot continue because the changed context of India warrants a different approach and poses a challenge to the classical way of doing theology.

The classical way of doing theology speaks for itself, but what is happening now in India is that people have themselves taken up this vocation. People, having appropriated the gospel, reflect on it, and thus there is a reversal in the manner of doing theology; that is, ordinary theologically non-academic people reflect on the gospel because of the context in which they find their existence. For instance, living in an unjust, oppressive and marginalised situation, and reflecting on the gospel, an ordinary, non-academic person raises the question: what has my unjust situation to do with the fact that God is a just God? In doing so, he reflects on a quite different level and this reflection requires recognition as being theological reflection, but the fascinating question is: where are the theologians who are ready to listen to these ordinary people, and who would question their own understanding? This has been attempted in varying degrees. It is the Dalit theology which is stressing the importance of recognising ordinary people's reflection as theological reflection.

Contextual theological approaches in India already existed before the emergence of the Dalit theology but they have not been considered and recognised as being theological reflections. Only now are they recognised as theological reflections and as such these approaches are only now coming into the mainstream. The present-day India is characterised by suffering. Large numbers of Indian Dalits are caught up in oppressive political, social, economic and religious conditions. They suffer hunger, poverty, under-development, despair and hopelessness. What has Christ to say in these specific situations of suffering in India? This is the same question that ordinary Dalits in India raise as they reflect on their faith, although reflection takes place on different levels, that is, the experiences people have in their everyday life get reflected in their faith. In other words, theology in India today springs out of the actual, concrete, day-to-day life situations of the *ochlos*.

Dalit study, once relegated to squiggles in the margins and faint traces on the fringes of academia, has now emerged as one of the most productive and creative correctives to dominant ways of interpreting history, understanding economics, probing sociology, studying culture, investigating globalisation, exposing racism, unlocking accepted anthropological 'truths' and indeed reconfiguring the whole gamut of social sciences.The field of Christian theology has not lagged behind. The pioneering efforts of people like Arvind P. Nirmal, in a range of evocative and iconoclastic writings, firmly placed Dalit theology and Dalit hermeneutics not as another 'branch' in the study of theology, but as a discipline,which while developing its own methods of inquiry, massively impacted on the whole theological enterprise and the life of the Indian Church.[3]

Dalit studies are now firmly established as an indispensable aspect of all attempts to understand and analyse the complexities of Indian society. For too long, there seemed to be an almost embarrassed silence when it came to fleshing out the harsh experiences of Dalit communities in independent India. One could speak of a resurgence of Dalit pride, and the increasing recognition of the vital role played by Dalit communities in the political landscape of India which have resulted in the flourishing of studies dealing with the variety and range of the Dalit experience.To the growing literature interrogating various aspects of the Dalit experience and the Dalit realities in India must be added more books.

A major book edited by S.M. Michael[4] contains a number of very important essays and articles investigating various issues in depth. Thus, we have articles looking back at how Indian society, in coming to terms with stratification, worked out a theory of untouchability. John C. Webster carefully responds to the question regarding 'Who is a Dalit' in a nuanced essay, which reflects his years of research and writing on this topic. Historical realities are fleshed out in essays dealing with the interaction and critique of Brahmin power (Mahesh Gavaskar Phule) and an analysis of Ambedkar's understanding of religion and the role played by Buddhism in the Dalit movement (Timothy Fitzgerald). The expectations of the Dalitsand their legitimate demands are specified in an essay regarding how society can be re-ordered in India, in terms of a Dalit vision (S. M. Michael), and the contribution and interrogation of mainstream sociology by the Dalit movement (Gopal Guru). The importance of a revamp of present sociological discourse in India is also indicated (S.Selvan).

There are fascinating and stimulating studies in delineating the realities of marginalised communities in various contexts – the *Adivasi's* in South Gujarat and the attempts at Hinduisation (Arjun Patel); Mahar Women in Ahmednagar District (Traude Pillai-Vetschera); A Comparative Study of Black American and Dalit Liberation (K.P. Singh); An Examination of the Phenomenon of Demon Possession in Catholic Communities (Robert Deliege). The collection also includes major articles on various aspects of Dalit realities within the framework of the Indian economic realities, including an analysis by Ambedkar of economic policy and its impact on the Dalit (Gail Omvedt); how the new economic policy forces the Dalits to bear the brunt of liberalisation (B.L.Mungekar); an analysis of the development paradigm in relation to Dalit employment (S.P.Punalekar); and how employment functions as a vehicle of social mobility (Richard Pais).

The reason for giving this overview of the contents of Michael's book is to show the broad array of the issues under consideration. This also serves to specify the magnitude of the task of addressing and problematising centuries of deliberate injustice and sanctioned marginalisation of the Dalit communities in India. *Dalits in Modern India: Vision and Value*indicates that despite all that the Dalit communities have had to experience, and in spite of the travails they had to undergo, and notwithstanding the tragedies that have become part of their lived reality, nevertheless there remains an optimism that change is possible and that far from allowing the oppressive forces to silence Dalit aspirations and hopes.

This collection raises several issues that demand urgent

attention and response. In the introduction, Michael has done a commendable job of highlighting the background on which the essays are built and also offers a historical overview of the ideology of the terminology. Terminology is constantly in a process of being interrogated and refined and one must continue to be aware of this. Interrogating terminology prevents words and concepts, as well as real people with real emotions, from being frozen in time and space, and constantly alerts us to the power of the politics of representation.

One must also take into consideration the fact that the so-called foundational texts and their interpretation have a power and reach far beyond that envisaged or even anticipated. One must recognise this and be prepared to perceive how meanings have been generated and values reinforced. This of course raises the question of the role of Sanskrit and the Sanskrit texts as being primary agents in reinforcing the ideology of Dalit enslavement.The texts are there to be read and re-read. It is when one understands the processes that created a context where enslavement was legitimised that the movement towards liberation is possible.

The emergence of Ambedkar as an icon of Dalit suffering and hope has led to a rise in interest in his immense and wide-ranging contribution not only to the Dalit cause, but also to his role in the emergence of the Indian nation state. The immensity and the magnitude of his achievements still have much to offer the committed researcher. Aspects of such contributions, which are indicated in various places in the essays, offer extremely valuable analysis and also point to directions in which Ambedkarian studies could profitably go by Gail Omvedt who speculates that Ambedkar would have welcomed aspects of globalisation if it would help in the process of Dalit emancipation and would promote the process of moving towards equality. Such ways of thinking cannot be simply dismissed, but need to be investigated, using Ambedkarian categories of understanding the mechanism of state intervention in promoting social and economic justice. The second book edited by H. Kotani[5], Professor of History at the Tokyo Metropolitan University, is an outstanding example of cross-cultural historical investigation, where those coming from a particular location and from a specific situation, in this case specialists in South Asian Studies at various universities in Japan, offer an invigorating and fertile analysis of historical and contextual studies of Dalit life.

A brief indication of the assortment of essays collected and the topics covered are given here: in the section on 'Untouchability in History', there are essays on tracing the reality of social discrimination from ancient India to the medieval period, indicating how the ruling classes benefited from the transfer of discriminatory discourse to actual social practice (Gen'ichi Tamazaki); an analysis of references to the untouchables in Tamil inscriptions and historical resources in Tamilnadu exploring neglected yet indispensable sources (Noboru Karashima); a comprehensive survey of the social and economic decline of the Chamar community in Rajasthan from the middle of the seventeenth to the beginning of the nineteenth centuries (Masanori Sato).

A survey of the *Ati Sudra* (Scheduled Castes) castes in the Medieval Deccan, clearly pointing out the deep ambivalence that lay at the heart of their interaction with other castes and amongst themselves (Hiroyuki Kotani). Kotani also offers a fine overview of the legal status of the depressed castes under British colonial rule to start the next section, which deals with the theme of the position and positioning of the depressed castes during the colonial period. The nomenclature is faithful to the period represented and the period is enfleshed through the description of the economic change in South Indian villages and its impact on the untouchables in a context when there was great water scarcity (Tsukasa Mizushima); in addition there is the description of conflict and controversy among the Mahars in Bombay Presidency over hereditary patrimony (Hiroyuki Kotani).

The concluding section on the liberation movements has five essays; an introductory overview and analysis of movements among the depressed castes seeking liberation (Masao Naito); a case study, rich in statistical data, of the *Taya* community in British Malabar, showing the connections and inter-connections with other social and ideological movements of that time (Toshie Awaya); the rhetoric of anti-untouchability and the anti-untouchability movements in the Maharashtra of the late nineteenth century and early twentieth century, including studies of a wide spectrum of influential leaders (Masao Naito); an essay demonstrating the significant contribution of Jogendranath Mandal, within the framework of the movement toward Partition (Masayuki Usuda); and a final essay on how elections at the Gram *Panchayat* (rural village)level in Bengal in 1993 led to debates on the politics of naming and the policies of social and economic benefits (Masahiko Togawa). Sathianthan Clarke[6] did his research on Dalit Religion and Dalit Culture. Jesuratnam's[7]sresearch explores Dalit Hermeneutics in relation to reading the Old Testament, particularly the Psalms.Katti Padma Rao[8] did scholarly research on 'Caste and Alternative Culture'.

These essays offer us a large mass of data which we need to enter into and interact with in the wider discourse on Dalit realities and Dalit liberation in India today. While it is easy to speak in generalities and engage in over-simplifications, the importance of this book lies in the display of thorough and detailed analysis which forms the seed-bed on which scholarship on Dalit issues can continue to grow.What strikes one is the scrupulous attention to detail that characterises each contribution. This is evident in the scope of information provided and the richness of the literature quoted and used. Ongoing scholarship on the caste system and its discontents is well served by the contributions. There is no over-simplistic problematising of caste realities that are then addressed with prescriptive formulae. This book succeeds indemonstrating how pioneering and dedicated academic work can serve as an instrument ofDalit liberation.

The study of Dalit theology was first introduced to the curriculum of Tamilnadu theological seminaries as an optional subject. Later, in the 1990s when the Senate of Serampore curriculum and syllabus were revised, it was made a basic course, with the idea that one of the subaltern groups whose perspectives should influence our study of theology could be Dalits. Work has been done on Dalit and Dalit Christian theology by Saral K. Chatterjee, M.E. Prabhakar, B.C. Moses, B.N. Banerjee, Antony Raj, Jose Kannaaikal, Abraham Ayrookuzhiel, Arvind P. Nirmal, V.Devasahayam and others. Within theological circles Franklyn J. Balasundaram,[9]Professor of History of Christianity at the United Theological College, Bangalore,has written several research articles and book reviews and also produced a well-documented historical research on 'Dalits and Christian Mission in the Tamil Country';former Bishop of Madras Diocese, the late M. Azariah, has written several research articles andpublishedmany books on Dalits and Dalit Christians in India. His book 'Mission in Christ's Way in India Today' exposed the 'unchristian side' of the Indian Church and portrayed Dalits as 'wounded psyche'.

At the doctoral level, too, this orientation has been seen: Fr. Jerry wrote on E.V.R. Pericarp, Fr. Antony Raj, on Dalit Christians,[10] Fr. Arokiadoss on Dr. Ambedkar and Fr. Joseph Chittiparampil on 'Caste and Culture, its Discontents and Politics of Culture'. Fr Maria Arulraja's research on 'Jesus: A Dalit' is a well-researched hermeneutical study from a sociological perspective on the Gospels. Anthony Raj Thumma did his research on Dalit Liberation theology from an Ambedkarian Perspective. A Spaniard, Mrs. Mary Celia, wrote her doctoral dissertation on a comparative study of Dalit theology and Basque theology. Research papers and dissertations on the Masters and Bachelor theology level are numerous. All this leads to a methodological point that the Dalit theology, which at one stage was accused of being a narrow theological '*ism*', of relevance only to those who had the 'pathos' experience, or were in empathetic or sympathetic agreement with it, draws its strength from the rich and complex inter-connections with the methodological possibilities thrown up by epistemological inquiry in the spectrum of fields of knowledge. In other words, the strength of Dalit theology lies precisely in the possibility of its inter-disciplinary alliance, something that needs to be acknowledged and fostered.

Dalit theology is an indigenous theology since it emerges out of the Indian context and out of the self-generated and self-directed Dalit consciousness. The rising consciousness and the yearning for release from an inhuman captivity is the cause for the genesis of Dalit theology.It is built on the historical heritage and living experiences of the Dalits. Their staunch faith in God as the liberator and their community consciousness geared the Dalits to make Dalit theology possible. It is also the theological expression of the Dalits in their struggle for social change in order to have a meaningful life in society. It aims to provide useful strategies to achieve their goals ofliberty, equality and fraternity.Dalit theology is an alternative form of theological endeavour. It has radically broken with the dominant theological tradition that is Indian Christian theology, which has failed to take account of the sufferings and hopes of the Dalits. It arose as a counter-theology when the philosophical-theological approach of Indian Christian theology became futile and ineffectual to fulfil the aspirations of the Dalits.

Dalit theology is a counter-theology. It is a critique based on the authentic Biblical opposition to the principles and practices of casteism and the institution of untouchability which are rooted in the religious traditions of Hinduism and defended under the shadows of Hindu doctrines.It questions as well as criticises the Hindu doctrines such as purity and pollution theories which ultimately alienate and reduce the Dalit masses to the bottom of the social pyramid.

Dalit theology is also theocentric because it expresses the saving action and liberating presence of God. It takes God as well as Jesus Christ as the launching pad in its theological process. It projects God's encounter with the oppressed and interprets Him as the one who acts against social ostracisation, economic exploitation and cultural subjugation. It reveals the liberating power of God in Jesus Christ who responds to the cry of the poor, the oppressed, the dehumanised and the alienated.

Dalit theology is biased in favour of the Dalits because it insists, and makes an urgent claim, that they ought to be treated properly since they are created in the image of God, like all other beings. Dalit theology is a unique theology since it deals with a particular people; this is the theology of the Dalits, by the Dalits and for the Dalits. In other words, the Dalits are the victims and at the same time they are the authors and originators of the Dalit theology. Moreover, it is articulated with the language and expression of the Dalits. It uses predominantly the stories, songs, proverbs and folk-lore of the Dalit people and interprets their history and culture with an aim to create a faith to live by and act for their release. Dalit theology is the result of a particular way of doing theology, because it puts into practice the theological objectives to challenge and eradicate the cruel injustices, harsh treatments and prolonged oppression faced by the Dalit masses. It is also conscientising the Dalits in the context of their sufferings and struggles to build a new social order. It further creates awareness among them that their position in life is not simply to undergo sufferings as their destiny but to take responsibility and to involve themselves in social change in order to transform their miserable, degraded and lowly existence.

Dalit theology can also be called liberative theology. It can even be regarded as Indian Liberation Theology because it is neither an academic discipline nor an intellectual activity with little or no direct contact with the realities. On the contrary, it activates the suffering masses to pursue and to accomplish their liberation. In other words, it provides a platform for vigorous action to attain their liberation. Dalit theology is both inclusive and exclusive. Although it is in favour of a specific community, it includes other religious traditions and movements which are engaged in the struggles for justice. In other words, it widens its concerns to take account of the experiences of the other oppressed and marginalised groups and envisages the oneness of all suffering humanity without the boundaries of religion, language and culture so that all the oppressed can unitedly participate in their liberation.

The primary goal of Dalit theology is not only socio-economic reformation but also to regain dignity, equality, liberty, fraternity and justice for the Dalits within the Indian Church, as well as in Indian society. In other words, it desires to root out the 'non-humanness' and the state of being 'no-people', for the Dalits are created in the same image of God and have the same spiritual dignity as all God's children in all God's *Oikoumane*.

Dalit Theology grew to its present form through a process of doing theology from a Dalit perspective, but by the end of the 20th century this process came to a standstill. By that time the majority of the early Dalit thinkers, activists and supporting institutions either were weakenedor, for a variety of reasons, had abandoned the process.One reason behind this situation was the absence of clear-cutdirection and guidelines. The process of doing Dalit Theology had not discovered for itself any clear-cut methodology. It is true that the priority for the first-generation Dalit theologians was to achieve the goal;namely, to realise full humanity. But even to reach that goal, they needed systematic thinking and organising of the many means. Here lies the issue of Reconsidering the scope and methodology of Dalit Theology, which is supposed to enable the process of liberation for the Dalits. As we entered the 21st century, more and more Dalit theologians (Dalits and non-Dalits) have become aware of this gap or weakness of the process of doing Dalit Theology.

Doing Dalit theology from a Dalit perspective has slowed down and it is stagnating. It may be so, because either we do not have enough theologians who are willing to enter into the process of doing theology from a Dalit perspective or Dalit Theology is unable to build the bases or the common ground to articulate Dalit Theology creatively. The motivation for this study is the search for a common ground or base for theology from the Dalit perspective; it is an exercise related to the methodology of doing Dalit Theology and to widening the scope of doing Dalit Theology.

This book, content-wise as well as geographically, has necessarily four limitations. First of all, it does not intend to cover all the Dalit theological approaches which have emerged in India. There are other contextual Dalit theological approaches such as Anthony Raj Thumma's 'Dalit Liberation Theology from Ambedkarian perspective',[11] Jerry's 'Dalit Liberation from E.V.R. Periyar's perspective', and 'Dalit Liberation from Gandhian perspective'[12] and so on. There are regional Dalit theological approaches from various parts of India as well. This study limits itself only to the Dalit theological perspectives that fall within the scope generally accepted by Indian Dalit theologians.

Secondly, this book does not intend to cover one particular part or region of India, one particular Church or one particular theology.Rather it refers generally to India as a whole nation, the Indian Church as an institution, and Indian theology as a theology which has emerged within the wider contextual reality of India.

Thirdly, it does not intend to cover the broad subject of the origin and development of castes in India and also the functional approach of castes, sub-castes and their inner divisions.

Fourthly, it does not intend to reconstruct an alternative to

Dalit Theology but to reconsider its scope and method so that it may become an endeavour for establishing a coherent and dynamic theological enterprise.

This study aims to provide a profile of Dalit Theology by looking at its history, development, thought, and some of the theologians that shape it. It begins with an analysis of Indian reality and its existing context in general, and Dalits' reality in particular. This is to show the complexities involved in the enterprise of theologising and doing theology in India. Dalits' contextual and confessional realities are the starting point.A special attempt is made to study the Indian oppressive social structures and marginalisation. This is followed by examining the theological strands of Indian Christian theology and Indian liberation theology.

This study has four major components in its scope: 1. Modern theological thought and its influence upon Dalit theology.2.Ideological identity and the impetus provided by international liberation movements for Dalit liberation.3. Dalit Theology's contents, scope, method and relevance, discussed critically in the light of present day Dalit realities. 4. A proposal is made to reconsider Dalit Theology's scope and method towards a relevant theology of Dalit liberation, which is suggested for future direction as an alternative or complement to the current Dalit theological debate.Former President of India V.V. Giri said in his address to the Indian National Council of Historical Research during its founding:

> A proper historical perspective is necessary to understand the real significance of the many political, social and economic changes that are taking place in the present day world.[13]

So, a suitable perspective is necessary for this particular subject. I have approached this research from the Dalit people's perspective. It is a subaltern approach. This kind of perspective is employed in the research of the past because it is believed that it will provide a sense of identity to the marginalised community. It gives them an awareness and understanding about themselves. It gives memories and images to nourish the collective ego, build self-confidence and provide an awareness of self-consciousness to the present reality and identity. An awareness of one's historical identity, achieved through a critical examination of the past, helps as a refuge against the domination of prejudice. It also servesas a tool in making responsible decisions about the kind of vision of itself society should live by.[14]

Endnotes

1. R. Tagore, *Gitanjali*, New York, Macmillan, 1918, poem 10.
2. 'Function aims and understanding of theology in the German Churches', *CCA Consultation*, 1976.
3. J.J. Sebastian, 'Creative Exploration: Arvind P. Nirmal's Ongoing Contribution to Christian Theology', *Bangalore Theological Forum*, vol.XXX1, no. 2, December 1999, pp. 44-52.
4. S.M. Michael (ed.), *Dalits in Modern India: Vision and Values,* New Delhi, Vistar Publications, 1999.
5. H. Kotani (ed.), *Caste System, Untouchability and the Depressed. Japanese Studies on South Asia No.1.*New Delhi, Manohar, 1997.
6. S. Clarke, *Dalits and Christianity: Subaltern Religion and Liberation Theology in India,* New Delhi, Oxford University Press, 1999.
7. K. Jesuratnam, "Towards a Dalit Liberative Hermeneutics: Re-reading The Psalms of Lament," Bangalore Theological Forum, Volume 34, Number 1, June 2002, pp 1-34
8. R.K. Padma, *Caste and Alternative Culture,* Madras, Gurukul Lutheran Theological College & Research Institute, 1995.
9. F.J. Balasundaram, *EATWOT in Asia; The Prophetic Voices of Asia* Vol. I & II. F.J. Balasundaram (ed.), *Martyrs in the Christian History*. F.J. Balasundaram (co-edited) *Asian Expressions of Christian Commitment.*

10. A.S.J. Raj, *Children of a Lesser God*, Madurai, DCLM Publications, 1992.
11. A. Thumma, *Dalit Liberation Theology: Ambedkarian Perspective*, Delhi, ISPCK, 2000.
12. I.S.J. Jesudasan, *Gandhian Theology of Liberation*, Maryknoll, Orbis Books, 1984.
13. Ministry of Education and Social Welfare, *The Indian Council of Historical Research: Aim and Objects*, New Delhi, 1972, p. 262.
14. J.C. Webster, *An Introduction to History*, Madras, The Macmillan Company of Indian Ltd, 1977, p. 165.

CHAPTER 1

A Context for Theologising in India: An Analysis of Dalits' Reality

Indian Christian theology seeks to discern, illuminate and support the people's struggle for human wholeness in freedom and dignity. Its endeavour is to make a meaningful contribution to the march of Indian people towards human fullness in a just society. It seeks to be of service to the Indian people in their common search for full humanity in an open fellowship. It also asserts that an academic type of theology divorced from action for change is irrelevant.Along with the oppressed communities elsewhere, theologians are prepared for a radical break in theological methodology in order that commitment to the oppressed and to their struggle for freedom, justice, and fellowship be the first act of theology. This commitment is implied in, and demanded by, faith-commitment to God in Jesus Christ.

One has to understand that this means serious critical reflection on the reality of India, which includes the praxis of secular and religious movements as well as the theologian's own lifestyle, ideology and configuration. It demands solidarity with the poor and the oppressed, the yielding of all the resources to serve the cause for their liberation from all that confines – hunger and social bondage no less than alienation from God and neighbours. Theology will therefore take local, grassroots action, experience and thought into account. Hence, theologising in India requires that Indian Christian theologians have to fulfil a function vis-à-vis the Christian community as well as the entire national community.

To do theology in India it is imperative to recognise the crucial character of the times and realise that what is at stake is the very life of Indians, even the physical life of the masses – to say nothing of the quality of their life, or of their participation in culture, or of space for that creativity. The situation is complex, but in my discussions I found the problem of poverty and of caste particularly urgent and deserving of emphasis. Clearly related to these are questions concerning women's status and rights and the orientation and organisation of social structures and educational systems.These problems cannot be addressed, however, without due consideration of the people's movements and stirrings from below, as well as the situation of religious plurality and the social role played by religious symbols. Hence social,political, economic and religious analysis is an essential preliminary to theological evaluation.[1]

Caste, an age-old social hierarchy, enjoys sanction of Hindu religion. It stratifies and discriminates 200 million Dalits in India. The purity and pollution concept, based on Varna theory and geared up by the fourfold creation theory of Hinduism as defined in Rig Veda bred casteism and untouchability that dehumanises Dalits to undergo social exclusion, occupational segregation, economic and political power deprivation. The *Varnashradharma* formulates where Dalits should reside, their occupation, access to resources and powers, whom to marry and where to be buried. It denies Dalits the basic human rights to touch and to be touched and forces them to remain as untouchables, to live mainly as manual scavengers, sweepers, gutter/drainage cleaners, cobblers, cremators, drum beaters for the funerals of dominant castes. Thus, Dalits are deprived of human dignity and denied human rights and privileges that are being enjoyed by non-Dalits.Here, I begin by clarifying the often misunderstood term, as it has a long history.Shudras – Untouchables - Dalits:these three terms are usually used interchangeably. Basically, they refer to a common phenomenon. However, there are some differences. Historically they refer to three phases in the history of those who have been classified as the lowest castes of India.

This category comes from the *Vedas* (the sacred texts of the Hindus). The word 'Hindu' also needs an explanation. The name Hindu is itself a foreign name. It was given by the Muslims to the natives for the purpose of distinguishing themselves. It does not occur in any Sanskrit work prior to the Muslim invasion. They did not feel the necessity of a common name because they had no conception of their having constituted a community. Hindu society as such does not exist. It is only a collection of castes. Each caste is conscious of its existence. Its survival is the be all and end all of its existence. Castes do not even form a federation. A caste has no feeling that it is affiliated to other castes except when there is a Hindu-Muslim riot. On all other occasions each caste endeavours to segregate itself and to distinguish itself from other castes. Each caste not only dines among itself and marries among itself, but each caste prescribes its own distinctive dress.

The Vedas classified everyone into four castes. Ambedkar explained this thus;

1. According to the Brahmins, the *Vedas* have defined what an ideal society is and the *Vedas* being infallible, that is the only ideal society which man can accept.
2. The ideal society prescribed by the *Vedas* is known by the name *Chaturvarna* (fourfold colour division).
3. Such a society, according to the *Vedas*, must satisfy three conditions.
4. It must be composed of four classes, *Brahmins, Kshatriyas, Vaishyas* and *Shudras*.
5. The interrelations of these classes must be regulated

by the principle of graded inequality. In other words, all these classes are not to be on equal level but to be one above the other, in point of status, rights and privileges.

6. The Brahmins were placed at the top; the *Kshatriyas* were placed below the Brahmins but above the *Vaishyas*; the Vaishyas were placed below the *Kshatriyas* but above the Shudras and the Shudras were placed the lowest of all.
7. The third feature of *Chaturvarna* was that each class must engage itself in an occupation assigned to it. The Brahmins' occupation was to learn, teach and officiate at religious ceremonies. The *Kshatriyas*' occupation was to bear arms and to fight. The occupation of the *Vaishyas* was trade and business. The Shudras' occupation was to do menial service for all the three superior classes.
8. No class is to transgress and trench upon the occupation of the other classes.[2]

At this stage *Shudras* still enjoyed some rights. The right to collect food from villagers, the right to collect corn from each villager at the harvest seasons and the right to appropriate the dead animals belonging to the villagers.[3]The period of Buddhism in India, which was also one of the richest in India and in world history, came to an end with the collapse of Buddhism and the rebuilding of Hinduism. The reason for the collapse, Ambedkar says, was the Muslim invasion and the slaughter of Buddhist monks.[4]

The period of revivalism of Hinduism was marked by great tensions between the low castes and Brahmins. The Brahmins tried to establish their hegemony as the superior caste and to have their position accepted by all. The Low Castes rejected this. This internal struggle had determined the characterisation of the untouchables even by the colonial officers of the British

Empire. The distinguishing features of the untouchables, according to the Census Commissioner in 1911, are these: 'they deny the supremacy of Brahmins, do not receive Mantra from a Brahmin or otherwise recognised Hindu Guru, deny the authority of Vedas, do not worship Hindu Gods, are not served by good Brahmins as family priests, have no Brahmin priests at all, are denied access to interior of Hindu temples, cause pollution (a) by touch, or (b) within a certain distance, bury their dead and eat beef and do not reverence the cow'.[5] Thus while this period was marked by the imposition of the *Veda*s' doctrine and at least considering Shudras as lower in the ladder of Hindu caste structure, the notion of untouchability resulted in creating total outcasts.

Dalits are called untouchables. The concept of untouchability developed from the ideas of purity and pollution, whether occupational or ceremonial, which are found to have been a practice of untouchability. Physically this meant ousting the untouchables even from their habitats and pushing them into a ghetto. Ambedkar called them, 'people of the Indian ghetto'. All forms of contact were forbidden by the use of rules of untouchability. Untouchability has been abolished in law and its practice in any form is forbidden in Article 17 of the Constitution of India. Yet after 68 years of Independence, the Dalits in India are discriminated against as impure, lower and lesser humans. Multiple deprivations, cumulative marginalisation, structural inequalities and widespread impoverishment mark the lives of Dalits. State and societal violations of Dalit human rights, historical isolation, social segregation, economic exploitation and political suppression have all contributed to the plight of Dalits.

The practice of untouchability, imposed on Dalits to affirm their inferior status and socio-economic marginalisation, is one of the most oppressive and traumatic aspects of Indian cultural memory; sadly enough, it still continues to segregate them from others. Designated in the traditional society as polluting the other castes, Dalits are made to settle outside the village without any access to basic civic necessities. In traditional practice their physical contact, even their shadow, was considered polluting.The practice took a perverse and inhuman form when the untouchables were made to tie earthen pot around their necks and a broom behind, so that the earth should not be polluted by their sputum and footprints. Of course, this polluting designation of the untouchables did not stop the high caste from using them as menial slave labourers, paying them a pittance as a constant reminder of the master's benevolence.[6]

Thus, Dalits are confronted with a peculiar form of slavery, in which the slave labourer was kept inhumanly segregated and inferior and the high caste master extracted maximum labour without taking an adequate responsibility for his slave labourer. Moreover, the Brahminical *dharma*, through the religious code *Manusmriti*, systematised perennial slavery in the lives of untouchables, by closing all avenues of social and economic prosperity. The concept of 'Purity and Pollution' is part and parcel of the Indian psyche and is culturally expressed through customs and practices and justified by Hindu scriptures Vedas.

Modern technology, industrialisation and urbanisation have failed to bring any positive change in the lives of Dalits. These forces have not provided the basis for their independence from enslaving, oppression and exploitation of the rural social situation. Despite legislative initiatives and various policy efforts, the Dalits continue to remain abjectly poor, subject to forced labour, discrimination, economic exploitation and brutal socio-religious atrocities.In the State of Maharashtra Mahars were the field labouring caste and, within the division of labour, were general village servants responsible for removing dead cattle, sweeping village roads and acting as village watchmen and so on.[7] In everyday life situations Dalits are subjected to segregation, insult, humiliation and frustration. They are cheated, insulted and used by the so-called caste community.

The discrimination and marginalisation experienced by Dalits in the villages restates their identity as Dalits forever.

Untouchability continues to be practised in many forms, reinforcing an iniquitous social hierarchy and allowing for the continuing humiliation of Dalits.'It does not matter whether a Dalit is a professor in a university, a bureaucrat in India's several administrative services, a public servant, an official in a private firm or a clerk, a coolie, a scavenger or a sweeper, he/she is a victim of a subtle hidden apartheid. Dalits are not allowed to wear footwear while they walk through the streets of a high caste community and even if they happen to meet any caste man in any part of the village Dalits have to remove their footwear and then salute the caste men.While in rural areas Dalits cannot enter the higher caste section of villages, visit the same temples, drink water or tea from the same cups or glasses, in urban centres caste operates in more subtle ways in recruitment for jobs, promotions and career advancements'.[8]

Boundary making and pollution avoidance have become tasks that consume much public and private energy. Even now in Christian churches in some places Dalits are given a particular place to sit for worship. Even the burial ground is separate for Dalits. Most upper caste people avoid having a Dalit prepare their food, for fear of being polluted, but they use them to clean their toilets, cowsheds and streets. Untouchables are those who suffer from various forms of economic, social, religious and political disabilities, many of which are traditionally prescribed and socially enforced and controlled by higher castes. Thus, untouchables are those castes which are subject to all kinds of oppression and marginalisation and pushed to the periphery in every walk of life such as social, economic, religious and political - in other words, this community have been denied their right to livewith their human dignity and not evenallowed see the shadow of a higher caste. They performthe lowest and most menial kinds of occupations, have been placedinthe lowest position in the caste hierarchical society and are deprived ofall forms of human rights.

One can understand various forms of denial, suffering, humiliation and insult inflicted on Dalits which split the psyche of their human personality. This insulting treatment of Dalits forced them to live in a subhuman, subordinated position. For Dalits, survival from day to day becomes imperative at the cost of sacrificing their human dignity and human rights. Challenging the status quo of the so called high caste men and womenare resulting in violence and caste riots. By using these mechanisms of insult and atrocities of humiliation the caste-minded people try to keep control of the graded Indian society in all spheres of life.The untouchability practices are numerous on Dalits. They face harassment by a range of social exclusion practices. Caste practices segregates them from mainstream life. Dalits were forcedto dwell outside villages and denied access to common water resources, natural resources, village restaurants and burial grounds.[99]

The term Dalit means 'the oppressed', 'broken people'.Common to many Indian languages it is derived from the Sanskrit root '*dal*', which means to break, crack, open, split, scatter, crush and destroy. In the 19th century, Jotiba Phule, a revolutionary social reformer of Maharashtra, used the word 'Dalit' to describe the outcastes and untouchables as the oppressed and broken victims of the caste-ridden Indian society. Ambedkar used the term to denote the untouchables. Later, this term became applicable only to the members of the *Mahar*[10] community in Maharashtra. It is a term used by the Dalits themselves to denote their protest. This was a new term, coming into use only after the 1950s. In the 1970s, the Dalit Panthers of Maharashtra used the term very frequently to identify themselves as the broken people and broadened the connotation to include the Scheduled Castes, Scheduled Tribes, landless, poor peasants, women and all those economically exploited (in other words all the marginalised sections of Indian society).

Nowadays the term is mostly employed by rights activists

to denote the traditional untouchable communities of India. Thus in its wider usage the term includes within its fold everyone who is denied or deprived of his or her natural rights as a human being, whose dignity or self-respect is mauled and systematically violated, and who is exploited and reduced to an instrument for serving the interests of the exploiters. In a narrow sense, the term is used to connote the Scheduled Castes.

The movements that fought for the rights of the untouchables achieved much during the twentieth century, though the fundamental place for Dalits as a whole has not yet significantly changed. The struggle, however, has intensified and has been contested severely. The Dalits are today a formidable force. The resolving of this problem by a final and complete abandonment of the caste ideal of society is very much on the agenda. It can easily be said that the greatest enduring achievement of India in the twentieth century is the progress, though small, that has been made in liberating the Dalits. The primary contributors to this process are the Dalits themselves. The opposition to this change has been strong and continues to be so. As many Dalits became more confident and defiant, the violence used against them has become more severe. Such use of violence is itself evidence of the upper caste realisation that the contest is not going in their favour. It is beyond dispute that Ambedkar had contributed more than any other single individual to bring about this situation. It is quite obvious that Dalits have selected him as their symbol.

In the caste classification, society is divided into a number of hereditary, endogamous, ranked occupational castes.A caste is regarded either as a status or an occupational heredity, or an endogamous or ranked group, or all these together. Hierarchy, separation and interdependence were the determining factors of inter-caste relations. Hereditary specialisation, hierarchical organisation and reciprocal repulsion are the three principles by which the different castes are related to and distinguished from each other in the caste system. The Dalit communities were regarded as untouchables in the caste system and were relegated to the bottom of the caste hierarchy.

The Dalits have been historically identified by different nomenclatures in the caste society. They were called *Harijan* (Children of God), *Panchamas* (fifth Varna) *Avarnas* (Colourless people), *Chandala* (sinners), *Achhuts* (Filthy), *Pariahs* (untouchable),*Namasudras* (Who carries the name of Sudras) Unapproachables, Outcastes, Depressed Classes, Exterior Castes, Scheduled Castes, etc.[11] This characterising with different names itself reveals how the Dalits were historically and socially humiliated, stigmatised and dehumanised. Their identity was defined by the upper castes, and the Dalits had internalised this identity.

The Dalits have been treated as low caste groups, and their social relationships with other castes depended on the rules of the caste system. The caste system enforced various restrictions in matters of marriage, inter-dining, social intercourse and untouchability. The Dalits were regarded as inherently impure. The traditional and primary occupations of most of the Dalit group were tanning, scavenging, cobbling or sweeping, etc.: these occupations were most repulsive to the non-Dalits, and so the Dalits were segregated and lived at the outer edge of the villages. They were despised by the non-Dalits who considered their touch defiling, their way of life impure and their occupation polluting. In addition, the Dalits suffered many social disabilities such as harsh treatment, insult and violence, injustice and inequality, prohibition from public places, public roads, public wells and public bathing places, and discrimination in dress and address. And they were ranked at the very bottom of the social hierarchy. The Dalits were denied education and excluded from schools. Society was centred on the high castes, and they enjoyed all the rights and benefits with exclusive privileges and facilities, whereas the human rights of Dalits were violated and they lived in total subjugation with degraded status.

Dalitssuffer from the indignities of caste-apartheid, pollution, poverty and powerlessness. They continue to remain the 'broken people', victims of atrocities and violence and the most backward section of society. Prior to the 1980s, a number of socio-religious reform movements, anti-caste movements and other initiatives emerged from within and without to awaken and uplift the Dalits. Since the1980s, a new discourse on rights, a rights perspective to development and a series of campaigns for human rights began to take shape within the context of civil and political rights, economic, social and cultural rights and the rights of communities.

Social ostracism continues as the Dalits struggle to emerge as a powerful social force. Their recent awakening has enabled them to assert their civic rights. This is to assume equality in the social structure that is unequal and subordinates the lowest in the social rank.Assertions of equality and self-dignity evokean untoward response from the dominant castes. In the recent past the southern districts of Tamilnadu confronted a social situation where the caste people systematically consolidated their social power as dominant communities. With a political backing that is entrenched in money, power perpetuates the struggle against the dominated Dalits. Caste consciousness is vigorously revived which reveals itself inordinately against any assertion by Dalits of their social equality.

At present campaigns are in progress for the liberation of Dalits in India. The campaign for Dalit human rights emerged from the campaigns for human rights in India. This campaign seeks to enforce first and foremost the right of Dalits to be human and to be treated as humans with dignity, freedom, equality, recognition and respect, to put to an end the State and societal violation of Dalit human rights, and to press for a range of demands including the restoration of land to Dalits, the reservation of jobs in private bodies, etc. The campaign is a concerted initiative of Dalit organisations, human rights groups, and activists, who are working among Dalits in India.

Social discrimination paved the way for economic discrimination. There are various ways of assessing the economic strengths and weaknesses of a person or a community, strength and weakness being relative terms when studying a group of under-privileged people.Economists usually make an attempt at the outset to define poverty in order to enable them to quantify their content. One way of measuring poverty is to calculate what is essentially needed for survival: food and other basic necessities of life such as shelter, clothes and medicines.[12]Among the most shocking features of India is the poverty of the masses, often being nothing less than total destitution and misery, side by side with enormous wealth and affluence enjoyed by the few who form a thin stratum at the summit of India's social hierarchy. India's economic policies are not designed to deal with this gruesome reality; it caters to consumerist tastes and the profits and power of the privileged elitist class. Almost all the means of production – land, capital, technology – are owned and controlled by this small group.

Therefore it also has a grip on political power and manipulates the state apparatus, preventing it from taking effective steps to reform landownership, to create jobs, to restructure the educational and legal system of colonial legacy, to free bonded labour, or to improve the buying power of the lowest income groups. The result has been that, although the country is rich in natural, technical and labour potential and the national income has grown considerably through the several 'Five Year Plans', the condition of the Dalits has deteriorated. Around 87 % of the population lives below, at, or just above the poverty line. This has given rise to widespread embitterment and restlessness, which the ruling class meets by stepping up repression.

Economically, the rulers and their subordinates, the landlords, the moneylenders, etc. exploited the Dalits. The majority of them were landless agricultural labourers and they were the poorest of all castes. They were forced to perform the most inhuman tasks like scavenging, carrying night soil, removal of dead animals, etc. They were exploited and made to depend on the upper caste landlords for their livelihood.

The process of globalisation that shakes the whole world today affects the Dalits at their basic existence. 'Land, water and employment are the basic resources of livelihood for the poor. Anything that weakens the control of Dalits, Tribals and women on these resources, paves the way for their marginalisation and impoverishment'.[13]As the State abdicates its responsibilities towards Dalits, life has become a burden to them. The historical injustice meted out to them kept them away from the economic rat race. Today most of them are employed in the agricultural sector. In the new economic process agriculture is becoming unproductive which means a literal desertion of the Dalits both by the government and society. As the traditional sources of income and new possibilities for employment are at stake, Dalits are impoverished to the core.[14] This reveals their dehumanised existence that is devoid of social protection.The majority of the Dalits are agricultural labourers. According to a 1991 Census, 49.06% of Dalit workers were agricultural labourers with very meagre landholding or mostly landless. This indicates that virtually half of the Dalit workforce is in the unorganised sector. Over the decades there has been a decline in the percentage of Dalit cultivators and an increase in agricultural labourers, non-farming workers or casual labourers.

The reason behind the poor economic condition among Dalits and their heavy dependence on agriculture as labourers, is the failure of the State to implement the land reform legislations. The Dalits were kept away from their rightful claim to land distribution and hence are heavily dependent on the high caste landlords for their livelihood. Though the percentage of Dalits living below poverty has decreased over the years (see Table 5), in 1987 – 88, 44.70% of Dalits continue to live in poverty.

Table 1: Occupational Classification of Dalit Main Workers (1961–1991)[15]

Dalit Main Workers	1961		1971		1981		1991	
	Dalits	General	Dalits	General	Dalits	General	Dalits	General
Cultivators	37.7	52.78	27.87	43.38	28.17	41.53	25.44	39.74
Agricultural labourers	34.48	16.71	51.74	31.71	48.22	25.16	49.06	19.56
Household industry	6.56	6.38	3.33	3.55	3.31	3.99	2.41	2.56
Other works	21.20	24.13	17.05	20.76	20.30	29.32	23.09	38.14
Total	**100.00**	**100.00**	**100.00**	**100.00**	**100.00**	**100.00**	**100.00**	**100.00**

Table 2: Percentage of Dalits Living below Poverty[16]

Years	Dalits	Tribals	Total
1977–78	64.60	72.40	51.20
1983–84	53.10	58.40	40.40
1987–88	44.70	52.60	33.40

The Caste system uses natural resources for perpetuating itself. The example of Sukkaltheerth village in Karnataka will demonstrate this. When people of the village protested against the untouchability practice there, the dominant caste denied access to their land and dismissed Dalits from work. Dalits, having no other means of subsistence, bowed down to the demands of the dominant caste. Many times such a survival factor constrains the Dalits to the dictates of the dominant caste. This we can observe in the *Jajimani* system (hereditary master-servant relationship).[17]Hanumanthappa[18] described the conditions of Dalits in the following words: 'The Dalits are in different stages of socio-economic development and are engaged in divergent forms of work for their living. The practice of such traditional unclean occupations as scavenging, carrying night soil, removing dead animals, leather work, beating drums, etc. gave them a low position in the traditional caste hierarchy, and they are viewed as occupying the lowest rung of the social ladder. The vast majorities of the Dalits are landless and work as agricultural labourers and wage earners to eke out their livelihood. Dependence on upper class landowners for agricultural labour and perpetual subjugation, forces many of them to live as bonded labourers'. According to Mohan Razu, Dalit Human Right activist, Dalit Ethicist and Theologian:

> The growing gap between the rich and poor, the undue burden placed on the poor and oppression of marginalised communities has led to a situation of unrest and disquiet. Very often they erupt and they are labelled as caste and communal conflicts. It is also true that in most of these situations the Dalits and marginalised sectors are worst affected. The government has come down strongly on any dissent and protests.[19]

Caste has an economic and non-economic identity which plays a vital role in the polity of the Indian villages. The economic situation has structural links with the political situation. India's independence movement terminated in a transfer of power without a social revolution.A westernised elite with economic interests integrated into the interests of the outgoing colonial power became the successor to the British Raj.It has been to their advantage to keep practically everything unchanged. This new bourgeoisie – together with the industrialists, the landlords, the plantation owners, and the professional politicians – monopolises political power and controls political and economic policies and processes.Local self-governing bodies either do not function at all or are manipulated by the wealthy class.

Melavallavu, a small hamlet 30 kilometres south of

Madurai in Tamilnadu saw the violent murder of six Dalits in May 1997. The offence of the Dalits was the assertion of political rights in a democratic country. One of the six Dalits was elected as the president of the local body[20] and the high caste people could not stand the leadership of their erstwhile untouchable brother. Even after a year the culprits of the crime have not been arrested and the lives of the families of these Dalits are still under constant threat. Political rights are still a distant dream to the Dalits of India, although India did have a Dalit President once.[21]

The masses are fast becoming cynical and losing faith in the political system that has proved incapable of meeting the real problems. Within a global new imperialist framework, India's political decisions are controlled by those who control India's economic processes – namely the superpowers and their multinational corporations. India's parliamentary democracy was devised by its ruling class as a system where all the symbols of social democracy were preserved and elevated to the highest level of principle, but which also provided the formal groundwork for every form of repression and exploitation.

Politically, the caste character of the earlier kingdoms, the non-interference in caste matters of the British administration and the high caste domination of the democratic polity facilitated political patronage of the caste system and went against the interests of Dalits. Dalits have scant representation in national politics. In local administration Dalits' representation is nil. The caste system, as a political power, conditions the consciousness of the Dalits to submit themselves to the lower status offered in society. In the villages, the traditional administration council was dominated by the high castes,who imposed differential scales of punishment on the basis of caste, and the Dalits were victims of injustice. For example, if a Brahmin killed a low caste man, he was at most fined. But if a low caste man killed a Brahmin, he lost his life. The Dalits were utterly powerless and lived a life of servitude to the non-Dalits. Denial of political rights marks deeper implications of economic deprivation.

Traditionally, religions in India, notwithstanding notable exceptions at various points in Indian history, have acted as bastions of legitimation for the power, privileges and exploitative practices of upper caste and upper class.The caste system too – born of conquest, enslavement, an imposed vertical division of labour, and racial prejudices – received religious legitimisation at the hands of priestly groups. In societies at the mythical stage, myth was part of the means of production.The claim was that there was no wealth without sacrifice and that such sacrifice has had an impact on the cosmos, but it was only the priestly group that had knowledge and control of sacrificial technology. Through its use this group emerged rich and powerful. Ritual technology defined ritual purity and pollution – untouchability, by which the enslaved were disqualified and excluded not only from cult but from ownership of land as well.

Based on religion the Dalits were denied entry into temples. They were kept at a distance from the temple while their offerings were taken. Religious ideology gave priority to Brahmins, and the Brahmins dominated in all matters pertaining to ritual and worship. They were the guardians of Hinduism, interpreters of scriptures, authors of philosophy and priests of the temple. They refused to serve the Dalits and the Dalits suffered religious discrimination.

The Christian religion was no exception. In Christianity too, the exploiters have become rich. Some Indian Churches have accommodated caste within themselves, making a mockery of the gospel.The Movement for liberation has also to reckon with side-tracking pieties and gurus, with domestic, charismatic and evangelical trends that seek to capture radical student organisations, and with the gap between the Church's radical words and stance on the one hand and its feeble, ineffectual deeds on the other. The Indian Church – not the

85% of Indian Christians, who are poor, passive, and alienated, but the Bishops and the organisational institutions – has not yet made a clear option for the poor. Often decisions are made in the light of a theology and spirituality that is colonial and anaesthetic.

Although Christianity is an egalitarian religion, the caste system found its way into it in India. Dalit Christians within the church were discriminated against and were denied powers within the ecclesiastical structure. Though Dalit Christians constituted approximately 70% of the Indian Christian population they were marginalised and ignored until recently. To illustrate this let me quote what Archbishop George Zur, Apostolic Pro-Nuncio to India said while inaugurating the Catholic Bishops Conference of India in 1991:

> Though Catholics of the lower caste and tribes form 60 per cent of Church membership they have no place in decision-making. Scheduled caste converts are treated as lower caste not only by high caste Hindus but by high caste Christians too. In rural areas they cannot own or rent houses, however well-placed they may be. Separate places are marked out for them in the parish churches and burial grounds. Inter-caste marriages are frowned upon and caste tags are still appended to the Christian names of high caste people. Casteism is rampant among the clergy and the religious. Though Dalit Christians make 65 percent of the 10 million Christians in the South, less than 4 percent of the parishes are entrusted to Dalit priests. There are no Dalitsamong 13 Catholic Bishops of Tamilnadu or among the Vicars-general and rectors of seminaries and directors of social assistance centres.[22]

The situation in the Protestant Church is no different except that some Dalits have been elevated to Bishopric and other positions of power recently. Many Dalit Christian leaders refer to the thrice-alienated situation of the Dalit Christians in India, namely, discrimination within the Church, discrimination by Hindu culture and discrimination by the State, as they are denied Scheduled Caste status in the Constitution and the related privileges which come with that status. Historically, the Dalits have been discriminated against, enslaved, victimised, stigmatised, dehumanised and marginalised. They were socially and physically segregated; their identity was defined by the non-Dalits with negative images; they were abused in word and deed; they were denied education; their human rights were violated; and they were denied economic opportunities and lived in utter poverty and backwardness.

Thus, the history of Dalits is a history of centuries of suffering, oppression, exploitation, humiliation, helplessness and powerlessness. They are the victims of historical and societal violation of their human rights by the State and the upper castes. According to the 1991 Census, the population of Dalits in India is 138.2 million (excluding Jammu and Kashmir), which is 16.48 per cent of the total population (see Table 3). The vast majority (81.28%) of the Dalits live in rural areas.

Table 3: Population of Dalits (in million)[23]

Dalits		Tribals		Others		Total	
Population	%	Population	%	Population	%	Population	%
138.2	16.48	67.8	8.08	632.6	75.44	838.6	100

In the village of Gandadevi, in the Sivagangai district of Tamilnadu, the Dalits wanted to participate in the chariot procession of the village feast. The caste Hindus united together to oppose the decision of the Dalits and that brought the village feast to an end. Nobody could take the chariot procession as the district chief administrator issued a special order to stop everything in order to avoid communal conflicts. Assertion of religious rights by the Dalits meets with the same plight as that of other rights. It is a historical process in which they lost their 'religio-cultural self-identity as a separate group by losing control over their gods, places of worship and the right to administer to their own people's religious needs'.[24] The losses of cultural identity hasten the debasement of the Dalits. By removing the Dalits from the central stage of cultural celebrations the high caste communities furthered their vested interests. Hence all these deprivations: cultural, social, educational, economic, political, religious, affective and cognitive, half-hearted implementation of the reservation policy and development schemes, and above all large scale state and societal violation of Dalit human rights haveallcontributed to the marginalisation of Dalits.

Socio-economic discrimination forbids the formation of human capital such as education and other cultural symbols. UNICEF says to be illiterate is to be excluded.When a Dalit was asked why she did not send her son to school, she answered: 'My son is not going to be a district administrator (District Collector), so why bother?' For this Dalit, education is a gateway for status and lucrative employment which she feels is closed to her kind. The attitude of this Dalit woman reflects the position of the Dalits in general. This section examines the kind of educational discrimination perpetrated on the Dalit community.

Table 4: Literacy Rate of Dalits (1961–1991)[25]

Years	Dalits			General		
	Male	Female	Total	Male	Female	Total
1961	16.96	3.29	10.27	37.36	12.95	24.02
1971	22.39	6.44	14.67	39.52	18.72	29.46
1981	31.12	10.93	21.38	46.89	29.85	43.67
1991	49.91	23.76	37.41	64.20	39.29	52.21

On the educational front, the Dalits lag behind the general population of India. The general literacy rate in 1991 was 52.21 percent, while the literacy among Dalits was only 37.41

percent.In 2004,according to the Government of India Report, the literacy rate of Dalits was only 54.70%.Table 4 indicates that 62.59% of Dalits remain illiterate. Many of them do not complete even their primary education. Nearly a third of Dalit children in the age group of 6 to 11 years do not get an opportunity to enrol in primary schools. Of those who enrol, 78.88% of Dalit children drop out by the secondary stage. This is because these children are engaged either as child labourers, rag pickers, wage earners, or domestic workers. Maybe education, as they see it, does not promise them a good future either. Even after completing school they are unable to obtain employment. Bribes are also a deterring factor. With the rise in the level of education in general, the enrolment of Dalits declines. The following table shows the decline in enrolment by stages of Dalit children:

Table 5: Enrolment by Stages of Dalit Children (1994–95)[26] in millions

Stages	Dalits			Tribals			Others		
	Boys	Girls	Total	Boys	Girls	Total	Boys	Girls	Total
Pri-mary	1.00	0.75	1.80	0.54	0.36	0.09	6.20	4.70	10.90
Middle	0.35	0.21	0.56	0.15	0.08	0.23	2.50	1.50	4.00
Secon-dary	0.20	0.08	0.29	0.07	0.04	0.11	1.60	0.08	2.40
Higher Edu cation	0.031	0.01	0.042	0.01	0.004	0.01	0.31	0.16	0.47

Occupations, as castes, are ranked with social status, and with levels of purity and pollution. There is some agreement within and across social fields on which occupations are considered prestigious. Historically the Dalits have been assigned menial work and have been forced to perpetuate those occupations hereditarily down the generations. Prominent among them are manual scavenging, clearing dead animals and carcasses, grave digging, drumming and dancing for various

Hindu religious festivals and other occasions such as death, marriage etc.Dalits are also involved in various agricultural operations and earth work, as messengers and as night watch and ward.[27] At least two thirds of the bonded labourers in India are Dalits. Of the more than 250, 0000 bonded labourers in India, 83.2% belong to Dalits and Tribal groups.[28] Even after 68 years of Independence, the Dalits in India are far away from the fundamental rights of freedom to choose one's occupation, vocation, profession, trade and business. When they refuseto perform demeaning tasks, they are threatened with physical abuse and social boycotts.

In Gujarat and many other places, the Dalit labourers were forced to leave employment which they had taken up outside their village for better wages. They were forced by the higher caste people to come back to their village and made to work on their fields for the whole day without food and water. The majority of the Dalits continue to perform their traditional occupation. Lack of education and discrimination in seeking other forms of employment force the Dalits to do demeaning and menial tasks determined by the caste system. By denying them any other asset or livelihood, they have been forced to continue these religiously polluting occupations.According to the 2001 Census Dalits constitute 16.6% of the population. According to the Government of India report in 2004, 77.01% Dalits remain as landless agricultural labourers; 51% sweepers and only 16% are in Government employment, even then in lower and middles class positions.[29]

India is a welfare state committed to the welfare and development of its people in general and of the vulnerable sections of society in particular. The rhetoric is for promotingsocial justice and empowerment to the disadvantaged and marginalised sections of the society. In reality, the Dalits have been systematically deprived and marginalised when it comes to the question of their just share in the benefits of development. Due to the paternalistic attitude of the State, the top-down model of development, the apathy of the administration, half-hearted implementation, etc., the Dalits, especially in rural areas, have not been provided with the basic amenities as is shown in Table 6. The Table shows that in 1991, only 1.86% of Dalits in rural areas had the facilities of safe water, electricity and toilet, and 32.14% had none of these facilities.

Table 6: Percentage of Amenities Available to Dalits[30]

No	Amenities	Dalits	
		Rural	Urban
1	Safe Drinking Water	59.84	80.59
2	Electricity	21.84	56.32
3	Toilet	5.15	38.28
4	Safe water and Electricity	14.71	47.60
5	Electricity and toilet	2.76	32.94
6	Safe water and toilet	3.35	32.34
7	Safe water, electricity and toilet	1.86	28.08
8	None of the above facilities	32.14	9.62
9	Cow-dung cake	24.78	6.29
10	Coal/coke/lignite	1.43	11.14
11	Charcoal	0.44	2.42
12	Firewood	67.69	45.83
13	Kerosene	0.66	21.89
14	Cooking gas	0.70	10.23

The 2001 Census quotes 21.4% of Dalit villages only having electricity; 19.5% have to walk for miles for a drinking water facility; 42.8% have only household goods; and 36.25% in rural areas live below the poverty line.[31]

The government policy of protective discrimination in favour of Dalits has become a burning issue in India. Laws granting Dalits special provision for government jobs benefit only a small percentage of Dalits. Half-hearted implementation of the reservation policy is another reason for the marginalisation of Dalits. With the exception of a minority who have benefited and are co-opted, reserved vacancies for Dalits in various States are seldom filled on the pretext that suitable candidates are not available. And in Central Government Services, there is clear-cut discrimination in recruiting Dalits for A, B and C grades as are seen in Table 7 below. In the E grade, i.e. the sweepers (manual scavengers) category, we see the maximum representation of Dalits (40.37%) indicating the reinforcement of demeaning tasks allocated to the Dalits.[32]

Table 7: Percentage Representation of Dalits in Central Government Services[33]

Grades	Dalit Representation			
	1971	1991	1994	1996
A	2.58	9.09	10.25	11.50
B	4.06	11.82	12.06	11.98
C	9.59	15.65	15.73	15.24
D	10.37	21.24	20.46	20.16
E	-	-	-	40.37

The 1986–87 annual Report of the Commissioner of Scheduled Castes/Scheduled Tribes indicated that the Dalits were attacked, harassed, assaulted and even massacred mainly on grounds of unresolved land disputes related to allotment of government land distribution of surplus land to the landless Dalit families, tensions and bitterness created on account of non-payment or underpayment of minimum wages, and resentment against the manifestation of awareness among Dalits about their rights and privileges guaranteed by the constitution. In the majority of cases, those attackers were enforcement police in connivance with the higher caste people.

The awareness generated by Dalit organisations and the support of various constitutional safeguards, special legislations, affirmative action policies and programmes of Government have gradually empowered, if not adequately, the Dalit youth who with resentment and anger have raised their voice against inhuman untouchability practices and other socio-economic deprivations. The uprising, assertion and challenge of Dalits were seen as an act of disobedience or rebellion against the traditional and hegemonies authority of non-Dalits.As a result, they resort to crude forms of physical violence that range from murder to maiming limbs, social/economicboycotts, damaging and looting properties, naked parading and raping of Dalit women. The Table below gives the total reported and recorded atrocities and violence on Dalits for three years. An equal number of crimes may not have been reported or recorded.

Table 8: Atrocities and Violence against Dalits[34]

No	Crime-heads	1993	1994	1995
1	Murder	510	546	571
2	Dacoit	102	78	70
3	Robbery	197	258	218
4	Arson	369	533	500
5	Kidnapping and Abduction	246	251	276
6	Rape	798	992	873
7	Violation of PCR Act 1995	2,531	1,731	1,528
8	Hurt	-	4,542	4,544
9	Violation of SC/ST Atrocities Act 1989	-	14,938	13,925
10	Others	20,220	10,038	10,492
	Total	**24,973**	**33,908**	**32,997**

The official Indian crime statistcs, averaged over the period 2001–2005 denoted 27 atrocities against Dalits every day; 13 Dalits murdered every week; 5 Dalits' homes or possessions burnt every week; 6 Dalits kidnapped or abducted every week; 3 Dalit women raped every day; 11 Dalits beaten every day and a crime committed against a Dalit every 18 minutes. The practice of untouchability has been the root cause for the atrocities committed against the Dalits. Violence against Dalits ranged from denial of entry into a temple to physical violence, setting Dalit houses on fire, sexual violence including rape of Dalit women and girls, forceful eviction of the Dalits from their lawfully owned land, using force to repress the voice of dissent from Dalits, and so on. Often complaints against atrocitiesare either not registered or, if registered, go uninvestigated. Often offences againstDalits have been committed with direct connivance between the police and the administration.[35]

The constitutional commitments of the State to the Dalits havenot been realised, and the laws designed to ensure that Dalits enjoyed equal rights and protection are seldom enforced. The Protection of Civil Rights Act 1995 was enacted to enforce the abolition of untouchability in the Constitution. However untouchability, in its varied forms and shades, is practised by the caste society to dehumanise the Dalits. In 1989, the Scheduled Castes and Scheduled Tribes (Prevention of Atrocities) Act was enacted to address other forms of human rights violation of Dalits. In 1995, the government of India enacted accompanying rules for the Atrocities Act, the Scheduled Castes and Scheduled Tribes Prevention of Atrocities Rules, 1995. Although a potentially powerful piece of legislation, the implementation of the Act of 1989was hampered by the lack of political will, lack of willingness on the part of the enforcement machinery and absence of steps to make the Dalits themselves aware of this Act and rights thereunder.

According to the Indian National Crime Bureau Report 2007, the total number of persons facing trial in courts for the crimes committed against Dalits is 235,560. Out of these 9048are under murder charges, 6748 for rape,2240 for kidnapping and abduction, 831 for dacoitary, 695 for robbery, 2509 for arson, 31195 for hurt, 5250 crimes under Protection of Civil Rights Act,90934crimes under Scheduled Caste / Scheduled Tribes (Prevention Of Atrocities) Act and 86110 for other crimes[36]. The recent annual report presented in March 2011 in the Indian Parliament quotes 38,943 cases as having been registered against the perpetrators but the conviction rate was only 31.4%.[37] While these figures prove the volume of physical violence on Dalits, they are simply a 'tip of an iceberg' as these were all only notified cases. An ocean of crimes is not taken to police and court by Dalits, who fear and continue to fear further persecution in the form of false counter cases against them or unfair trial. The impunity being enjoyed by both the perpetrators of violence and the erring officials who violate and neglect their bounden duty is enormous.[38]

Women's value is often considered only in their relationship to men – usually as wives, sisters and mothers – rather than as persons and individuals in their own right.[39] In male-dominated societies, both modern and traditional women are seen as 'other', and women's experiences of discrimination, subordination and domination are not taken account of. Women are treated as the property of men and valued only in association in relation with their male counterpart.[40]Gail Omvedt, a feminist sociologist, quotes the words of a song by Kamla Bhain:

> Every woman in this country is dishonoured, degraded,
>
> With your hand on your heart, say, how can such a country be free?
>
> In this country, they say, there are goddesses without number,
>
> Tell me, have they loosened even a link of our chains?
>
> Have we gained anything of honour from the veil?
>
> Beneath the veil we have remained smothered, beneath the veil we burned...[41]

The condition of Dalit women is particularly deplorable. They face the triple burden of caste, class and gender.[42]Dalit women are thus thrice oppressed victims of centuries of social, political, economic, cultural and religious pressures. Dalit women in India live an insecure existence combining dismal poverty with pulverising labour in the fields/workplaces and in the home – abused and used, powerless and exploited.[43]They are subjected to physical abuse, denied basic human rights, and have been systematically brain-washed into accepting their inferior status in Indian society.[44] They constitute the major workforce, doing hard manual labour and engaging in agricultural operations.On the job, whether in agriculture, construction, industry or elsewhere in the unorganised sector, their exposure to outdoor work and interaction with cunning employers make them vulnerable to sexual exploitation, as attimestheirown andtheir family's survival are at stake. Caste plays a vital role in defining the status of women in society.[45]

Sexual purity of women is directly linked to the purity of the caste. This suggests that female sexuality presents a threat to those with 'purity of blood',i.e. the higher castes. The caste-based Indian society generally believes that it is through women and not men that the purity of caste is ensured and preserved. Dalit girls are forced to become prostitutes for upper caste patrons. Cases of rape, especially of power rape,[46] reveal a more sinister aspect of this same depersonalisation of Dalit women on the basis of their gender and caste. Men from dominant castes have raped Dalit women not only because such women are poor, work outside the home and so become vulnerable, but also because raping them has rarely been punished. In addition, however, the rape of Dalit women has been used as a way to humiliate or punish Dalit men by sexually violating the women under their protection. In fact, rape has proven to be such a powerful tool of social oppression that Dalit women have often been the chief targets in inter-caste and communal conflicts.[47]

In short, the dominant tradition gives to Dalit women a status, role, identity, and self-image which only compounds their problems as women and offers them little, if anything, positive in return. Dalit women are raped as a form of restitution, i.e. as part of an effort by upper caste leaders to suppress movements to demand minimum wages, to settle sharecropping disputes, or to reclaim lost land. To crush Dalit uprisings the landlords and the police use sexual abuse and other forms of violence against Dalit women. Dalit women are arrested and tortured as a means of punishing their male relatives.

Dalit women's sexuality has been subjugated to various kinds of interpretations. On the one hand, some have tried to suggest that, because of their comparative economic independence, they enjoy autonomy or control over their sexuality; whereas the caste-ridden Indian social order has construed and justified them as instruments of upper caste perverted sexual pleasure.[48] The *Devadasi* system,[49] which legitimises sexual violence and discrimination against Dalit women, is in fact an attempt to control and enslave Dalit women's sexuality by giving it religious sanction.

In some areas sexual violence is linked to debt bondage. Dalit women are made to eat human excreta; they are paraded naked in public, gang-raped, etc. Thus, their human rights are violated. The lack of law enforcement leaves many Dalit women unable to approach the legal system to seek redress. Even when cases are registered, the lack of appropriate investigation, or the judge's own caste and gender biases, can lead to acquittal, regardless of the availability of evidence or witnesses. The women's movement has also been an uncertain ally, largely because of its dominant caste leadership who define women's issues in dominant caste terms and tend to ignore the role of caste in the oppression of Dalit women.[50]

The plight of Dalits within Christianity is no better, if not the same. Christianity propagates equality but it practises caste discrimination among Christians. Christianity made its presence in India in the 1st century with the arrival of St. Thomas, one of the disciples of Jesus.[51] The early missionaries from Syria,

Portugal, Italy and Spain converted mostly Brahmins, other dominant castes and fisher people.[52] The gates of Christianity were opened wideronly in the 17thand 18th centuries for others[53]. Dalits started embracing Christianity through mass conversion mainly after the arrival of Protestant missionaries from 1706 onwards who were involved in educational, social and health services among them.[54] Today, in all mainline churches – Roman Catholic, Protestant, Church of South India and Church of North India, in Lutheran Churches and Pentecostals – irrespective of denominations, Dalits constitute around 70% of the total of Christians.[55] Though forminga majority among Christians, Dalits mainly rooted in rural areas which are still the heart of India[56]continue to suffer the shackle of untouchability practices and face discrimination and oppression at the hands of minority non Dalit Christians within church.[57]

Caste practice is more visible and vibrant in rural and less visible in urban congregations. Largely, Dalit Christians live in exclusion and are treated unequally in worshipping, sharing Eucharist, getting space in church activities and in burial grounds. Inter dining and inter caste marriages among Dalit and non-Dalit Christians are still largely an unrealised dream, although stray incidents of inter-caste marriages take place out of love affairs among the educated youth. Revd Fr. Antony Raj, in his study *Discrimination against Dalit Christians in Tamil Nadu* (1989), lists the following discriminatory practices which still continue to remain in many churches:

> Two chapels are constructed – one for the non Dalits and other for the Dalits; in some parishes liturgical services are conducted separately; separate seating arrangements are made within the same chapel; Dalits are usually seated in the two aisles of the church; even if there are benches or chairs, Dalits are asked to take seats on the floor; the existence of two separate cemeteries, two separate funeral trucks to carry the dead bodies;

> two separate queues to receive the sacred body of Christ; Dalits are asked to receive communion only after non Dalits; Dalit is forbidden to be an altar boy at the sacred liturgy; non-Dalits restrict the corpus Christi procession, palm Sunday procession and other processions only to their streets; Dalits are not invited to participate in the washing of feet ceremony during Maundy Thursdays; for fear of equal participation in the celebration of the parish saint, the parish council decides not to ask any contribution from Dalits for such festivals; the feast of the village patron saint is celebrated separately; most of the civic amenities like hospital and school etc., are centred around the upper castes' residences; Dalit Christians are seldom allowed to assist the priests in reading scriptures; not allowed proportionately in the choir; in cemeteries walls are raised to separate Dalit Christians graves from the upper caste ones.[58]

A very glaring example of today's burning issue is that the church chariot carrying the statue of Mother Mary has been denied and prevented to be carried into the Dalit Christian area of Eraiyur village of Tamilnadu.A wall dividing burial spaces of Dalit and non-Dalit Christians in a cemetery in Tiruchirappalli, a corporation in Tamilnadu, is another outstanding example.

Like Dalits of other faiths, Dalit Christians are also termed as impure, polluted and forced to carry out the filthy jobs, viz manual scavenging, sweeping, gutter / sewage cleaning, garbage removing, cobbling and cremating the dead bodies as a service to non Dalits.[59] This reality continues even today and Dalit Christians are forced to undertake the same oldpolluting jobs.[60]Therefore, Ambedkar, said: 'Christianity has not succeeded in dissolving the feeling of caste from among the converts of Christians. There are Brahmin Christians and non-

Brahmin Christians. Among non-Brahmin Christians, there are, Maratha Christians, Mahar Christians, Mang Christians, Bhangi Christians, Pariah Christians, MalaChristians and Madiga Christians. They would not marry or inter-dine. They are as much caste ridden as the Hindus are'.

Some Visible Caste practices that Dalit Christians face today:

- Christians are divided by caste.
- Non Dalit Christians carry suffixed caste names to their names as a matter of pride and caste identity.
- Invisible different seating positions are in place for Dalits and non Dalits inside church in village churches.
- Preference is given to non-Dalits in all ministerial acts including serving of Eucharist.
- Inter dining among Christians in village-based churches is still a problem.
- Inter caste marriage among Dalit Christians the non Christians, still a dream.
- Church leadership both clergy and lay are by and large in the hands of the so called upper caste Christians except in some Dalit dioceses
- Bishops, priests, nuns, pastors, catechists and all committee members are mostly nonDalits. Sextons, gardeners and cemetery watchmen are mainly Dalits.
- Dalit priests and pastors are posted in unimportant and poor village churches, while non Dalits are posted in urbanised and affluent churches
- Dalit priests and pastors are prohibited from postings in certain churches where non Dalit dominate.
- Dalit youths do not share the same space and opportunities on a par with the non-Dalit youth
- Church festivals are planned, organised and celebrated by non Dalits and Dalits are forced to give their share

of money but to undertake all menial work like cleaning and sweeping during festivals.

- Pulling Church chariots to the abode of Christian Dalit areas is still a matter of dispute.
- Cemetery is divided or invisibly separated.
- Church institutions are invariably in the hands of the nonDalits minority.
- The administrators and beneficiaries of church based educational and health institutions are mostly nonDalits.
- Church properties are by and large occupied, administered and managed by non Dalits.
- Church based educational institutions lost the missionary zeal and admit students on merit by which the affluent and non Dalits of all faiths are the maximum beneficiaries.
- Higher education opportunities are mostly provided to non-Dalit Christians in seminaries and theological institutions.
- Seminaries and theological colleges are overcrowded with only non-Dalit Christians in terms of staff and students, except one or two institutions.
- Christian Dalit women, except fora few elite, are still neglected, ignored and sidelined in all aspects and spheres of church and church-related activities.
- Rural based Dalit Christians do not get adequate pastoral care.
- Church as a democratic institution - its politics, elections, power positions, administrations, managementsis fully and purely decided by caste.
- Church is not able to address the issue of social exclusion by caste and, on the contraryit perpetuates the same.[61]

The other major exclusion within the Church hierarchy is that Dalits suffer to get access to power positions.[62]NonDalits, largely, do not want to share power with Dalits, ranging from the ecclesiological hierarchy to admission to the Christian institutions mainly educational and health.An obvious example is, 'out of 156 Catholic Bishops in India 150 Bishops belong to the upper caste community. Only six belong to the Dalit community. Out of 12500 Catholic Priests only 600 are from the Dalit community.While 75% members are from the Dalit community, 25% of the upper caste Christian clergy and laity have complete control over the Dalits, the untouchable Christians.[63] Among approximately 40,000 Christian educational and health institutions, majority beneficiaries are not from Scheduled Castes or Christians of Scheduled Castes Origin'.[64] In the name of 'merit and excellence in education', these institutions cater and serve to the needs of mainly non-Dalits and to a lesser degree of elite Dalit Christians. This is the same situation that occurs in the hospitals of higher ranksrun by Christians. Those who can afford to pay for costly treatments alone are engaged in such hospitals.Thus, the Christian institutions are managed largely by non-Dalits and have become institutions for the welfare of dominant caste and class while the poorest of the poor, especially the rural Dalit Christians, are largely neglected, ignored and sidelined.[65]

Vincent Manoharan argues that, 'a noteworthy change took place in the recent past in certain dioceses of the Protestant Churches and a very few in the catholic church, where the Church leadership has reached the hands of Dalits, who serve as Bishops, Secretaries, Treasurers, committee members and Institution heads. But this counts only a positional change; but structural change is still a distant dream'[66].He reiterates that 'historically non Dalits were in the advantageous positions in terms of socio, economic and political spheres and they were the first ones to embrace Christianity. Therefore naturally they were the first ones to occupy and enjoy these positions of church hierarchy and all related institutions which legacy still continues'.[67]

For example in Church of South India, although almost all 22 dioceses are predominantly Dalit represented, still the majority are under the power dominance of non Dalits. Of course, in some dioceses Dalits have wielded power positions. But largely they – both clergy and layare urban-based, educated and elite. The grass root level Dalit Christians who form the majority both among Catholics and Protestants still remain as excluded and oppressed. The same is the case with minority rights that are guaranteed by the Constitution. The minority rights are enjoyed by non-Dalit Christians in both the Catholic and Protestant Churches and also by a sizable elite of Dalit Christians in the Protestant Churches. This situation needs to be changed for the poor and discriminated, rural based Dalit Christians to inherit their rights and privileges.

In addition to Casteism, the worst forms of corruption, nepotism, manipulation and victimisation are the present-day visible values of the Church. Church leadership is decided by caste affiliation and corrupt practices.Any challenging voice against caste or corrupt practices is silenced with victimisation. Unfortunately and sadly, Christian Dalit leadership is also not able to escape from these vindictive motives and practices in terms of suppressing the legitimate voices within the church.

Over the last two decades, large scale violence has been unleashed on Christians by the Hindu fundamentalist forces, by way of warning and stopping conversions. The worst affected have been the rural-based Dalit Christians and Christian Tribals. In the urban areas, comparatively, more than physical violence, damage had been caused mainly to church structures or institution buildings. But in the rural areas the Hindu chauvinists unleashed physical violence, razing down prayer halls, their small thatched roof huts and homes and setting fire to their properties. Khandamol in Orissa was a recent example where the Dalit Christians and Tribals were targeted by the Hindu fundamentalist forces. Dalit Christians, despite their other oppressions, sufferviolations and violence from the hands of Hindu hooligans. The affected Dalit Christians are not able to get access to justice by invoking special legislations that are in place for protecting Dalits, as constitutionally they are not counted as Scheduled Castes.They face differential treatment by the State owing to their change in faith. Dalit Christians were denied the benefit of the positive discrimination measures, rights and privileges ensured by the Constitution of India, special legislations and development programmes enjoyed by the Hindu, Sikh and Buddhist Dalits, in the name of Scheduled Caste.[68]

Dalit Christians are on a democratic warpath and are challenging the Indian Government to scrap the Presidential order of 1950 which abrogated their right to be called a Scheduled Caste, to enjoy the protection of Constitutional safeguards and all anti-discrimination laws and to avail themselves of the benefits from all Governmental socio economic and political programmes, schemes and measures.[69] Of course, non-Dalit leadership of the Church supports the struggle of Dalit Christians against the state for their constitutional rights. But the same leaders are not adequately in favour of addressing the issue of caste within the church. Thus, Dalit Christians suffer quadruple oppression. First, by the non Dalits of other faiths; second, by the non Dalits of Christian faith; third, by the state exclusion[70] and fourth, by the Hindu fascist forces.

Dalit reality is a unique social phenomenon. It includes a category of people who are socially ostracised, culturally debased and economically deprived. Their case cannot be reduced to any particular social problem such as poverty or discrimination. Antony Raj remarks, 'There is a lack of understanding of Dalitness. It has a material and ideological dimension. They are economically deprived and socially ostracised. But that is only the tip of the iceberg. At the level of consciousness, every Dalit feels that he is not wanted in his country and in his Church.'[71] According to Azariah, they are 'no-people'.[72]

Such, in outline, is India's present reality – disenfranchisement of the Dalit at all levels calls for the emergence of theologising in India from a different perspective. To theologise is to interpret this reality in the light of the tradition of God's liberating action in India's history in order to lead to renewed humankind.The contexts for theologising in India are the authentic life experiences of these marginalised people, their struggles, their failures and successes, their conflicts and contradictions, their dreams and hopes, and their comradeship with people of other faiths and ideologies etc.John Parratt supports the above argument and points out that,

> The social, political and economic contexts form a 'given' for theologians, which they cannot ignore without risk or becoming irrelevant to their people. Whether they begin from the usually accepted sources of Christian tradition and then seek to apply these to their own context (the traditional way of doing theology) or whether they reverse this process and begin by analysing the context before seeking to relate it to these sources of tradition (the method, among others, of liberation theology) is a question and challenge about which there is no unanimity. However, to devalue or, worse, to ignore the social, political and economic structures in which we work is seriously to limit the practical usefulness of our theological thinking.[73]

Endnotes

1. J. Parratt, *A Guide to Doing Theology*, SPCK, 1969, p. 59.
2. *Buddha and His Dhamma* was published 1957 one year after Ambedkar's death. It is a long exposition in which Ambedkar attempted to give 'a clear and consistent statement of the life and teachings of the Buddha' as he said in the introduction to the book.

3. B.R. Ambedkar, *The Untouchables*, 1sted, Bheem Patrika Publications, 1948.
4. Ibid.
5. *Census of India 1911*, p. 46.
6. G. Shah, *Dalits and the State*, published for Centre for Rural Studies, Lal Bahadur Shastri National Academy of Administration, Mysore, by Concept Publish Company, 2000.
7. Ibid.
8. Pinto, 1999, p. 1.
9. A study in 2006 by Human Rights organisation (*SHASHI HUMAN RIGHTS WATCH* – Special Report, Hyderabad, India, 2006) has revealed the existence of more than 124 forms of visible and invisible untouchability practices in the socio, economic and political life of 200 million Dalits in India. To quote a few from the report:

   Discrimination In Government Services: 37.8% of the villages, Dalits to sit separately in government schools; 27.6% of villages, prevented from entering police stations; 25.7% of villages, prevented to public retails shops; 33% of the villages, public health workers refuse to visit Dalit homes; 23.5% of Dalit helmets, mails not delivered to their home; 14.4% of villages, not permitted to enter Local Government Buildings; 12% of the villages, denied access to water resources.

   In Market Access : 35% of villages surveyed, barred access to local markets; 47% of village co-operatives, Dalits prevented from selling milk, and 25% of villages, prevent Dalits from buying milk.

   In Work : 25% villages, Dalits paid lower wages, worked long hours, delayed payment, suffer verbal and physical abuse; 37% of villages, wages paid in distance to avoid physical contact.

   In Religion and Rites :64% of villages, Temple entries restricted; almost 50% of villages, no access to cremation grounds.

   In Private Sphere : 73% of villages, not allowed to enter non-Dalit homes; 70% of villages, no inter dinning; 35.8% of villages denied entry for village shops.

In Religion and Rites : 64% of Dalits restricted from entering Hindu Temples; almost 50% of villages, Dalits prevented from accessing cremation grounds.

In Private Sphere : 73% of villages, not permitted to enter non-Dalit homes; 70% of villages, Dalits and non-Dalits cannot eat together, 35.8% of Dalits denied entry into village shops.

10. Mahars are Dalits in Maharashtra State in the south-western part of India.
11. The Scheduled Castes represent the victims of untouchability. They were called 'exterior castes' or 'Depressed Classes' before the 1935 Government of India Act. Ambedkar preferred the term 'Untouchables' and Gandhi 'Harijans'; today, 'Scheduled Castes' is widely used in Government official correspondence. Most of the Scheduled Castes have begun to call themselves 'Dalits' which means 'downtrodden or oppressed'.
12. A. Raj, *Children of a Lesser God*, DCLM Publications, 1992, p. 13.
13. VAK Report, 'Grassroots Impact of Globalisation', *Integral Liberation*, September 1997, p. 148.
14. A. Pinto, 'Dalits and Globalisation', *Integral Liberation*, September 1997, pp. 153-154.
15. National Commission for SC and ST, *Annual Report* 1993-94, p. 57.
16. *Eighth Five Year Plan 1992*, p. 420.
17. Forced Dalits labourers to work for landlord.
18. The former Chairperson of the National Commission for Scheduled Castes and Scheduled Tribes.
19. J.M. Razu, *Globalisation and Its Impact on Dalits,* unpublished paper, p. 11.
20. Which is known as local *panchayat.*
21. Mr. Kocher Raman Narayanan, Vice President of India, 21 August 1992 to 24 July 1997; President of India - 25 July 1997 to 25 July 2002.
22. J. Massey, 'Dalits in India: Religion as a Source of Bondage

or Liberation with Special Reference to Christians', *Manohar*, 1995, p. 82.

23. *Census of India 1991-1993*, p. 11.
24. A.M.A. Ayrookuzhiel, 'The Religious Factor in Dalit Liberation', in Beda's and J. Massey (eds.), *Dalit Solidarity*, ISPCK, 1995, p. 128.
25. *Census of India 1961-1991.*
26. *Report of the Ministry of Human Resource Development 1995.*
27. J.F. Balasundaram, *Introducing the Dalits*, unpublished paper, p. 1.
28. D.L.N. Berwa, 'Human Rights – A Dalit Perspective', *Asian Dalit Solidarity*, ISPCK, 2000, p. 53.
29. Report of Sub Group – I on Assessment of Prevailing Situation in respect of Scheduled Castes and Scheduled Tribes for certain Socio-Economic Indicators, prepared and released by the Office of the Registrar General, Census, Government of India in November 2004.
30. *Census of India 1991.*
31. Report of Sub Group – I.
32. Protective discrimination in favour of Scheduled Castes, Scheduled Tribes and Backward Castes.
33. Eighth Five Year Plan 1992, 419. See also India 200. Publications Division, Ministry of Information and Broadcasting. 268.
34. Government of India 1997. *Crime in India 1995*, National Crime Records Bureau, Ministry of Home Affairs, p. 260.
35. D.L.N. Bewra, 'Human Rights – Dalit Perspective', *Asian Dalit Solidarity*, pp. 53–60. And also for detailed information, see 'Dalits Human Rights in Modern India Honourable Chairman and Members of Sub- commission on Human Rights', *Asian Dalit Solidarity*, pp. 44-51.
36. Home Affairs Report, 2007.
37. Presented in Indian Parliament on 16th March 2011 by the Minister for Social Justice Enforcement.
38. 'Crime in India', National Crime Record Bureau, Ministry of Home Affairs, Government of India, New Delhi, 2008.

39. J. Parratt, *A Guide to Doing Theology*, SPCK, London, p. 61.
40. J. Parratt, quoting Marianne Katppo, *Compassionate and Free*, WCC, 1976.
41. G. Omvedt, *Dalit Visions,* Orient Longman Ltd, 1995, p. 83.
42. Quoted by Aruna Gnanadason, 'Dalit Women – The Dalit of the Dalit', in J. Massey (ed.) *Indigenous People: Dalits,* ISPCK, 1994, pp. 167–176.
43. Ibid
44. J. Parratt, *A Guide to Doing Theology*, 1969, p. 61.
45. J. Muthumary, *Dalit Women in India*, unpublished paper, p. 1. (Muthumary is a Dalit woman, working as a Professor at The Centre for Advanced Studies in Botany, University of Madras.)
46. This has been defined as the 'rape of helpless women by men in position of authority' by Rehana Ghadially (ed.), 'Violence', *Women in Indian Society: A Reader*, Sage Publications, 1988, p. 149.
47. S. Abdulali, 'Rape in India: An Empirical Picture', *Women in Indian Society*, pp. 196 - 206. See also: G. Dietrich, *Reflections on the Women's Movement in India: Religion, Ecology, Development*. Horizon India Books, 1992, pp. 73–93; R. Manorama, 'Dalit Women: Downtrodden among the Downtrodden', in J. Massey (ed.), *Indigenous People: Dalits, Dalit Issues in Today's Theological Debate*. ISPCK, 1994, pp. 165–166.
48. J. Massey (ed.), *Indigenous People: Dalits,* ISPCK, 1994.
49. Temple prostitution for sexual pleasure of temple priests.
50. See G. Dietrich, *Reflections on the Women's Movement in India: Religion, Ecology, Development,* 1992.
51. S. Duraisamy, *Christianity in India*, CLS, 1986, p. 3.
52. C.B. Firth, *An Introduction To Indian Church History,* New Delhi, ISPCK, 1998, pp. 58, 110 - 113.
53. S. Duraisamy, *Christianity in India*, CLS, Chennai, 1986, pp.24-27; J. Massey, *Roots of Dalit History, Christianity, Theology and Spirituality*, ISPCK, Delhi, 1996, pp. 54-72.
54. S. Duraisamy, *Christianity in India*, CLS, Chennai, 1986, pp.

24-27; M. Larbeer, 'Dalit Identity-A Theological Reflection', in V. Devasahayam (ed.), *The Frontiers of Dalit Theology.*

55. J.C.B. Webster, 'From Indian church to Indian theology: An attempt at theological construction', in A.P. Nirmal (ed.), *A Reader in Dalit Theology*, Madras, Gurukul, 1992, p. 27.

56. Satish Deshpande and Geetika Bapna, 'Dalits in the Muslim and Christian Communities', a Status Report for Minorities Commission of India, 2008, p. 25.

57. M.R. Arulraja, *Jesus the Dalit,* USA, DCENCCC, 1996, p. 163.

58. S. Lourdusamy, *Towards Empowerment of Dalit Christians*, New Delhi: Centre for Subaltern Studies, 2005.

59. V. Devasahayam, 'Pollution, poverty and powerlessness', in A.P. Nirmal (ed.), *A Reader in Dalit Theology*, pp. 1–4. Also see, J.C.B. Webster, 'From Indian Church to Indian Theology, An attempt at Theological Construction', in A.P. Nirmal (ed.), *A Reader in Dalit Theology*, p. 96.

60. S. Deshpande and G. Bapna, 'Dalits in the Muslim and Christian Communities', a Status Report for Minorities Commission of India, 2008, pp. 7–11.

61. Collected during the Field Study of Rev. Dr. J.Vincent Manoharan in the state of Tamilnadu – Oct 2010 to Jan 2012.

62. M. John, *Dalit Christian Liberation Movement in Dalit Movements in South India*, edited by M. Thangaraj, University of Madras, 2007, p.115.

63. http://www.dalitchristian.com Html/arulappa.htm – Problems and struggles (accessed 8 April 2009).

64. F.C. Thomas, *Multiple Discrimination: Special Characteristics of the Situation of Dalit Christians*, New Delhi, 2009,p.2.

65. Ibid.

66. Vincent Manoharan, *Caste Discrimination Still a Menace in the Indian Church*, unpublished paper, p. 7.

67. Ibid, p. 7.

68. Ibid, pp. 3-4.

69. F.C. Thomas, Multiple Discrimination: Special characteristics of the situation of Dalit Christians,2009, p. 1.
70. M.E. Prabhakar, 'The Search for a Dalit Theology', in A.P. Nirmal (ed.), *A Reader in Dalit Theology*, Gurukul Lutheran Theological College & Research Institute, Madras, 1991, pp. 42–43 See also the report A Research on Dalit Christians in India, by Elze Sietzema-Riemer, submitted to ICCO, 2009, pp. 8–15.
71. A. Raj, 'Disobedience. A Legitimate Act for Dalit Liberation', in N.P. Arvind (ed.), *Towards a Common Dalit Ideology,* Chennai, GLTC, 1990, p. 47.
72. M. Azariah, *Mission in Christ's Way in India Today*, Madras, CSI & CLS, 1989, p. 93.
73. J. Parratt, *A Guide to Doing Theology,* London, SPCK, 1969, p. 66.

CHAPTER 2

Indian Christian Theology

In this chapter an attempt is made to examine certain unique marks of Indian Christian theological thinking during the 19th and 20th centuries with a view to noticing its theological identity.It is not the intention of this book to deal with all the Indian Christian theologians and their theological standpoints which are mostly associated with and developed from Hindu philosophical traditions. Hence a select few Indian Christian theologies are examined and analysed to find out whether this Indian Christian theology is relevant to India's own environment already seen in Chapter One.

Christian theology in India illustrates some of the important insights of reflection on the whole history of Christian thought down the centuries. On the one hand it is the confirmation of the insight that there is no perennial theology, no formulation of any doctrine universally relevant. This insight has been affirmed by several western theologians who have reflected on the meaning and role of theology. John Dillenberger puts it as follows:

> Theology, too, is inextricably immersed in the problem of changing orientations and cultural shifts. That all genuine theological statements contain truth is not thereby denied, but the radical contingency of all theological work is affirmed. Both the statement that cultural shifts cannot be explained, and that the theology is relative to the

> situation, can be interpreted as matters for despair or for hope. Such approaches are psychologically difficult to accept for those who must be sure and a sense of laziness for those who must be assured of certain results. It is a source of hope for those for whom the situational aspects of truth provide multitudinous facets by which truth may be known.[1]

Jaroslav Pelikan discussing the problem of doctrinal change refers to a traditional patristic view that change is something that can happen only to heretical doctrines and says,

> Unfortunately for the simplicity of such a criterion, the closer one studies the various texts, the more evident does change become, with the result that none of the Fathers appear to have been exempt from the inexorable reality of change. By strange but unique irony the dogmatic method of treating the phenomenon of theological change can move with great rapidity into the very relativism it seeks to avoid.[2]

He concludes by saying,

> The continuity of Christians with one another both within a period of history and between periods is neither identical with doctrinal agreement nor separable from it, but it is a function of that unity which the Church finds not in its members but in its lord... There is ecumenicity in time as well as ecumenicity in space and this calls for a doctrine of the unity of the Church that will take up into itself both the fact of theological variety and the fact of doctrinal change.[3]

On the other hand, even while recognising changes and variations in theology, the historic development of theology raises the question of identity and continuity of the faith that theology seeks to understand and interpret. In what sense are the faith and apostolic affirmations about the uniqueness and finality of Jesus Christ normative and unchangeable? The apostolic confession that Jesus of Nazareth is the Christ, the one in and through whom we have the saving knowledge of God is the substance of what theology seeks to interpret. It is the meaning of this confession which has to be brought out in a challenging manner in the formulations made on the context of different social, political cultural and philosophical backgrounds.

Many Indian thinkers have set their minds to the need of expressing and proclaiming the Christian faith in a way that would be intelligible to the Indian people. For this purpose they have not only used the Indian languages, but Indian concepts that were found useful. Indian theologians are indebted to Robin Boyd who attempted to trace the history and development of Indian Christian theology in his book, 'An Introduction to Indian Christian Theology'[4] (1969). Marcus Ward's 'Our Theological Task: An Introduction to the study of Theology in India'[5] is an earlier book (1946) which grapples with the problem of theology in a particular cultural setting and theology in its universal character.The essence of the Christian faith is universal, unchanging and is the same for all people at all times, Ward calls this 'dogma'. The elucidation of it in a particular cultural context may differ from culture to culture, and he calls this 'doctrine'. He draws clearly the distinction between dogma and doctrine. The problem of the universal and particular, the permanent and the changing in religious faith is to be faced. Bultmann also faced this problem in his study of New Testament theology and resorted to resolve it by a process of demythologisation. In the Indian scene Chenchiah sought after the *raw fact of Christ* from which he could raise the edifice of an Indian Christian theology. He realised that until he found the *raw fact of Christ* he could not clothe him with Indian garments.

Chenchiah was not prepared to believe that everything in

India was bad and therefore to be shunned by the Christian convert. A fresh look into the New Testament reveals that its writers have used the Jewish, Hellenistic and Roman concepts to understand and interpret their faith in Jesus Christ, and in witnessing to the Gospel of redemption to the people of Palestine, Asia Minor and Europe. Christianity, of course, began in a Jewish religious and cultural environment with Hebrew and Aramaic vocabulary, and in a background of Semitic hopes and longings.When the Gospel was preached to the people of Greek cultural and philosophical background in Antioch and later in Europe they had to use different vocabulary and concepts and relate it to their religious longings and fulfilment. The problem they faced in witnessing the Gospel to the people of their day and in those lands is the same as those faced by the Indian Christians.How are we to bear witness to the Gospel to the Indian people in their religious, philosophical and cultural environment? How are we to make it intelligible to them? How are we to lead them to worship in a natural way? How are we to develop a Christian style of living which will not isolate the Indian Christian from his countrymen? These are the questions that set in motion a rethinking of the Christian faith in a way that would be understandable to the Indian people, and at the same time true to what God has done in Christ Jesus to all mankind.

Another factor we have to bear in mind is the plurality of religious and cultural traditions in India. There are numerous philosophical systems. Therefore, within India itself, we may expect not one Indian Christian theology, but theologies. Various philosophical systems and religious insights may be allowed to bring out the manifold wisdom of God as revealed in Jesus Christ. In India we are bound to have a plurality of approach. Boyd in his survey of Indian Christian theology has pointed out various strands of Indian thought and life which different Christian theologians have found useful and valuable to understand the wisdom of God in Christ – strands such as the *Advaitic* represented by Brahmabandab Upadhyaya, the Theistic and the *Bhakti* traditions represented by Appasamy and Chakkarai, the mystical by Sadhu Sundar Singh, Aurobindo's concept of the spiritual evolution represented by Chenchiah. Indian Christian theology as it seeks its own identity is bound to be enriched by a plurality of visions.

Some individual Christian thinkers and theologians, however, from time to time, felt the need for effectively relating the gospel message to the soil of India and this resulted in the development of various concepts and theological approaches. Confronted with Indian religions, cultural and philosophical situations many missionaries from the west recognised the need to modify a totally negative approach to other faiths and cultures with which the western Christian mission had started. Earlier they had assumed that it was the theological formulations made in the West which the Indian Church also should accept. It took a long process before the attitude could be effectively challenged and a more dynamic and contextual approach adopted.

In India, this process was pioneered by Roman Catholic Jesuit Robert De Nobili who had worked in India since 1605. He was one of the earliest to raise the question of adopting indigenous forms for expressing the Christian faith.[6]The traditional policy of his mission was that the more Indians discarded their ancestral customs and the closer they adhered to Portuguese ways the better Christians they would be. But De Nobili said it was unjust to require people to change their national customs and give up caste and other forms of social and cultural life. The only way to make Christianity acceptable to caste Hindus was to present it as a universal religion, not as the religion of the *parangis*. He wanted to replace Latin with Sanskrit. He advocated Christian participation in Hindu festivals. His approach, however, was primarily directed to making Christianity look less objectionable in external forms. He made no attempt to modify any part of his theology of his time. He simply rejected the Hindu practice of the repetition of the divine names as a prescription from the Devil and ridiculed the doctrines of *Karma* and rebirth. He hesitated to associate even with the missionaries working among the Dalits, because of his fear that his association would jeopardise his aim to convert the high caste Brahmins.

The first Protestant Missionary, Bartholomew Zieganbalg, who arrived in India in 1706, also shared the prejudices and assumptions of European Christians of that time, and in his meetings with the Brahmins he used terms such as 'you heathens', 'your blindness', 'the bondage of idolatry', 'gross ignorance', ' extremity of madness' etc. Robinson mentioned Zieganbalg in his writing, and according to him, after Zieganbalg's study of Hindu scriptures, his attitudes clearly changed. In 1710 in his unprinted 'Remarkable Voyage', he wrote,

> I do not reject everything they teach, rather rejoice, that for the heathen long ago a small light of the Gospel began to shine. He wanted his reader in Europe to see how far they had come by the light for their reason in the Knowledge of God and of the natural order, and how by their natural powers, they often shame many Christians by their upright life, also showing a much greater striving for the future life.[7]

Such sensitivity to facts did not find much encouragement from the official sponsors of the Missions. What A.H. Franke said conveys the general attitude which the Western Christian Missions have had for a long time. The Missionaries were sent out to exterminate heathenism in India, not to spread heathen nonsense all over Europe.[8] This shows the spirit of confidence not only about the pre-eminence of the Gospel of Jesus Christ but also about the inflexibilityof the doctrines held by them.

The knowledge and interpretation of the Indian religious

scriptures by orientalists like Max Muller, Paul Deussen, A.A. Macdonald, Berridale Keith and others did have an impact on Christian Missionary thinking. But while this started a process of rethinking of the Christian approach to other faiths, few missionary theologians considered it necessary to revise their formulations of the basic Christian doctrines.Even for a scholar like J.N. Farquhar, whose thesis was that the Christ fulfils the unfulfilled longings and aspirations of Hinduism, the positive appraisal of several aspects of Hindu faith and practice was based on the acceptance of the traditional Christian doctrines as the criteria for evaluation. This was true also with several other Missionary theologians in India such as T.E. Slater, Sidney Cave, E.W. Thompson and A.G. Hogg.

J.S. Hayland,[9] writing in the 'Young Men of India' in August 1927 assumed that India did not possess any heritage comparable to what was contributed by Plato and Socrates and that by accepting Christianity, India would also be accepting the Hebrew-Greek-Roman cultural values.

With regard to the caste system, the Western missionaries accepted it as a social reality like the class distinctions in Europe. As a result, they did not do much to eradicate the social inequality based on the caste system. They taught the Christian theology of equality of all men before God but failed to remove the prevailing social inequality.Another reason which restricted the missionaries to fight against casteism was the threat from the high caste Christians. They threatened the missionaries that they may leave the Church if segregation between them and the Dalits was abolished. In such a situation, the missionaries yielded to such pressures and concentrated on the theology of saving souls rather than of social justice and social transformation.[10]

Missionaries' theologies not only shaped Indian theology but also of their western theological patterns in Indian Church's architectural outlook. The missionaries built cross shaped churches where high castes occupied the central part while the

Dalits were assigned to the wings as their place. The Eucharist was distributed to the Dalits only after the participation of the high castes. Sometimes the missionaries used separate cups for the Dalits at the Eucharist celebration. Many a time the Church was washed after the Dalits took part in the worship.[11]Indian Church has been affected by caste discrimination and purity and pollution ideologies even at the Eucharistic table where they supposed to affirm oneness in Christ!

As far as Indian Christian Theology is concerned, it has its own peculiarities. During its formative years Indian Christian theology had received intellectual, philosophical and ideological support and response from many quarters of the theological circle both within the Church and outside the Church. There were many Indian non-Christian intellectuals and thinkers from outside the Church who contributed immensely to the formation and shape of the Indian Christian theology, a few of their contributions are analysed here.

Raja Ram Mohan Roy belonged to the *Brahmo Samaj* movement which stood for a radical reform of Hindu religion and society. He had come under the influence of Western rationalism and Unitarian Christianity. His most significant book *The Precepts of Jesus* is evidence of the appeal the person and the teachings of Jesus had for him and his faith that a moral reform of Hinduism could be brought about by calling people to accept the teachings of Jesus as the moral expression of their faith in one God. The doctrines of the divinity of Christ, the Holy Spirit, Trinity, and Atonement as presented by the missionary theologians of the time, particularly the Serampore trio, appeared to him irrational and he rejected them. At the same time the centrality of place he gave to Jesus' ethical teachings in his movement and his acceptance of the titles like 'Son of God'; the doctrines of the Virgin birth and the resurrection, interpreting them in his own rationalistic manner, is evident of depth of faith which, though far removed from the traditional form, has great theological significance in India.

Keshub Chandra Sen made Jesus Christ even more central to his faith and experience than Ram Mohan Roy had done. His form of the *Brahmo Samaj* was known as the 'Church of the New Dispensation' and much resembled the Christian Church including the rights of initiation and communion. His interpretation of the person and work of Christ and the doctrine of the Trinity also came much closer to orthodox Christian doctrines than that of Ram Mohan Roy. He used the concepts of Logos involved in creation, the evolutionary process and in its final perfection. Even though some of his statements about the work of Christ sounded like the moral influence theories, he also called Jesus Christ the Mediator and spoke of the 'atoning medium'. In an appealing speech he said, 'Behold I am reconciled to all through the blood of him crucified. Fellow countrymen be ye also reconciled through him'. He definitely moved away from Ram Mohan Roy's Unitarian interpretation of the Brahman and expounded a Trinitarian doctrine relating the Trinity to the Indian description of Brahman as *Sachitananda* (*Sat, Chit, Ananda*). For him the confession of God as the Father, Son and the Holy Spirit also implied the whole philosophy of Salvation because it means a God who comes down to humanity and carries it up to heaven.Despite all this he was not regarded as a Christian, nor would he call himself a Christian. This was because the criterion for Christian orthodoxy and membership in the Church had been derived from the formulations of the West and the Church in India, which Keshub Chandra Sen described as denationalizedand had no freedom to reformulate.

Many Indian Christian thinkers have set their minds to meet the need of expressing and proclaiming Christian faith in a way that would be intelligible to the Indians. For this purpose they have not only used the Indian languages, but Indian concepts that they found useful. The need for an Indian interpretation of the Christian faith rose from the fact that

Christian theology in India was dominated by Western formulations and imposed on the Christian Church in India. The Church organisation, Church architecture, liturgies, music etc. followed the western pattern, with the result, that the Church and the Christian community looked like a foreign pocket on Indian soil. An Indian citizen existing as a foreigner in his own native land in thinking and in lifestyle raised naturally, a crisis in identity.

The attempt by Indian theologians to establish an Indian theology/Christology is not entirely a recent effort. In fact, the chain of Indian Christians, who have tried to separate the Christian faith from its Western forms of expression, has not been interrupted since the turn of the century. In the latter part of the 19th century and in the first part of the 20th century, rethinking theology by Indians assumed great significance. Among individual thinkers in India,were for example Brahmabandab Upadhyaya, A.J. Appasamy, Chenchiah and Chakkarai.

While individual Christian thinkers challenged the theological approach of the Missions and Missionaries and called for new approaches, this challenge was intensified in the context of the International Missionary Council meeting at Tambaram, 1938, in India. This time, the challenge came from a lay group called Madras Rethinking Group of which Chenchiah was the exponent. This group published a book entitled 'Rethinking Christianity', as a response to Kraemer's 'The Christian Message in a Non-ChristianWorld'.[12] They challenged the presence of Western theology and stressed the importance of restating Christian faith in Indian terms and Indian religious experiences.

Appasamy and Chakkarai gave the highest place to Scripture as the supreme *pramana*. However, they do not seem to accept the Scripture uncritically or blindly. They seem to search for what the Bible seeks to convey and its concurrence to personal experience. Chenchiah raised the question of the authority of the Old Testament and whether it is necessary for Indian theology. His use of the New Testament was to get at the raw fact of Christ. It is not an uncritical acceptance of Scripture as it is but a seeking to understand God revealing himself in and through the Scripture. Among the *pramanas* of Hindu thinkers, besides experience and Scripture, a place is given for *yukti*. The mind is not passive in understanding either the Scripture or experience. Indian theologians have accepted all the *pramanas* as valid and accept them as sources of theology. Appasamy adds a fourth one namely the Church. He regards the teachings of the Church as a source of theological reflection and gives it second place in his group of four *pramana*s. What he intends is not merely to give uncritical acceptance of the faith as traditionally handed down but to recognise the fact that God reveals himself not only to individuals but also to groups of believers. Thus we see the acceptance of four *pramanas*, not independently and exclusively but interdependent of each other, as a source of Indian Christian theology.

Theology certainly and basically includes a belief in God. In Indian Christian theology there has emerged a concept of God which reconciles certain contrasting views of Brahman. In Hindu religious thinking there are terms such as *Brahman* and *Isvara*. The one is absolute, impersonal or suprapersonal; the other is personal and inferior. In the context of absolute monistic thinking the personal aspect is subordinate and is only symbolical and hence unreal. There are terms such as *nirguna* (no-wish and no-character) as applied to the absolute and *saguna* (all wish and character) as applied to *Isvara*. The absolute Brahman is unknown and unknowable and at the same time there is God who is known and worshipped: the *Avyakat* (ignorance), and the *Vykta* (knowledge). Brahmabandhab is at pains to clasp these two apparently different views into a meaningful understanding of the One Brahman, as absolutely personal, as *nirguna-saguna*, the one who is both hidden and revealed. Appasamy holds that there are ranges in God which we cannot see but God has revealed Himself sufficiently and adequately in Jesus Christ for the redemption and liberation of man and society. What we see in Jesus is the guarantee of what lies beyond. This comprehensive view ofBrahman satisfies and answers the deep quest of man for intellectual understanding and spiritual satisfaction.

The doctrine of the Trinity has been very difficult to understand for the Indian minds of non-Christians and to the Christians as well. Brahmabandhab Upadhyaya has taken the concept of *sachitananada* and found in it a useful framework to understand and expound the being of God as a Trinity. Western exposition of Trinity as 'Three persons in One' has often imperilled the unity of godhead. In any case the Greek and Latin expressions used to explain Trinity and which have found their way into the creeds have no relevance to the Indian mind. Upadhyaya, in using the Indian concept of *sachitananda*, preserved the unity of God and raised it to the highest level of that which is absolutely personal.

Indian Christian theologians seem to develop Christology in terms of *Chit* (logos) of *sachitananda.* This is clearly seen in Brahmabandhab, *Chit* as the word by whose *sakti* (power) the world was created from *Sat* (nothingness). This is a point of view reminiscent of Johannine logos Christology. Chakkarai however, prefers to use the word *avatara* (incarnation), while safeguarding the reality and uniqueness of Christ.The relation between Christ and God is a crucial issue, whether the relation is a metaphysical one, or only a moral one (identity of will and purpose). Appasamy is inclined to accept the latter. Indian Christology has to grapple with this problem and perhaps the solution has to be sought along the lines of the *satchitananda* doctrine.

Closely related to the above is the issue of unity of the personhood of Jesus. Western theology has sought to explain it in terms of the two-nature doctrine, which raises more problems than it seeks to solve. The concept of *purushatva* (personality) as expounded by Devanandan may give us some insights to our understanding of the God-man. When developed this may be another point of identity in Indian Christology. The historicity of Jesus Christ has been a problem in the Indian context. In Indian systems of thought, history is not so important. Principle is of more value than the person. The Indian Christian theologians have stressed the reality and history of the Incarnation. Docetic tendencies have been resisted and the real humanity of Jesus has been stressed.

Chakkarai considers the humanity of Jesus as permanent. According to him the Logos having become man in Christ, remains as God-man for ever. He considers this permanent humanity as dynamic, working in the world of today. This thought is further explored in terms of its implication to the socio-political struggles of Indian people.

Chenchiah, influenced by the evolutionary concept of Sri.Aurobindo, considers the fact of Christ as a new emergence in the order of creation. In this emergence, he sees unity of the person of the God-man. To quote him, 'The fact of Christ is the birth of a new order in creation. It is the emergence of life, not bound by *Karma* of man, not tainted by sin, not humbled by death, of man triumphant, glorious, partaking of the immortal nature of God, of a new race in creation, Sons of God'.[13] Indian Christian theology interprets Jesus as god-man, permanently and dynamically human. But none of these Christologies are relevant to the situation of the Dalits, who, like all oppressed groups engaged in liberation theology, need to understand Christ in terms relative to their experiences of oppression.

In dealing with Christ's work in traditional doctrines of atonement, the Cross has been central. All the traditional theories of atonement have dealt with what Christ did on the cross, in terms of sacrifice, satisfaction, penal substitution etc. The Indian Christian theologians, however, have been inclined to look at the whole fact of Christ, the whole Christ event as redemptive – the incarnation, life, death and resurrection. For Chenchiah the birth of Jesus was more important than the death of Christ. According to him, redemption is effected not by the death of Christ but by the larger life. 'Salvation is not sinlessness but lifefulness'. Christification,[14] or reproducing Christ in one's life is salvation. According to him 'true evangelism consists in reproducing Jesus. By rejecting the juridical interpretations of atonement, Chenchiah brings out: Christ saves us in what He is; Faith-union with Christ is the essential basis of Christian Life; and Salvation is regarded positively as lifefulness rather than sinlessness. Chenchiah's emphasis on the raw fact of Christ, particularly the birth, the resurrection and Pentecost, needs to be supplemented by Chakkarai's *darsana* (vision) of the Cross. The Cross marks the place where sinful human beings meet God. According to him the Cross in some mysterious way opens a channel in the heart of man by which the divine *sakti* (Power) flows into man and renews him. The sufferings of Christ turn into an active energy for spiritual restoration.

This group of theologians challenged the presence of Western theology and stressed the importance of resting Christian faith in Indian categories, liberating Christian doctrines from the language of Greek philosophy and the categories of Western thought and culture. They tried to liberate Indian Christian theology from being captive to Western theology but unfortunately they used Indian Hindu Brahminical – philosophical methodology in their theological articulation.

There were three more theologians whose writings lay down patterns or templates for an Indian Christian Theology. We are going to use these three ecumenical Indian Christian theologians: Panikkar, Samaratha and Thomas to indicate the gradual trend from a metaphysical understanding to a secular or social consciousness within present-day Indian Theology.In the 1950s, after the Second World War, countries in Asia attained national liberation and with this change, the Mission–Church relationship also changed. The Mission became a task of the Christian Church in India. In this context, Christianity was still seen as a foreign religion and a much more powerful challenge was posed by Indian religions and cultures. In the face of such a serious challenge, the Church in India realised that its mission has to account for, on the one hand, the faith once given for all received through the different theological formulations of the past and on the other, the discernment of the reality of Christ on the different frontiers of the church's mission. The Church's evangelistic and missionary task on the frontier, where meeting with the people of other living faiths was unavoidable, meant not only carrying the reality of Christ to the people of other faiths but also being witness to the reality of the Gospel of Christ in the frontier situation or even in the other faiths. This realisation gave birth to another approach called the Dialogue approach. A significant contribution in this direction came from two important Indian theologians namely, P.D. Devanandan[15] and Raymond Pannikar.

In 1964, the 'Unknown Christ of Hinduism' appeared by the Roman Catholic Raymond Panikkar, who is a philosopher of religions.[16] 'The Acknowledged Christ of the Indian Renaissance' by M.M. Thomas appeared in English in the year 1969[17]. 'The Hindu Response to the Unbound Christ' by Stanley J. Samartha, was published in 1970.[18] The Unknown Christ, The Unbound Christ, The Acknowledged Christ, three times the name of Christ is connected with participial adjectives. He is unknown in Hinduism, or better unrecognised, although, one may add that His presence cannot really be overlooked. Only the blind spot has to be found, that point discovered, at which Christian Faith and Hindu philosophy meet. He is universal or unbound: even as the Hindu can hardly avoid being aware of His presence, also the Hindu has to come to terms with Him. He is acknowledged. It is a recognised fact that the reformation in Hinduism owes a large debt to the Person of Christ.

A Roman Catholic theologian, born to a Hindu father and a Spanish Roman Catholic mother, Raymond Panikkar was brought up in close acquaintance with both Hinduism and Christianity. He shares the fruit of his theological reflection in several of his writings, particularly in two of his books, the 'Unknown Christ of Hinduism' and 'The Trinity and World Religions'.Both these books combine the technical terminology of Thomistic Philosophy and Vedanta. In a spirit of genuine dialogue he seeks to understand Hinduism from within and come to the conclusion that Christ is already present in Hinduism, though he is not known as Christ. He says that:

> Christ has not unveiled his whole face, has not yet completed his mission there. He still has to grow up to be recognised. Moreover, he still has to be crucified there, dying with Hinduism as he died with Judaism and with the Hellenistic religions in order to rise again, as the same Christ (who is already in Hinduism) but then as a risen Hinduism, as Christianity.[19]

Similarly in his book 'The Trinity and World Religions', which he describes as a meditation rather than erudite study, he expounds the three traditional *margas* of Hinduism, namely the *Karma marga*, the *Bhakti marga*, and *Janana marga* as being related to the three persons of the Trinity, the Father, the Son and the Holy Spirit. He describes the synthesis of these *margas* as a theAndric synthesis which according to him helps both a deepening of the understanding of the Trinitarian Christian faith and recognition of the possibility of such a synthesis in other faiths though the key to the fullness of revelation of the Trinity is Christ.

In the methods of dialogue implied in Panikkar's writings the emphasis is on the common ground of the interiority of the religious experience. Such recognition of the reality of the presence of Christ is certainly an important and legitimate starting point for dialogue. However, for the dialogue approach to be truly faithful to the mission of Jesus Christ it cannot be exclusively limited to the sphere of interiority of religious experience. Personal as well as corporate religious experience has to be related to the total human experience, including the social and political struggles of the human community. Panikkar is deeply concerned with the quality of the 'and' in the relationship between Hinduism 'and' Christianity. From the Christian point of view, it has to be maintained that Christ is the Universal Redeemer and that there is no redemption apart from Him.

In Samartha's 'The Hindu Response to the Unbound Christ' Samartha considers the precondition for a theology/Christology in India with reference to the present situation: 'What does it mean to confess Jesus Christ as Lord and Saviour in the India of today?' and in what way does our own time ask for a new and useful Christology?[20] It is significant that Samartha chooses to adopt the thought-forms of the *Advaita* in its classical and modern interpretations, even though some work has already been done towards an interpretation of Christ through *Bhakti* tradition. The fact that both Hindu and Christian thinkers prefer the *Vedanta* tradition is particularly significant. While it is quite possible in India to have several theologies/Christologies existing side by side, it appears however, that with regard to Hinduism, a Christology using the *Advaita* concept would be more important for many Indian Christian theologians.[21]

'Indian Christian theology in the context of Nation Building' is how M.M. Thomas defines his theological approach to our time. Theology is thus 'cited' as the attempt to describe what kind of a contribution the group of Christians in a particular situation and at a particular period in history by reason of their faith can offer. 'The Christian nationalists explore the meaning and relevance of Jesus Christ in relation to the national awakening to new life.'[22] Thomas stresses that in contrast to an individualistic-spiritual understanding of the gospel, its message is rather that of reconciling relationships, of restoring the relationship to God and of men among each other with the result that human society is given a new quality.

The Christian representatives among the Indian Nationalists saw the Church and Society from this point of view.Just those 'Christian values', which have made their impact through western Liberal Humanism or through Christian religion on Indian social life and its religious foundations are precisely the values associated with the idea of *koinonia* or fellowship in which men are reborn in Christ.[23]

This way of understanding the Gospel has proved itself in the attitude of Indian Christians concerning the great problem of caste and Thomas gives an exciting glimpse into the controversy which took place concerning this question. Already mentioned in an earlier part of this chapter, the Roman Catholic missionary to India, Roberto de Nobili, permitted the caste-system to be continued within the Christian Church on the basis that the Church belongs to a higher order than society, whereas the classical Protestant missionary view considered the caste-system as the greatest evil in India, from which the convert had to be saved. The reverse side of a history of conversions, which wanted to wipe out even the cultural heritage of the past, has been that a refuge was offered to the convert, which took its pattern from the Western way of life.In other words, the protagonists of the integration of the Church into the caste-system, like for example, Brahmobandab Upadhyaya at the beginning of the 20th century, and Manilal Parek in the middle of the 20th century, were particularly sensitive to the missionary way which resulted in a near fusion of the Christian faith and Western culture.

They were afraid that by this a disservice was being done to the cause of Christ in India. Their aim was to establish in principle the right atmosphere for the Christian religion to combine with any other culture just as it had done with the Europeans. In spite of the legitimacy of the demand that India should be left to find her own way of dealing with the challenge of Christ, M.M.Thomas's strong criticism of their attitudes is that they are not doing it any better than the West, and even make the same mistake by misunderstanding the Christian Faith to bea transcendental crowning of a 'sacerdotal hierarchy,' thus denying its socio-critical reference, instead of drawing the socio-ethical consequences of the Gospel in such a way that the *Agape*-Ethic of the New Testament can change the cultural norms. Thomas' reproach, that this would empty the Gospel of its socio-ethical content, is right.

Manilal Parek's theology which says that, 'an inward belief in Christ should be sufficient and such outward acts as those of Baptism and Holy Communion should not be required of Christians'[24] is strongly opposed by other Indian Christians like S.K. Datta, S.K. Rudra, K.T. Paul and V.S. Azariah. For them the Church of the New Testament is just that fellowship, in which the barriers of caste and race are overcome. Further, a situation in which Christians of a higher caste refuse to receive communion together with the outcaste, becomes an unbearable one. The Indian church is not only in danger of taking over the Western division of the Church but even to multiply these by a number of other divisions. The Christian nationalists see here the double danger for the equality and dignity of humankind, as well as for the idea of national unity.

At a point which concerns the concrete living together or not living together of countless Indians, the question is asked what contribution the Christian could make towards the special consciousness of a radically changing country. The qualified minority of the Church is expected to produce models of community living which might effect a change of consciousness in those living around them. Therefore, our thinking about the question of how Christ could become indigenous in India does not move in the other-worldly areas of metaphysical theology but in tracking down and finding out the social consequences of the Incarnation.

One can, as S.K. Rudra does, join in the longing of the Hindu for the true, the eternal, the unchangeable and speak of God as the absolute *Brahman* (God) without attribute – *Nirguna*

Brahman – who then *SagunaBrahman*, as *Brahman* in relation, enters into a relationship with the world, making himself known to the world as the *Logos*, Christ. Man achieves then his destiny by union with Christ, Christ the Word made Flesh, by what is called abiding in Christ. What then does our abiding in Him and His abiding in us mean concretely? 'Organised forces are thus set into operation making for solidarity, the Christ-life within the individual linking him to all humanity and creating organic forms, corporate bodies, inspired with a single spirit and life. The organic forms are charged with vital resistance to evil in every shape and are penetrated with living energies of goodness. In this way, an ever increasing and widening social progress in all directions becomes the direct issue of the union of the individual with God in Christ. When at last humanity has found its centre in Christ, the Son, a fully organised human society embracing the entire world in one common brotherhood will be both possible and practicable'.[25]

Although this concept of the living organism may strike us as somewhat romantic nowadays, it should be noted that the seed of a political theology is to be found in this approach already formulated before the First World War. Rudra points out that Christology must start 'right from the bottom', so that it may be possible to describe the mystery and the majesty of God not as the Unknowable, not as Power or the Unattainable, but as the Love which overcomes death.[26] Surely, this is a theology, which is aware of the minority situation of the Church in quite a modern way, which has understood that the condition of life, its context of reality, has to be seen in the sign of the Cross.

One could of course object and say that this is no different from what the Neo-*Vedantins*[27]used to do: they interpreted the Hindu scriptures ideologically, in order to establish from them the necessity of the unity of India. Similarly, the Bible is being used here in order to establish for Indian Christians the need to engage themselves in the new social processes of the National

Independence Movement. This should, however, not be mistaken, for this is no inept attempt at being just friendly with all; on the contrary, it should be noted how critical of the Churches this position must have appeared to the Christian congregation of different denominations, who were themselves caught in this spirit of narrow groupism. In any case, such a theology would be a better way for action than those apologetic attempts, which offer to a Hinduism awakened to a new self-awareness and identity.The theology of the Christian Nationalists simply preferred a living ethos born out of faith to the formulation of the credo out of faith. It is exactly this one-sided accent on ethics over dogma, which shows the courage to be heretical which M.M. Thomas considers essential, if theology on the frontier of the life of society is to be relevant.[28]

This tendency, which was analysed by Thomas, found its clearest expression in a vision of C.F. Andrews the friend of Gandhi. Andrews described his vision as follows: 'One morning about noonday while I was thinking of these things, lying on a chair on the veranda, I saw in front of me the face of a man in a vision. I was not sleeping; my eyes were quite open. It was that poor runaway coolie I had seen in Natal. As I was looking, the face seemed to change in front of me and appeared as the face of Jesus Christ. He seemed to look into my face for a long time and then the vision faded away.[29]

Anyone who sees in this Christology for India, a Christology of the Son of Man, who suffers in every shameful treatment of even the least of his brothers, the capitulation of faith to an ethic of a self-sufficient humanism, should then understand that for Andrews, Christ has become not less central, but more universal, not less divine, but more so, because more universally human, as the pattern of all that is best in Asia as well as in Europe.[30]Having found the point where the biblical understanding of Christ and the Indian situation coincide, the difference between a metaphysical consciousness and a Christology arising out of a social consciousness becomes very clear. It becomes, therefore, the unavoidable task of a Christology for India to analyse the conflicting situation between the secular forces urging on the processes of social change on the one hand and the religious forces blocking this consciousness on the other hand; to uncover harmonising tendencies, like those determining Samartha's approach and to disallow such trends as we find in Panikkar, that is the exclusion of the social consciousness. Somehow no theology seems to manage without looking for a partner to form an alliance. It is still the temptation of theology to choose for her partner simply that which is religion, but this is no longer possible. If this temptation could be renounced, it would also do away with the uneasy feeling that a partner has been asked to join in a dialogue, without his having indicated any wish to do so.[31]

Thomas enquires about the role which a particular pattern of understanding would play in the situation, to which the Gospel is supposed to be taken. Without making it explicit, he nevertheless raises the question whether an Indian philosophy and religion are able to give the necessary pre-understanding for the gospel. The fact that he does not explicitly put the question emphasises the much more important concern the tremendous significance for the future of theology of patterns of secular humanism which have become worldwide in our generation through the development of science and the impact of technology and ideas of social justic

It has been argued by many contemporary theologians that the process of secularisation and the secular human patterns of understanding existence, are in themselves the product of the ferment of the Gospel working on the mythical and metaphysical patterns, transforming them. If this is true, then Bonhoeffer's idea of the Church speaking of God and Christ in a 'secular fashion' and the theologies of 'Secular Christianity' have a new universality and relevance.According to M.M. Thomas, 'we are only at the beginning of building up a theology with the secular mind of our time. Perhaps even here, perhaps here more than elsewhere, it is necessary to emphasis the additional character of understanding in faith.'[32] 'The living theology' for which Thomas proposes the criterion of contextualism, realisation through Laity and the courage to stand with one-sidedness on the frontier of dialogue with the world, can only happen if the practising Church frees herself from her deeper dependence on Western theology, so far still a bourgeois scholarship, and at the same time frees herself from the strong pull of Indian metaphysics.

However, Indian Christian theology has failed to heed the life situation of the Dalits. It failed to take into account the sufferings, aspirations and hopes of the Dalits who are the main body in the Indian Church. The age-old cry of the Dalits was not at all taken into consideration in the shaping of Indian Christian theology. In short, Indian Christian theology neither recognised the sufferings and struggles of the Dalits nor regarded their history and heritage as having any theological significance. On the contrary, Indian Christian theology was philosophical in its thinking and was concerned with the vertical dimension of God and man and the doctrines related with it.

The roots of the current Indian Christian theology lie in the experiences of converts of this century and the last century, predominantly from the upper strata of Indian society.For example: Upadhyaya, from a Bengali Brahmin family; Sadhu Sundar Singh, from a high caste, welloff Sikh Punjabi family; Nehemiah Gore, a Marathi Brahmin; H.A. Krishna Pillai, a high caste *vaishnavite*non-Brah*min,* Narayana Vaman Tilak; P. Chenchiah, son of a well-known upper caste lawyer from Andhra; V. Chakkarai from the *Chetty* caste[33]; a non-Brahmin upper caste in Tamilnadu; and so on.[34]

They aimed to interpret the Christian precepts in line with the Hindu philosophy which was familiar to them because they found it as the most adequate medium for the propagation of the Christian gospel. These thinkers and their experiences and search were very different from those of an average Christian in India because all of them came from either a high caste or their families were rich. So, after they became Christians, their immediate concerns were not the same as thousands of those who became Christians who were both poor and belonged to the lower strata of Indian society. These high caste converts' immediate concern was how they should relate or interpret their new faith or experiences in Indian thought forms, i.e. based on the Brahminic religion and culture in which they had grown up. Their major pre-occupation was searching for an indigenous expression of Christianity, which forms an important element in Indian Christian theology.

Indian Christian theology did not address itself to or reflect the issues which the majority of Christians faced either before or after they became Christians especially the Dalits. The current Indian Christian theologies have failed to apply the gospel to the situation of the down-trodden, and continue to ignore these issues, because their understanding and experience were quite different from that of the Dalits. They incorporated the Brahminic philosophy in which they were brought up but failed to identify the reality of the Dalits.Here, it is not proposed to reject these known Brahminic expressions of theologies including the current Indian Christian theology or their usefulness.According to M.M. Thomas, 'Living theology is the manner in which a church confesses its faith and establishes its historical existence in dialogue with its own environment', 'Indian Christian theology' is not really relevant to its own environment i.e. the living situations of the majority of the people. Hence it was arguably felt byDalit theologians that there is a need to work out another expression of Indian Christian theology which would be relevant to the living situation of the vast majority of people especially of the Dalits.

Endnotes

1. J. Dillenberger, *Contours of Faith-Changing Forms of Christian Thought,* Abingdon Press, Nashville, 1969, p. 22.
2. J. Pelikan, *Historical Theology– Continuity and Change in Christian Doctrine,* Hutchinson, 1971, p. 26.
3. Ibid, p. 161.
4. R. Boyd, *An Introduction to Indian Christian Theology,* CLS, Madras, 1969.
5. M.A. Ward, *Our Theological Task: An Introduction to the Study of Theology in India,* CLS, Madras, 1946.
6. J.L. Miranda, *The Introduction of Christianity into the Heart of India: Father Robert De Nobili's Mission,* Trichinopoly, 1923, p. 22.
7. S. Robinson, *Early Protestant Missionaries in India,* unpublished paper, presented at a colloquium on Indian Missions held at Southern Asia Christian College, Madras, 1997, p. 4.
8. Ibid, p. 5.
9. Known to be a very sympathetic missionary to India and Indian culture.
10. T. Aruldoss, *Dalit Theology,* Sivakasi, Alfa Technic Prints, 1998, pp. 15–16.
11. Ibid, p.16.
12. H. Kraemer, *The Christian Message in a non-Christian World,* Edinburgh House Press, London, 1938.
13. A. Sudarisanam (ed.), *Rethinking Christianity*, CLS Press, Madras, 1938, p. 166.
14. This word is coined and used by an Indian Christian theologian Revd. V.P. Thomas in his writings.
15. P.D. Devanandan, *The Gospel and the Hindu Intellectual*, CISRS, 1959; *Christian Concern in Hinduism*, SCM, 1959; *Preparation for Dialogue*, CISRS, 1964.
16. R. Panikkar, *The Unknown Christ of Hinduism*,Darton, Longman & Todd, 1964.

17. M.M. Thomas, *The Acknowledged Christ of the Indian Renaissance*, CISRS/CLS, Madras & Bangalore, 1969.
18. S.J. Samartha, *The Hindu Response to Unbound Christ*, CLS, Madras for CISRS, Bangalore, 1974.
19. R. Panikkar, *The Unknown Christ of Hinduism*, p. 17.
20. J.S. Samartha, *The Hindu Response to the Unbound Christ*, CLS, Madras, 1974, p. 146.
21. Ibid.
22. M.M. Thomas, *The Acknowledged Christ of Indian Renaissance*, p. 270. Here the English term 'Nationalist' does not carry the negative meaning which the word has in Europe nowadays.
23. Ibid, p. 260.
24. Ibid,p. 266.
25. Ibid,p. 273.
26. Ibid,p. 274.
27. The modern followers of Vedanta teaching.
28. M.M. Thomas, *The Acknowledged Christ of Indian Renaissance*, p. 275, 280ff.
29. Ibid, p. 279.
30. Ibid.
31. C.M. Rogers, 'Hindu-Christian Dialogue Postponed',*Dialogue between Men of Living Faiths*,WCC Publications, 1971, 21ff.
32. M.M. Thomas, *The Acknowledged Christ of Indian Renaissance*, p. 313.
33. Business community from Vysa caste.
34. J. Massey, 'Ingredients for a Dalit Theology', in James Massey (ed.), *Indigenous People: Dalits,* ISPCK, Delhi, 1994, p. 339.

CHAPTER 3

The Influence of Modern Theological Thoughts and Dalit Theology

During the twenty years between1948–1968[1] the world at large underwent major changes. After the Second World War the USA became powerful and richer. The decolonisation process began around 1945; countries in Asia headed towards national independence and attempted the 'nation-building' process. The newly independent non-aligned countries sought regional or Third World status[2] and this began with the Bandung Conference in 1955.[3] The Cold War and arms race heightened tensions between the First and Second Worlds, their confrontation most often taking place in the Third World. More than 60% of nuclear testing was done in the Pacific. During this period remarkable things began to take place in the Third World. This is demonstrated in the following paragraphs:

In the 1960s the global situation became serious and the world set the agenda for Churches.[4] The hopes raised by the election of the young John F. Kennedy as President of the United States in 1961 were dashed by his assassination two years later. The Berlin wall was built. The free speech movement broke out at Berkeley. Students and factory workers took to the street barricades in Paris. Cultural revolution was proclaimed by violent young Red Armies in China, while North American society became bitterly divided over civil rights and the Vietnam war, and tens of thousands of disillusioned young people dropped out in communes, loosely connected with which was 'the Jesus movement'. Militarism became a way of life in Africa and Brazil.

Technological development reached, so to say, its height with its blessings and dangers in the West. The need for accelerated development in the Third World – Asia, Africa and Latin America – and for fundamental changes in the relationships between those countries and the advanced industrial nations became more urgent. In summary, it was a period of conflicts. There was general prosperity in the West at the expense of the Third World countries on one hand and struggles for development and survival of the Third World on the other. There was confusion also in the churches. Bishop John Robinson's confrontational book *Honest to God* was published in 1963. Liberation theologies began to spread from Latin America throughout the world; the charismatic movement grew in strength and stature. In such a situation, churches had to rethink more and more their role and this process led the World Council of Churches,[5] the Roman Catholic Church and also the Evangelicals to come out with clear theological perspectives on social issues.

Challenged by the Cold War's hard ideological conflict between liberalism and communism and the agenda presented by the world at large, the World Council of Churches had to deal with questions of Church and Society. Although this process began much earlier,[6] in the years after World War II, the process deepened.The WCC came into existence in 1948 with its Assembly in Amsterdam. Since then, the WCC has contributed greatly to the development of ecumenical social thinking and sought to keep abreast of social questions. At Amsterdam it came out with a definition of *Responsible Society*.[7]In 1952, the world missionary movement faced a crisis. Missionaries had been expelled from that 'jewel' of missions – China.Facing squarely the 'contagion and power of rival and revolutionary faiths', the delegates to the Willingen Conference of the International Missionary Council renewed their confidence in the providence of God. They also identified as issues for further study the relationship of the church and the significance of eschatology for mission and the relation of the mission to the Reign of God.[8]

In The Evanston Assembly new lines of study were opened up, especially in relation to the social questions which the Church was confronting in Asia, Africa and Latin America. Thus, the concept of *Responsible Society* was replaced by the notion of *Rapid Social Change*.[9]Evanston paved the way for the creation of the department of 'Church and Society' in 1955.[10] So its central theme became: *The Common Christian Responsibility towards Areas of Rapid Social Change.* This work kept the Church and Society department busy in the 1950s but in the 1960s it became evident to the WCC that the problems of the developing countries could not be solved unless the structure of the world's economic order was radically changed.[11]

The Third General Assembly of the WCC was held in 1961 at New Delhi, where the International Missionary Council was integrated with the WCC. The theme of the New Delhi Assembly was *Jesus Christ, the Light of the World*, which dealt with the social involvement of the Christian church. This New Delhi Assembly gave an impetus to the social involvement of Christian churches in India. M.M.Thomas[12] had been invited to the New Delhi Assembly of WCC to give a talk on 'The Challenge to the Churches in the New Nations of Africa and Asia'.[13] M. M. Thomas later quoted Kathleen Bliss's statement about the WCC New Delhi Assembly, that:

> The message of New Delhi was intended to talk to local congregations not about their domestic life but about their conversation with the world around them. It pointed to the historical-theological fact that the collapse of the centrality of the West had led, not to disintegration of the church but to its renewal and to new dimensions of the Christian

> witness, not to the paralysis of humanity but to the opening of new possibilities for it.[14]

The Central Committee elected at New Delhi appointed M.M.Thomas to be the Chairperson of the Working Committee of the department of Church and Society in the WCC.[15] After the WCC's Assembly in New Delhi, it became apparent that further progress in ecumenical social thought required a world-wide conference on Church and Society and the Central Committee meeting in Paris in 1962 approved the proposal for such a meeting and authorised the department of Church and Society to begin preparations for it. This conference became a landmark in the social theological thought partly represented by the WCC.

The WCC – sponsored World Conference on Church and Society was held at Geneva from 12 to 26 July 1966. The Conference theme was Christians in the Technical and Social Revolutions of our Time'.[16] Four hundred and twenty participants took part in the conference, representing 80 nations and 164 churches.[17] The majority were men: professionals, economists, political leaders, social workers, businessmen, social and physical scientists; the rest were theologians and church leaders; and almost half were from Asia, Africa and Latin America.[18] M.M.Thomas was the Chairperson of both the planning committee and of the conference.[19] The Geneva conference was different from all previous ecumenical conferences in the sense that churches of Asia, Africa and Latin America that belonged to the WCC were represented to an extent that was out of proportion to the size of the churches of those continents. This helped enlarge the ecumenical dialogue.

The purpose of the conference was to examine 'the accelerating technological developments of our time, the liberation of peoples from diverse kinds of dominance collectively with their new potential of fuller life, the growing division between the rich and the poor countries, the conflicting interests and consequent power struggles of the nations in an increasingly independent world'.[20] The widening gap between the rich and poor nations pervaded the debate of the whole conference. A revolutionary proposal involving the displacing of those in power by illegal and probably violent means was voiced. Third World delegates recommended the rejection of structures of the global economy and colonialism. The conference concluded thus:

> The Church as a body must speak to society on behalf of the oppressed... It demands identification with the oppressed... It should restore the dignity of the oppressed... the alleviation of human suffering and achievement of the abundant life for all have a primary claim on Christian bodies. This must include energetic work towards the elimination of social causes of suffering as well as care for the victims of injustice and misfortune... Corporate ecumenical planning and action are desirable in attacking the problems of suffering and injustice... If the Christian community wishes to live out its faith in the worldwide community, it must put its weight on the side of the oppressed.[21]

Thus, the World Conference on Church and Society gave to the WCC a clear track into the future and helped strengthen the emergence of a theology in favour of the oppressed and the poor.[22]

The concept of *Missio Dei* was developed during the 1960s. Johannes Christian Hoekendijk[23] is often appreciated as an influential figure behind the so-called worldly theology that was the trend in the ecumenical movement of the 1960s. He was very much attached to the campaign against *ecclesio*centrism, longed to embrace the secular world as the arena of God's action and insisted on a desacralised mission in which 'shalom' rather than 'church' was the key word. At the 1960 conference of the World Student Christian Federation in Strasbourg, Hoekendijk urged participants to desacralise the church and to recognise that Christianity is a secular movement; the evangelical participants called these ideas 'extravagant nonsense'.[24]

Bert Hoedemaker indicates that 'Mission' came to mean for Hoekendijk the vicarious existence of the whole people of God for the whole world, presence and service wherever thedivine initiative, with regard to the world, manifests itself in history and witnesses as a postscript to the 'self-evident' movement of the message toward the poor.[25]There are three important documents, which gave a clear concept of *Missio Dei*. First was 'The Confession of 1967', made by the United Presbyterian Church in the United States of America. It emphasised that in Jesus Christ, God was reconciling the world to Himself,[26] and that Jesus' suffering made the church sensitive to all the sufferings of humankind so that it could see the face of Christ in the faces of men and women in every kind of need.[27] It also said that the fact that Jesus Christ reconciled humanity to God made it plain that enslaving poverty in a world of opulence is an intolerable violation of God's good creation. Because Jesus was in solidarity with the needy and exploited by identifying Himself with them, the cause of the world's poor is the cause of His disciples.... A church which is unconcerned with poverty, or avoids responsibility in economic affairs, or is partial to one social class only, or respects gratitude for its beneficence makes a mockery of reconciliation and offers no acceptable worship to God.[28]

The second document drafted by the Uppsala Assembly of the WCC (1968), under the theological influence of Dietrich Bonhoeffer and secular theology, encouraged the church to engage in revolutionary activity for the betterment of human society and to seek its unity through solidarity with those struggling for equality (Uppsala, sec. II).[29]J.C. Hoekendijk laid strong emphasis on God's work in the world and gave what some have viewed as missiologically radical views on *Missio Dei* as used by Karl Hartenstein at Willingen in 1952.[30]The idea of God's activity in the world and its structures independent of the Church[31] and the de-sacralising of mission, including its de-clericalising, became part of a stream of changing attitudes which converged at the Uppsala meeting of the WCC in 1968.[32]

Thirdly, 'Salvation and Social Justice', the report of Section II of the Bangkok Conference of the WCC (1973), defines the Mission of God as follows:

> As evil works both in personal life and in exploitative social structures, which humiliate humankind, so God's justice manifests itself both in the justification of the sinner and in social and political justice.... Therefore, we see the struggles for economic justice, political freedom and cultural renewal as elements in the total liberation of the world through the mission of God.... This comprehensive notion of salvation demands of the whole of the people of God a matching comprehensive approach to their participation in salvation.[33]

Thus, the report says,

> Without the salvation of the churches from their captivity in the interests of dominating classes, races and nations, there can be no saving church. Without liberation of the churches and Christians from their complicity with structural injustice and violence, there can be no liberating church for mankind.[34]

At this juncture it is explained what it is to be involved in God's mission in today's world with special reference to Asian realities, Dhyanachand Carr argues that:

> To be involved in God's Mission can be simply described as a wholehearted effort to be continuously in partnership with God to translate the prayer 'Thy Kingdom come and thy will be done

> on earth...' into action with empowerment from God. This will further mean to live in Christ with people, especially the suffering and struggling people of Asia. For our witness through words needs to be evidenced through our life.[35]

The Roman Catholic Church could not ignore the agenda presented by the world. Its response came specifically in its option for the poor and the oppressed.[36]

The first Pontifical social document, which deals with the problems of the working class, is the encyclical Rerum Novarum of Pope Leo XIII written in 1891 in the face of the onslaught of socialist ideas. Until the election of Pope John XXIII, the Roman Catholic Church by and large remained closed to the world and its problems. But the arrival of Pope John XXIII to his Papal throne in 1958 signified the beginning of a new era for the Roman Catholic Church. In calling for Vatican Council II, he inaugurated a new approach to social problems that depended on a new methodology.[37] He began to speak of the need to discern the signs of the times. Vatican II was inaugurated on 12 October 1962.[38] On the basis of his famous encyclicalsMater et Magistra and Pacem in Terris, Vatican Council II produced documents which emphasised the social involvement of the Christian church for the welfare of the oppressed peoples: Great numbers of people are acutely conscious of being deprived of the world's goods through injustice and unfair distribution and are vehemently demanding their share of them.[39]

The Church desires nothing more ardently than to develop itself untrammelled in the service of all men under any regime, which recognises the basic rights of the person and the family and the needs of the common good.[40]The Council, before its intermission due to Pope John XXIII's death, sought dialogue with the other churches. Pope Paul VI succeeded Pope John on 21 June 1963 and declared at once that he intended to continue the Council in the spirit of his predecessor. Vatican

Council II, which met again under Pope Paul VI, made as its own the widespread demand for renewal, openness and dialogue.[41] Thus, openness to the world, renewal in liturgy and dialogue with other Christians soon came to be stressed by the Council.[42]

However, the most important document which the Council produced was the *Pastoral Constitution of the Church in the Modern World (Gaudim et Spes).*[43] In this the Council declared its views on the great problems of the time. This was the only text which did not have a draft. Various groups drew it up during the Council proceedings. In other words, this text arose out of the realisation that the Church could not remain preoccupied with itself but had to face up to the problems of our time.[44] The opening statement of *Gaudium et Spes* also contained a hint, not fully worked out in the rest of the document but pregnant with the future, that the poor were to be privileged in the Church.[45] Thus, with Vatican Council II, the Roman Catholic Church turned towards the world. Vatican II was a serious attempt on the part of the Roman Catholic Church to look at the world as a whole. The same spirit was reflected in Pope Paul VI's Social Encyclical Letter *Populorum Progression* (1967):

> Its express aim was to throw the light of the gospel on the social question of our time... Christian communities throughout the world had the duty of scrutinizing the 'signs of the times' in their own situation... They could only be discovered through patient work, in which the human sciences would play a part, in collaboration with others involved in the same field.[46]

Vatican II, particularly its Pastoral Constitution on the Church in the Modern World, recognised the social problems of humanity and the difficulties of individualist morality in dealing with these issues. It urged the local churches to use the social sciences to understand their specific conditions and pledged the Church's commitment to overcome them. Vatican II provided a basis for understanding the relationship between the evangelical mission of the Church and the commitment to human liberation and opened the way for liberation theology. This came in the form of the Medellin Conference of the Latin American Bishops (CELAM) in 1968.

The Second General Conference of the Latin American Bishops was held in Medellin, Columbia, in 1968.[47] Medellin referred to such factors as: various forms of marginal living; alienation; excessive inequality between different social classes; the continuing and increasing frustration of people's expectations; the oppressive exercise of repressive power by certain ruling segments; tensions resulting from the dependence of countries on some centre of economic powe the growing imbalance and perversion of international trade; the flight of economic and human resources; the evasion of taxes by various foreign companies; steadily rising indebtedness and flight of profit and dividends; international monopolies and the international imperialism of money; and political imperialism of whatever ideological stamp, and other social evils.[48] The Bishops acknowledged that 'our nations are not masters of their own resources and economic decisions'.[49]They also recognised that the fundamental issue was a condition of economic dependency entrenched in structural injustice as the root problem. The need was to 'conscientise' and towards this the church was to commit itself to an 'instructional ministry'.[50] The Bishops at Medellin called for a shift in theological method.With this analysis of Latin American reality, the Medellin Conference came out with a prophetic document. It referred to oppression as a situation of sin.[51] In its document XIV, Medellin took a clear option for the poor and the oppressed. It said:

> The poverty of the church and its members in Latin America ought to be a sign and a commitment – a sign of the inestimable value of the poor in the

eyes of God, an obligation of solidarity with those who suffer.[52]

Medellin saw the poor as the protagonists of history, the oppressed classes, Christ suffering in the poor. The poor are those who challenge the church and define its task.[53] The central idea of Medellin was that the entire church needed to be converted to take a preferential option for the poor, with a view to their liberation.[54] Although Medellin had its own limitations, it stressed the relevance of the Gospel to the suffering of the oppressed millions.[55] In summary, Medellin was clear and prophetic. Its message was that if the gospel was to be relevant it must be related to the suffering and oppression of the poor and the oppressed.[56] To evangelise the poor, Medellin said, was to incarnate the Gospel in time. This conference had a great impact on the Latin American continent and particularly helped to evolve a theology which its supporters claimed was true to the spirit of the gospel.

The Medellin conference was criticised by the Brazilian Hugo Assmann. His quarrel with the Medellin meeting was that in opting for what he called an 'analytical construct' the bishops had adopted, knowingly or unknowingly, 'an ethical and political stance'. The danger of all such thinking is that it evades the historical challenges: instead, 'love, a properly theological term, is indispensable in any political struggle for liberation'.[57] However, the great merit of Medellin was that it had been rooted in the reality of Latin American life as 'deeply conflictual' and it had given legitimatisation to movements for renewal.[58]

The Medellin conference (Catholics) and the World Conference on Church and Society (Ecumenicals) thus expressed their understanding of the Gospel message in identical terms, taking a clear and prophetic option for the poor and the oppressed; thus they helped to develop a new theological approach; and as a result, involvement in the struggles of the people to over-throw unjust economic and political structures was increasingly recognised as an essential dimension of participation in God's mission. It was in this climate that some theologians of the Third World – Asia, Africa and Latin America – Protestants and Catholics decided to meet together as an ecumenical body and attempt to consider theology from the perspective of the poor, marginalised and oppressed and the underside of history. As liberation theologians in Latin America took shelter in Vatican II in order to launch their revolutionary ideas into the theological arena, so Indian liberation theologians were also stimulated by it to fight for the human rights of the oppressed in India.

From the evangelical constituency, Billy Graham resolved for Christianity to respond to the social upheavals and radical revolt of the 1960s. He was convinced that the historic, crucified, resurrected and reigning Christ is Himself good news for the world, and that he speaks of alienated youths, the drug subculture, racial conflict, the breakdown of moral values, the cult of violence, the search for freedom and the longing for love. He determined not only to continue his own crusades, but also to encourage the evangelical constituency to unite in reaching out to the world for Christ. He was mainly responsible for convening the World Congress on Evangelism in Berlin in 1966. It was co-sponsored by the *Billy Graham Evangelistic Association* and *Christianity Today*. Its motto was *One Race, One Gospel, One Task*. Here an evangelical theological foundation for world evangelisation was established.It was followed by a series of regional conferences on evangelism in Singapore (1968), Minneapolis and Bogotá (1996) and Australia (1971). It seems the evangelical constituency had forced to accept change and the new waves came from liberal groups.

Theologically, Edinburgh 1910 (World Missionary Conference) was not so much a matter of doctrinal disagreement as apparent doctrinal indifference since doctrine was not on the agenda. Vital themes like the content of the Gospel, the theology of evangelism and the nature of the church were not discussed. The reason is that Randall Davidson, the Archbishop of Canterbury, as a condition of Anglican participation in Edinburgh, secured a promise from John R. Mott that doctrinal debate would be excluded. In consequence, the theological challenges of the day were not faced. And, during the decades which followed, theological liberalism entered into the structures of Western universities and seminaries and largely opened the gates for liberal thinking on the churches' mission.

The evangelicals felt that these two movements undermined the self-confidence which had characterised the Christian leaders who met in Edinburgh in 1910 and their successors. When the first assembly of the WCC convened in Amsterdam, mission was not at the top of their agenda. Some ecumenical pioneers tried hard to remedy this by securing at the Third assembly in New Delhi the integration of the International Missionary Council with the WCC. Then, it was said, when the IMC became the missionary arm of the WCC, mission would be at the heart of the Council's concerns and so of its member churches. In the event, however, the evangelicals felt that mission became marginalised by being largely reinterpreted in socio-political terms, thus the evangelicals felt that the vision of Edinburgh 1910 suffered an almost total eclipse.

In July 1974 the International Congress on World Evangelisation was held in Lausanne, Switzerland, and issued the Lausanne Covenant. The 2,700 participants who went to Lausanne represented over 150 nations and were from a wide diversity of denominational backgrounds. Approximately 50% were from so called Third World countries; over 4,000 Christians attended the Congress. Much of the agenda was dictated by Third World evangelical leaders. The Evangelical constituency felt that Lausanne I was a watershed in placing social justice within the purposes of the Church's mission.[59] Perhaps the single most important outcome of the 1974

Congress was the Lausanne Covenant. This 15-point document drafted by a committee chaired by John Stott (leader of the Anglican evangelicals), and signed by the great majority of participants, has been translated into many languages and distributed among church leaders throughout the world.

In July 1989, over 3000 participants from 170 countries met in Manila for the Lausanne II Congress and issued the Manila Manifesto. During the 15 years between the two congresses some smaller consultations were held on topics like Gospel and Culture, Evangelism and Social Responsibility, Simple Lifestyle, the Holy Spirit, and Conversions. These meetings and their reports have helped to develop the thinking of the Lausanne movement.The Manila Manifesto takes up the two congress themes, 'Proclaim Christ until He Comes' and 'Calling the Whole Church to Take the Whole Gospel to the Whole World'. Its first part is a series of 21 succinct affirmations. Its second part elaborates these in 12 sections, which are commended to churches alongside the Lausanne Covenant for study and action. Under the section The Gospel and Social Responsibility, the Manila Manifesto declared that:

> In a spirit of humility, we are to preach and teach, minister to the sick, feed the hungry, care for prisoners, help the disadvantaged and handicapped, and deliver the oppressed. While we acknowledge the diversity of spiritual gifts, callings and contexts, we also affirm that good news and good works are inseparable.
>
> Among the evils we deplore are destructive violence, including institutionalised violence, political corruption, all forms of exploitation of people and of the earth, the undermining of the family, abortion on demand, the drug traffic, and the abuse of human rights. In our concern for the poor, we are distressed by the burden of debt in the two-thirds world. We are also outraged by the

> inhuman conditions in which millions live, who bear God's image as we do.

In its concluding part the manifesto declared that:

> Our continuing commitment to social action is not a confusion of the Kingdom of God with a Christianised society. It is rather, recognition that the biblical gospel has inescapable social implications. True mission should always be incarnational. It necessitates entering humbly into other people's worlds, identifying with their social reality, their sorrow and suffering and their struggles for justice against oppressive powers. This cannot be done without personal sacrifices.[60]

What did Lausanne II mean for the definition of evangelical constituencies' new policies in world mission? Alan Nichols, Anglican Archdeacon of Melbourne, Australia said:

> Social concern is accepted now by virtually everyone as part of the Good News of Christ. It is no longer seen as an option, or as the specialist interest of a minority. And social concern includes working for structural justice and engaging in social and political action. The fifteen years since Lausanne I has seen a huge shift in thinking in this area. Evangelicals engaged in social action ministries need no longer be defensive.[61]

Paul Tillich introduced the idea of God as the ultimate ground of existence, breaking through the bourgeois self-sufficiency; abandoning the traditional view of God and the heteronomous faith, he advocated religious socialism.[62] A theme of Tillich's philosophy was 'unconsciousness'.[63] That true freedom is the realisation of one's own destiny, namely, of one's innate qualities; nature must be realised in personality, and personality must participate in nature. True reality must be grasped here and now; historical reality, namely, the personal action of volitional choice is the only unique reality. God is Being itself (*ipsum esse*). God is knowable in 'Him' self. God is not a being but the ground of being, the power of being, and being itself. God does not exist but he is the supernatural being.[64] 'He' is the name for that which concerns man ultimately. This God can be known by the relationship with our neighbours and so-called secular things. The knowledge of God consists in the daily life of drinking and eating, the doing of justiceand the plea for the poor and oppressed.[65] Indian theologians were attracted towards this idea of God, human, justice, poor and oppressed.

One root of secular theology as it is understood today lies with Dietrich Bonhoeffer. Bonhoeffer opened the way for a theology that would concern itself with contemporary political realities. He concentrated his theological reflection on the question of how to reinterpret the Gospel for the modern adult and proposed a secular religionless interpretation of the Scriptures.Bonhoeffer named the post-Christian era the 'post-Constantine era', which indicated that he understood the Christendom of the Post-Constantine concepts of Jesus as the Lamb of God, Redeemer, Son of God, True God and True Man, and humanity like God to be absolutely meaningless to the modern man. For him the word 'God' is dead to modern man. The concept of the supernatural, transcendent God is supposed to belong to the basic criteria of metaphysical thought, which is strange to the modern man, who does not recognise the concepts of supernaturalism and transcendentalism and discards the distinction of the secular and the sacred.[66]

According to Bonhoeffer, because modern man has come of age, he does not need God as a working hypothesis.[67] For Bonhoeffer, transcendentalism does not lie in that which exists beyond our sight and power but in our neighbour who is within reach; God is transcendent in the midst of our secular life.[68] Asian Contextual theologians appreciate Bonhoeffer and affirm Christian faith is a service of activity for one's neighbour[69] and salvation by man himself.[70] Humanity can be saved by man through charity to his neighbours. If that is the case, then where is the place for God's grace? For Bonhoeffer, Jesus is there only for others; His being there for others is the experience of transcendence; faith is participation in this being of Jesus; our relation to God is a new life in existence for others.[71]Influenced by Bonhoeffer's 'Religionless Christianity', such secular theologians as Thomas J.J. Altizer, William Hamilton, Harvey Cox and Paul van Buren declared the objectified God to be dead and affirmed that to be a Christian is to be a human.[72] For them, man's place is to stand with God in the midst of the world.

Hamilton discards any dualistic observation of the world.[73] He, like Bonhoeffer, emphasises the life for others. 'Reserve means a willingness to leave the other person alone, to let him be himself, apart from us... Respect means giving the other a full right to be apart from us, apart from society, alone'.[74] Defining 'goodness' he states, 'such goodness might well involve: gentleness, sensitivity to the needs and claims of others; willingness to be counted with the underdog in our society; opposition to all coercion, pompousness, injustice, restriction of legitimate freedom ...'[75]Paul van Burenmaintained that it has become impossible to believe in any reality apart from that which is open to the empirical investigation of science.[76] He understood the 'secular' as excluding any kind of transcendent reality.[77] And Harvey Coxunderstands 'God as being at work in secular history.[78] We are to seek for God and co-operate with Him in secular history, namely in the social and political ferments of our own time'.[79]

In the Indian sub-continent, S.K. George (1910–1960) and E.V. Mathew (1917–1971) were the prime advocates for secular theology. George articulated more clearly the Gandhian challenge to Christianity. In his writings he reflects extensively on Gandhi's life and work and present*Satyagraha*(Truth)and love in practice.The Cross is here reclaimed, George declared, as not only a working principle for life but also as a science of mass action for a new social order. George's own commitment to inter-religious understanding, to Christian theologising and to social justice shaped his life, which in poverty and suffering resembled the same cross.

E.V. Mathew was also closely associated with such leaders as P.D.Devanandan, M.M. Thomas and Russel Chandran. Described by his close colleagues as 'Prophet of Christian Secularism', Mathew continually urged the churches to promote secularism in India (take part in nation building) as the only way in which communal divisions could be reduced and politics desacralised. Yet he affirmed the heart of his beliefs in the conviction that God had acted decisively for the renewal of humanity and of society, in Jesus of Nazareth – 'the transcendent in the secular'. The demand of the Christian therefore was no less for radical personal change than it was for revolutionary change in unjust social and political structures.

The term Process Theology came into currency in the 1950s. It referred to the type of theology developed at Chicago especially under the influence of the philosophy of Alfred North Whitehead. But others readily adopted the term, for example, the followers of Teilhard de Chardin. Process theology seeks the salvation of all humanity. It acknowledges the global horizon as its ultimate concern. The understanding of human beings as indissolubly social is basic to process thought; in that regard, Teilhard de Chardin wrote that the eminently progressive group of Homo *Sapiens* was born in an atmosphere of socialisation.[80] Since Process Theology sees human beings as part of a wider community, which includes all creatures, the indivisible salvation of the whole world cannot be limited to humanity.[81]

According to Teilhard, human beings are designed to play at the centre of economic or evolutionary processes of development. In Teilhard is crystallised much of that hope in humanity which excited the dreams and struggles of Marx. One of the core principles shared by Marxism and Teilhard's evolutionism is that to be human means to change his/her own nature, to become someone he/she is not. Hence, evolutionism constitutes a way toward human transformation.[82] Marx had a rudimentary knowledge of the evolution of the human. He wrote, 'The whole of history is a preparation for man.... History itself is a real part of natural history, of the development of nature into man'.[83]Teilhard's thoughts are subsumed: man is a participant in evolution and a creature related to God.[84] Humanity is the self-consciousness of evolution, the axis and tip of evolution;[85] and it is 'in the science of evolution (so that evolution may show itself capable of functioning in a*hominized milieu*), God become the Prime Mover, Gatherer and consolidator, ahead of us, of evolution'.[86]

Three theologians of history, namely Friedrich Gogarten, Jurgen Moltmann and Wolfhart Pannenberg, are familiar to Indian Christian theologians. According to the Theology of History,[87] revelation is totally historical, and history is supposed to be a way of God's existence; in other words, history is a divine revelation.[88] Therefore, this theology of history does not know any concept of the transcendent.

Gogarten's view of Christian faith calls for radical demythologising and existential interpretation, which replaces the static concepts of traditional metaphysics with historical existential concepts. He understands secularisation as history making of human existence.[89] John Macquarie pointedly summarises Gogarten's concept of secularisation as follows:

> The Pauline notions of inheritance and sonship furnish a powerful inspiration to Gogarten. Once we were children 'under guardians and trustees' but now we 'received adoptions as sons.' As responsible sons who have now come of age, we have, so to speak, been given the key of the house. We are delivered from tutelage, and stand now in an adult relationship to the Father. This means that

> we have received the world for our use, and are no longer enslaved to its 'elemental spirits'.[90]

In India, Paul D. Devanandan[91] and M.M. Thomas[92] were two of the most noted post-independence thinkers who advocated a Theology of History. Devanandan's theology is primarily a theology of Christian participation in nation building and of dialogue between religious and secular faiths.[93] Thomas, through his prolific theological writing, represents a genuine attempt to present the Christian gospel within the framework of India's quest for 'fuller humanity'. His theological contribution emerged from the dialectic and dynamic interrelation between salvation, which is based on the life, death and resurrection of Jesus Christ, and the continuing process of humanisation, which finds expression in the religious and political movements in India. Both these theologians identified that the political ideologies and secular movements that strived toward humanisation within the ethos of nationalism and national integration became imperative to theology in India.

The humanism of Secular Theology became the seedbed in which Jurgen Moltmann's Theology of Hopeconvinced the necessity of doing theology. Georg Wilhelm Hegel understood that the death of God is experienced in 'the openness of history and the totality of experiences'.[94] Philosophically, the Theology of Hope found its immediate origin in the ideas of Ernst Bloch. Bloch's philosophy of the 'not yet' can be traced back through Karl Marx to Hegel.In his writings 'Evangelism and Liberation', Moltmann said that a cry for liberty is a common hope of humankind as well as nature.[95] The feast of freedom promised by the Liberator Jesus (Luke 4: 17–21) belongs to the future, not to the present. This feast is prepared only for the poor, namely the ones who have suffered from violence and injustice.[96] In connection with this feast, Jesus is the gate to the neighbour. To believe is to open oneself to God's future and to do it right now, the day of Jesus. This hope can be achieved by 'being-for-other', and 'being-with-other'.[97]

Moltmann defined people as the uneducated *ochlos (mass)* who cannot afford to learn or to observe the law. This 'ordinary people' is in contrast to the ruler. The ordinary people are the people of no position, uneducated and poor.[98] Jesus became one of the ordinary people and identified Himself with them. Thereby He can call them, 'my brethren'. Jesus presents Himself through the people.[99]Consequently, Moltmann emphasis that the people are subjects of the Messianic Reign, and that the hope in the midst of the struggle of people cannot appear until the people become the subjects of their own history.[100] The feast of liberty, namely the 'table fellowship' mission, expects that the Reign of God should be realized among the physically hungry and thirsty.[101]

Innocent and involuntary suffering can never be justified. It must be justified either by Theodicy, which explains it as necessary to God's purpose, or by anthropodicy, which explains it as necessary to some higher human purpose. Such justifications suppress the sense of moral outrage against evil, silence protest against it and therefore at the very least reduce the motive for relieving and overcoming suffering. At worst they justify infliction of innocent suffering by totalitarian regimes both theocratic and atheistic.[102]

An adequate theological response to the problem of suffering must contain an initiative for overcoming that suffering. It is not to justify suffering, it must, on the contrary, help to maintain the protest against suffering and convert it into an initiative for overcoming suffering. These two requirements are presupposed in Moltmann's approach to Theodicy.The determining centre of Moltmann's early theology was 'a dialectic of cross and resurrection'. Moltmann holds cross and resurrection together in a creative dialogue and tension so that the one continually informs the other. The connecting link that holds cross and resurrection together is Jesus – the crucified one who is raised from the dead. As the crucified one, Jesus identifies with the world's death but as the crucified one who is risen, He brings the promise of God's life to the world in its apparent abandonment by God.

In his work *The Crucified God* Moltmann moves back from the resurrection event of God's promise to the crucifixion event of God's love. Moltmann is trying to establish how God's promise reaches those to whom it is addressed, the godless and the godforsaken, i.e. sinners who suffer their own turning away from God and innocent sufferers who are victims of pointless suffering.[103] Moltmann's answer is in the cross, interpreted by Jesus' cry of dereliction. Jesus identifies with the godless and godforsaken. In love He suffers in solidarity with those who suffer. He meets their suffering with His voluntary fellow suffering. His resurrection is, therefore, the basis of hope for the suffering because it is the resurrection of one who has identified Himself with their condition, suffered with them and overcome. The suffering of Jesus does not sanction suffering. Rather, it demonstrates both God's solidarity with the suffering and God's commitment to liberate them from it.[104]

The solidarity in love through Jesus is God's act of solidarity with those who suffer because it is the suffering of the incarnate and Trinitarian God. By the cross God embraces the contradiction between the way the world is and the way God intends it to be and suffers its pain. The event of the cross involves the whole event of the Trinitarian being of God: The Son suffers in His love being forsaken by the Father as He dies. The Father suffers in His love the grief of the death of the Son.

The incarnate God identifies with the suffering of those He loves and, as those who suffer in loving solidarity with innocent sufferers must, He takes up and expresses their protest against their pointless suffering. In the cry of dereliction, the crucified Christ protests on behalf of all innocent sufferers. And the example He sets is not of fatalistic acceptance of suffering but of voluntary, loving identification with the desolate and the abandoned. Thus protest and moral outrage against suffering is not quelled but sustained by the cross, and becomes an essential element in that loving solidarity which the crucified Christ both practises and encourages in His followers.[105] The Cross, for Moltmann, is God's demonstrative act of solidarity by which He identifies with all human suffering. Arvind P.Nirmal's interpretation of 'New Man' activity in his book *Heuristic Exploration* is similar to what Moltmann has suggested as 'a passion for the people' for immediate implementation in his book *A Theology of Hope*.

Liberation theology is concerned with the socio-economic, politico-religious and racio-cultural situations of the people but these realities differ in each continent and country. When theology is not neutral, but concerned with integral liberation and praxis, different theologies of liberation emerge. These liberation theologies are commonly called 'Third World Liberation Theologies'. Theologians from each country display their own distinctive approaches to articulate the liberation of the people. The following are some of the main theologies ofliberation. Black Theology[106]; Hispanic Theology[107]; African Liberation Theology[108]; Feminist Theology[109] and Asian Theology of Liberation. Asian Theology of liberation has produced so many indigenous versions of local liberation theologies, such as: Water buffalo Theology;[110] Third Eye Theology;[111] Planetary Theology[112] and Minjung Theology.[113]

In this part, we shall consider two specific streams of theologies namely Latin American Liberation Theology and then the EATWOT[114] because these two theologies have very specific links with the Dalit Theology. In 1971 the original Spanish version of Gustavo Gutiérrez' book 'A Theology of Liberation' was published in Peru. The English translation appeared in America in 1973 and in Britain in 1974, subtitled, 'History, Politics and Salvation'. The background of the book is threefold: Latin America the 'Oppressed Continent', the Roman Catholic Church and its oppressive structure, and

Marxist economic theory. This is a fundamental text for liberation theology.[115]It seems this is the fullest and most thorough effort to understand biblical salvation in terms of the liberation of the oppressed. For a description of the theological methód proposed, J.L. Segundo's 'Liberation of Theology' has been judged to be even more significant. Chronologically, Latin American Liberation Theology followed the Theology of Hope; the Theology of Hope, influenced by Ernst Bloch[116] followed the Theology of the Death of God and Secular Theology; and the Death of God Theology and Secular Theology followed the theology of Dietrich Bonhoeffer.

Harvey Conn and Allan Killen refer to Bonhoeffer as a fundamental theological source of liberation theology. Gutiérrez, a representative of liberation theology, can be taken as an example in this regard. Quoting Bonhoeffer, he defines the meaning of liberation: 'Freedom is ... something one has for others.... Being free means being free for others, because the other has bound me to him, only in relationship with the other am I free'.[117]Bonhoeffer's formulations challenged the Protestant ghetto mentality and its alleged church-world dualism. It was Bonhoeffer who aided in seeing the relationship between faith and ideology and the demands of Christian discipleship.[118] In this respect, in order to understand the historical origin of liberation theology, it is necessary to go back to Bonhoeffer.[119]

There are other examples of Bonhoeffer's influence. Bonhoeffer's rejection of the absoluteness of the truth such as the Ten Commandments can be seen in José Miguez Bonino's denial of the existence of any form of eternal truth; truth can only be known through action.[120] Truth, for Miguez Bonino, is sparked by social action; man is to learn truth by becoming involved in the problems of poverty and oppression.[121] Bonhoeffer's idea of the changed world and corporate salvation in a Reign of God upon this earth comes out very clearly in Gustavo Gutiérrez's idea of the qualitative aspect of salvation.[122]

Bonhoeffer's 'Religionless Christianity', which emphasises that humans suffer in their identification with the secular world as Christ suffered, can be viewed as parallel with liberation theology's identification with the poor.[123]

Latin American Liberation Theology starts from a situation of economic dependence and social injustice. In other words, this theology is forged in a social context of extreme poverty in which millions of Latin Americans live. This theology has made use of Marxist tools of socio-economic analysis for the description and transformation of Latin American society and is concerned with the struggle to free those who are oppressed under unjust economic structures. The Latin American Church took seriously the social responsibility toward rapid social and cultural changes for the poor of the Third World. The church began to participate in the revolutionary process, namely, the class struggle.

The Theology of Liberation is an authentic product of Latin America. Beginning with historical reality rather than with Scripture or tradition, and drawing on the help of social sciences, it registers its spirited protest against the theologies of North America and Europe. Its best-known exponents apart from Gutiérrez are Ruben Alves (*Theology of Human Hope*) and Hugh Assmann (*Oppression – Liberation: A Challenge to Christians*). Orlando Costa distinguishes them by saying that 'if Alves is the prophet of the movement, and Assmann is the apologist, then Gutiérrez is the systematic theologian'.[124]About Gutiérrez, John Stott said:

> I admire the deep compassion of Gustavo Gutiérrez for the exploited, his insistence on solidarity with the poor, his emphasis on social 'praxis' instead of unpractical theorizing, and his call to the church for a more evangelical, more authentic, more concrete and more efficacious commitment to liberation.[125]

Latin American Liberation Theology's starting points,

socio-economic analysis, and revolutionarystruggle and solidarity with the oppressed, find an exact transition in Dalit Theology.However, Arvind P. Nirmal considers Latin American Liberation theology as yet another imported theology even though the context differs. He questions the uncritical acceptance of it.He questions but does not denigrate liberation theology. In fact, he believes that 'the whole of Christian theology needs to become dialogical in character and such a dialogue should not exclude a dialogue with liberation theology'.[126]However, he finds the Latin American Liberation Theology and its traditional doctrinaire Marxist analysis inadequate in the context of the socio-economic realities of India. However, its option for the poor and the oppressed is found to be useful. But it needs to be questioned because 'it neglected the caste factor which adds to the complexity of Indian socio-economic realities'.[127]The liberation theology that is emerging in the Asian context is not a replica of the Latin American liberation theology. It certainly uses Marxian tools of analysis and is something one needs to bear in mind.

EATWOT held its first theological conference at Dar-es-Salaam in 1976. It attempted a first survey of theological reflection in Africa, Asia and Latin America, and ended with the Dar-es-Salaam Manifesto, which can be considered the official birth certificate of Third World Theology.[128]All the Third World Liberation theologies find expressions under one umbrella, the EATWOT. Their statement speaks of the Third World context. The accent on liberation is loud and clear and they are consensus statements.Although each theology highlights its own contextual problems, the methodology used to theologise can be listed as follows: (i) commitment is the first act and theology is the second act, a commitment to prevent exploitation and oppression, and to promote justice and peace; (ii) theologians make an option for the liberation of the oppressed and are against unjust structures; (iii) a comprehensive social analysis of the economic, political, social, cultural and religious dimension is undertaken; (iv) the poor look at history from below and discover in history and in the Scriptures a God who liberates; and (v) Continual searching for a relevant theological language, practice and theory, action and reflection, discussion and prayer, involvement and contemplation constitutes a single process.[129]

It seems that there are certain drawbacks in the EATWOT movement. EATWOT was and is even now interested in developing methodically a theology that speaks with the voice of the poor and the marginalised in society. The question is who reads this methodical theological exposition and who needs it, except of course those who still find relevance in it.This certainly applies to all theologies. Should theological articulation be always systematic? If theology, as it is understood today, is done by the community of believers or by the community, then why should we be systematic and precise?EATWOT methodology, however revolutionary it may be, has not gone far enough. It has not yet fully spoken about specific oppressions such as caste in an Indian context, though it has made peripheral reference to it in the past.In other words, it is yet to come up with an adequate framework of analysis to this specific form of oppression such as caste. It is easier to speak about racism in the West but what about caste oppression in the Indian context? EATWOT's call for a radical break in epistemology which calls for engagement in critical reflection on the praxis of reality has somehow precluded the reality of Dalits in India. Has EATWOT had and does it still have class and caste interests? The pioneers of the EATWOT movement certainly seem to be visionaries. Then, how come they are still looking for an adequate framework of analysis for the past thirty years?

EATWOT's analysis begins with the emergence of capitalism, i.e., with the history of capitalism for the past 500 years or so.[130] There is nothing wrong with that because the present-day suffering of the Third World can be easily traced back to the era of colonialism. Why did they not go beyond? What would happen if we go beyond that demarcation? Should colonialism be the starting point? If we only refer to the Third World context, the answer is yes. But caste oppressions in India are older than colonialism. EATWOT's theological enterprise with regard to India in general and Dalits in particular should go beyond colonialism.

The Vatican Council II and the concept of *Missio Dei* are concerned with the social involvement of the Christian church in the service of all people who are subject to oppression and exploitation. This idea of the social involvement of the church can be traced back to Dietrich Bonhoeffer, on the one hand, and to Hegel on the other. Dalit theology came to emerge under the influence of these two.Dalit Theology learned from both Existential Theology and Secular Theology that God can be seen in our relationship with our neighbours within our reach; from Process theology came holistic humanism; from the Theology of History came the negation of transcendentalism; from Roman Catholic Theology came universal ecumenism and the idea of 'anonymous Christians'; from Latin American Liberation Theology came the application of the socio-economic hermeneutics to the social situation of evil structures and from EATWOT came the political concept of people and the socio-political conflict between the rulers and the ruled.

There are several reasons for Dalit theology to be able to make use of these theologies with harmony. First of all, practically speaking, Bonhoeffer is considered as the fountainhead of all liberation theological thoughts. His proposals of 'Religionless Christianity' and 'Discipleship for others' are the common foundation. The humanistic or human centred way of life is the major concern in these theologies. Secondly, concerned with the first reason, most of these modern theologies are focused on justification by works rather than by faith in Christ and His vicarious atonement. In their case, to believe is to do something for others in need, praxis rather than doctrine or theology. Thirdly, these theologies often do not start from scriptural text but from a situational context. They regard Scriptures as historical and sociological references. In fact, the core of these modern theological thoughts is the sociological hermeneutics, so to speak, the secularisation of the Gospel.

Considering this, one can see the need, origin and development of Dalit theology from historical perspectives. In subsequent chapters this study analyses how much Dalit theology is genuinely Indian in nature, significance and relevance as frequently maintained by Dalit theologians themselves, or how far one can rightly maintain that Dalit theology is a foreign thought system taken on by India.

Endnotes

1. Cf: World Conference on Church and Society, op.cit, 48–50. See also: Social Questions – The Responsible Society in World Perspective (a memorandum issued by the Study Department, WCC, Geneva, in preparation for the Second Assembly, 1953), pp. 1–5 (hereafter Social Questions – The Responsible Society).
2. According to the *Penguin Dictionary of the Third World Terms*, the term 'Third world' was first introduced by the French Economist and demographer Alfred Sauvy in an article published in 1952. The concept 'Third World' reflected the reality of the continents, which have been excluded from power in the world. This term has to embody the idea that this very exclusion has generated a set of common characteristics in the historical experience of the peoples of Asia, Africa, Latin America and the Middle East.
3. Twenty-nine free and independent nations' leaders of Asia and Africa came together at Bandung on 18 April 1955. Among the countries attending, to name some, were: India, China, Japan, Indonesia, Burma, Egypt, Turkey, the Philippines, Gold Coast, and Ethiopia. The Bandung Conference gave a sense of inter-regional solidarity not only to Asia, but also to the

Third World. Bandung was a movement in the sense that it not only affected the social, political, religious, and cultural and economics of Asian countries, but also created a movement in theological history the whole theological direction in the Third World came to be named after. In other words, in the given colonial and post-colonial experience of the nations in Asia, Bandung highlighted the challenge from the Asian context to theology.

4. The evangelicals called this the 'Guidelines for the Church's Global Task'.

5. Hereafter mentioned as WCC.

6. In the Ecumenical Movement represented by the protestant churches, concern for social issues began in the year 1925 with the Universal Christian Conference on Life and Work in Stockholm. It was succeeded by the World Conference on Church, Community and State, held in Oxford in 1937. Cf: World Conference on Church and Society, p. 6: Hooft, Vissert, W.A.Oldham's Method in Albrecht's in Ecumenical Perspectives Ecumenical Review, p. 3; Ibid, p. 99. Cf: Santa Ana, Julio de, The Economic Debate in the Ecumenical Movement.

7. 'Theology and Social Ethics,' *Study Encounter,* Vol II, No. 2, 1966, 78ff.

8. N. Thomas (ed.), *Readings in World Mission,* SPCK, 1995.

9. Potter, *Ecumenical Perspectives Ecumenical Review*, xii–xiii. Cf: *Social Questions – The Responsible Society*, p. 15; *Evanston to New Delhi 1954–1961* (Report of the Central Committee to the Third Assembly of the WCCs) Geneva: WCC Publications, 1961, p. 46 (hereafter *Evanston to New Delhi*).

10. *Evanston to New Delhi*, 1961, pp. 46–51.

11. V. Hooft, *Ecumenical Perspective*, Geneva: WCC Publications, 1961, p. 7

12. M. Mammen Thomas was the well-known Ecumenical Indian theologian and activist in Marxist and Socialist movements in Kerala, India.

13. M.M. Thomas, *My Ecumenical Journey,* Ecumenical

Publishing Centre Private Limited, 1990, p. 251. (See also *The New Delhi Report, The Third Assembly of the World Council of Churches 1961,* Association Press, 1962.)

14. Ibid, p. 252.
15. Ibid, p. 253.
16. Cf: *World Conference on Church and Society,* p. 6.
17. Ibid.
18. Ibid.
19. M.M. Thomas, *My Ecumenical Journey,* Ecumenical Publishing Centre Private Limited, 1990, p. 270.
20. *World Conference on Church and Society*, p. 6.
21. *World Conference on Church and Society*, pp.200–209, points 20, 23, 7 a, c & I.
22. For WCCs concern on social questions Cf: Pury, de Pascal, WCC, CCPD, 1962; *Ecumenical Studies leaflet* No 3, Geneva, WCC, 1954; de Viries, Egbert, *Man in Rapid Social Change*, SCM Press, 1961. Every Department in WCC stresses the central idea arising from its Assembly message. The Gospel as liberating word to the poor and oppressed is highlighted by all of them.
23. J.C. Hoekendijk was born in 1912 in Indonesia and spent his childhood in western Java, where his father was a missionary. At eighteen, he entered the missionary training school in Oegstgeest (the Netherlands), where after 6 years he was selected to pursue theological studies at the State University of Utrecht (1936-41). In 1940 Hoekendijk was ordained as missionary. He was a well-known theologian among the ecumenical circle.
24. B. Hoedemaker, 'The Legacy of J.C. Hoekendijk', *International Bulletin of Missionary Research,* vol. 19, no. 19, October 1995, p. 166.
25. Ibid, p. 169.
26. The Confession of 1967, *The Constitution of the United Presbyterian Church in the USA*, 9.07.
27. Ibid, 9.32.

28. Ibid, 9.46.
29. H.E. Fey (ed.), *The Ecumenical Advance*, The Westminster Press, 1970, p. 421.
30. D.J. Bosch, *Witness to the World,*John Knox Press, London, 1980, pp. 179–180.
31. D.J. Bosch, *Transforming Mission: Paradigm Shifts in Theology of Mission*, Maryknoll, 1991, p. 382.
32. J.C. Hoekendijk, *The Church Inside Out*, SCM, London, 1967.
33. *International Review of Missions,* vol. 62, 1973, p. 199.
34. Ibid, p. 200.
35. D. Carr (ed.), *Towards an Asian Theology of Hope. No 1. Reading the Bible with New Eyes,* Hong Kong, CCA, 1997.
36. The term *The Agenda of the World* came to be used widely in the WCC. The Roman Catholic Church used another term to describe the situation in the 60s. The term it used was *The Signs of the Times*. Cf: Hebblethwaite, *The Popes and Politics,* pp. 18 - 19.
37. Ibid, p. 18.
38. L. Vischer, 'The Ecumenical Movements and the Roman Catholic Church', in H.E. Fey (ed.), *The Ecumenical Advance,* SPCK, 1970, p. 330 (hereafter Fey, *The Ecumenical Advance*).
39. 'Pastoral Constitution on the Church in the Modern World', in A.P. Flannery (ed.), *Documents of Vatican II*, W.B. Eerdmans, 1984, p. 909.
40. Ibid, p. 943.
41. Fey, *The Ecumenical Advance,* p. 336.
42. Ibid,p.336.
43. Ibid, p.342.
44. Ibid.
45. Hebblethwaite, *The Popes and Politics*, p. 20. Cf: Also Vischer in Fey, *The Ecumenical Advance,* p. 342.
46. Vischer in Fey, *The Ecumenical Advance,* pp. 20–21; Pope Paul VI, Encyclical Letter *Populorum Progression*, 26 March 1967, AA 59, 1967, pp.257–299.

47. S. Torres, *Theology in the Americas, Documentation Series*, Doc. No. 7, 1 (hereafter mentioned as Torres), *Theology in the Americas, Documentation Series.*

48. Eagleson (ed.), *Declaration of the 80 in Christian and Socialism: Documentation of the Christians for Socialism Movement in Latin America*, Orbis Books, 1975, p. 100.

49. T. Yates, *Christian Mission in the Twentieth Century,* Cambridge University Press, 1994, p. 179.

50. Ibid. p.179

51. P. Lernmoux, 'The Long Path to Puebla', in E. John and S. Phillip (eds.), *Puebla and Beyond: Documentation and Commentary*, Orbis Books, 1979, p. 11. See also: D. Enrique, *History and the Theology of Liberation,* Orbis Books, 1979, p. 115.

52. Torres, *Theology in the Americas*, Documentation Series, p. 2.

53. Ibid. pp. 3, 8.

54. Torres, *Theology in the Americas*, Documentation Series, p. 11.

55. P.E. Berryman, "*Latin American Liberation Theology*" in *Theologyin the Americas*, pp. 21–51.

56. For other documents on Medellin, see M.P. Carvalho and D.S. des Volkes Gottes, *Information,* December 1978; Latin Bishops Expected to Keep to Centre, International Herald Tribune, Tuesday, 13, 1979, p. 3; *Puebla and Beyond,* op.cit, pp. 289–290; H. Assmann, *Practical Theology of Liberation,* Search Press Limited, 1975, pp. 45–53; S. Galileo, 'Liberation Theology and New Tasks Facing Christians', *Frontiers of theology in Latin America*, pp. 164–227.

57. H. Assmann, *A Practical Theology of Liberation,* Search Press Ltd, 1975, p. 85.

58. G. Gutierrez, *Theology of Liberation,* SCM, 1974, pp.136–137.

59. A. Nichols (ed.), *The Whole Gospel for the Whole World: Story of Lausanne II Congress on World Evangelization, Manila 1989, Lausanne Committee for World Evangelization*, Regal Books, 1989, pp. 14 - 15.

60. Ibid. p. 115.
61. Ibid, pp. 143-179
62. P. Tillich, *Systematic Theology*, 2 Vols, The University of Chicago Press, 1951, pp. 228, 235, 282.
63. Ibid, pp. 179, 261, 279.
64. Ibid, pp. 183–186, 243.
65. Ibid, pp. 21, 240: the meaning of God is understood in terms of man's relation to the ultimate concern.
66. N.D. Suh, *Theology at a Turning Point*, Korea Theological Study Institute, 1976, pp. 220–221.
67. Ibid. p. 223. Also see D. Bonhoeffer, *Letters and Papers from Prison*, Eberhard Bethge (ed.), Macmillan Publishing Co., 1972, p. 260.
68. N.D. Suh, *Theology at a Turning Point*, Korea Theological Study Institute, 1976, p. 226; Bonhoeffer, *Letters and Papers from Prison*, p. 381.
69. N.D. Suh, *Theology at a Turning Point*, Korea Theological Study Institute, 1976, p. 227.
70. *Theological Thought* (Spring 1979), p. 116.
71. Bonhoeffer, *Letters and Papers from Prison*, p. 381.
72. W. Hamilton, *The New Essence of Christianity,* Association Press, New York, 1966, p. 42.
73. Ibid., pp. 109–110.
74. Ibid., pp. 124–125.
75. Ibid., p. 132; the word 'underdog' is similar to 'Dalits'.
76. P.M. van Buren, *The Secular Meaning of the Gospel*, MacMillan Publishing Company, New York, 1963.
77. J. Macquarie, *God and Secularity*, The Westminster Press, Philadelphia, 1967, p. 21.
78. H. Cox, *The Secular City*, MacMillan Publishing Company, New York, 1965.
79. J. Macquarie, *God and Secularity*, p. 25.
80. P.Teilhard de Chardin, *Man's Place in Nature,* Harper & Row, 1956, p. 79.

81. J.B. Cobb Jr., *Process Theology as Political Theology*. The Westminster Press, Philadelphia, 1980, p. 15.
82. R. Lischer, *Marx and Theilhard,* Orbis Books, 1979, pp. 2–3.
83. T.B. Bottomore, 'Economic and Philosophical Manuscripts', in Erich Fromm (ed.), *Marx's Concept of Man,* Ungar, 1961, p. 137. Cited in Lischer, *Marx and Teilhard,* p. 5.
84. Lischer, *Marx and Theilhard*, p. 9.
85. N.D. Suh, *Theology at a Turning Point*, p. 327.
86. P.Teilhard. de Chardin, *Man's Place in Nature*, p. 121.
87. Theology of History, advocated by W. Pannenberg, insists that there is only indirect revelation through historical acts. This history in which revelation takes place is not a special redemptive revelation known only through faith.
88. W. Pannenberg, *Basic Questions in Theology*, Vol. 1, Fortress, 1970, pp. 15, 19, 98.
89. N.D. Suh, *Theology at Turning Point*, p. 397.
90. J. Macquarie, *God and Secularity*, p. 37.
91. For a thorough understanding of Devanandan's theological thought, see, Joachim Wietzke (ed.), *Paul D. Devanandan: Selected Writings with Introduction*, Vol. I and II, CLS, 1983 and 1986.
92. Among M.M. Thomas' work, the following are relevant: *Salvation and Humanization,* CLS, 1971; *Man and the Universe of Faiths,* CLS, 1975; *The Secular Ideologies of India and the Secular Meaning of Christ,* CLS, 1976; *Religion and Revolt of the Oppressed,* ISPCK, 1981; and *Risking Christ for Christ's Sake*, WCC, 1987.
93. M.M. Thomas, and P.T. Thomas, *Towards an Indian Christian Theology: Life and Thought of Some Pioneers,* Tiruvalla, The New Day Publications, 1992, p. 147.
94. K. Hamilton, 'Liberation Theology: An Overview', in C.E. Armerding (ed.), *Evangelicals & Liberation*, Baker Book House, 1977, pp. 2–4.
95. J. Moltmann, Evangelism and Liberation, *Christian Thought*, April, 1975, p. 106.

96. Ibid., pp. 107, 111.
97. Ibid., pp. 115–116.
98. J. Moltmann, The Hope in the Midst of the Struggle of Minjung, *Christian Thought*, April 1975, p. 122.
99. Ibid., 129.
100. Ibid., p. 135.
101. Ibid., p. 132.
102. R. Bauckham, *The Theology of Jurgen Moltmann*. T&T Clark, 1995, pp. 81–82.
103. Ibid., p. 85.
104. Ibid., p. 86.
105. Ibid., p. 88.
106. Some of the key themes and questions of Black theology are: Black Religion as a source of Black radicalism; spiritual as a key source of the prayer and social praxis of African-Americans; anthropological and historical treatment of ritual, cult sect, and role of religio-racial heritage for Africans of the Diaspora; sociology of religion; theodicy or the attempt to justify God's goodness in view of the evil racism; criticism of colour symbolism in white Western theology; the significance of Marxist categories in shaping an Afro-American revolutionary Christianity; Black Christian nationalism; Black theological ethic based on Christian agape; Black Women and ministry in the church; Black theology and feminist theology; Black theology as biblical theology; theological, catechetical and liturgical reflection from the Christian Perspective; and the religion of Caribbean an African theologies to Black theology. J.H. Cone, *For My People: Black Theology and the BlackChurch*, Orbis, 1984; W.R. Traynham, *Christian Faith in Black and White: A Primer in Theology from the Black Perspective*, Parameter Press, 1973.
107. The historical evolution of theological reflection from the unique Perspectives of Hispanics in the USA owes much to the Academy of Catholic Hispanic Theologian of the USA (ACHTUS). Their theological exploration is on culture rather than a systematic critique of the dominant USA society. See

V.P. Elizondo, *Galilean Journey: The Mexican-American promise,* Orbis Books, 1983.

108. There is a deluge of literature on the African Liberation theology. Kofi Appiah, K. and Torres, (eds) 'Final Communique', in *African Theology en Route: papers from the pan-African conference of Third World Theologians, Accra, December, December 17-23, 1997,* Accra, Ghana, Maryknoll, N.Y:Orbis Books. D. Tutu, 'The Theology of Liberation in Africa', *African Theology en Route,* pp. 162–168.

109. *The Dictionary of Theology*, pp. 391–392.

110. Water buffalo theology comes from Thailand. It says that most people spend most of their time with the water buffaloes in the rice field and this expresses their simplicity and poverty. The meaning of Christ's message is reflected in this contextual situation. For details see K. Koyama, *Ware buffalo Theology,* Orbis Books, 1974.

111. Third-Eye Theology is proposed by Taiwan Chinese Theologian C.S. Song. He puts forward a theology which can look at Christ with Asian eyes, with the third-eye of the Buddhist tradition, which is the eye of the heart that transcends reason and looks towards mystery. This is not an apolitical theology but a theology of the womb, which accompanies a process of the gestation of a new world. See C.S. Song, *Third Eye Theology: Theology in Formation in Asian Settings*, Orbis Books, 1986.

112. Tissa Balasurya considers the need for a global reorientation of theology on the basis of global agenda of problems on a planetary scale. The problems of economic and cultural domination are characterised by classism, racism, sexism, religious fundamentalism, etc. A Planetary theology faces the problems on a planetary scale with a view to an integral human liberation. See T. Balasurya, *Planetary Theology,* Orbis Books, 1984.

113. Minjung Theology has emerged from South Korea. Minjung is a Korean word which is produced by the combination of two Characters: *min*, which denotes people, and *jung*, which denotes mass. So Minjung denotes the mass of people, or

simply the masses, or even the people. The Minjung is the permanent reality of history which has the experience of the rise and fall of political powers. This theology arises out of the rediscovery that the Christian message has not only a religious dimension but also apolitical one. There is a very expressive word in Korean literature – Han, which is the collective sentiment of the oppressed people. Minjung theology seeks to give expression to the Han of the *minjung*, to the just indignation of the oppressed people both in the Communist regime of North Korea and the technocratic regime of South Korea. See *Commission on the Theological Concerns of the Christian conference of Asia, Minjung theology: People as the subjects of History,* Orbis Books, 1981. The main articles are written by Suh Nam-Dong, Kim Yong-Bock and Ahn Byung-Mu.

114. Ecumenical Association of Third World Theologians
115. T. Yates, *Christian Mission in the Twentieth Century,* p. 181.
116. The Paths of the Marxist philosopher Ernst Bloch and the protestant theologian Jurgen Moltmann crossed at the University of Tubingen in the 1960s.
117. D. Bonhoeffer, *Creation and Fall Temptation*, MacMillan Publishing Company, 1959, p. 36.
118. H.M. Conn, 'Theologies of Liberation: An Overview', in S.N. Gundry and A.F. Johnson (eds.), *Tensions in Contemporary Theology*, Moody Press, 1979, p. 350.
119. R.A. Killen, *The Theology of the Third World,* Reformed Theological Seminary, 1977, pp. 16–18.
120. Ibid., p. 118.
121. J.M. Bono, *Doing Theology in a Revolutionary Situation,* Fortress, 1980, p. 72.
122. G. Gutiérrez, *A Theology of Liberation,* Orbis Books, 1973, pp. 151–152.
123. Ibid, p. 300.
124. O. Costa, *The Church and Its Mission: A Shattering Critique from the Third World*, Coverdale, 1974, p. 223.

125. J. Stott, *Christian Mission in the Modern World,* Falcon, 1975, p. 92.
126. A.P. Nirmal, 'A Dialogue with Dalit Literature', in M.E. Prabhakar (ed.), *Towards a Dalit Theology,* ISPCK, 1988, p. 64.
127. Ibid., p. 65.
128. S. Torres and V. Fabella (ed.), The Emerging Gospel: Theology form the Underside of History, Papers form the Ecumenical Dialogue of the Third World Theologians, Dar-es-Salaam, 5–12 August 1976, Maryknoll, 1976.
129. S. Rayan, 'The Irruption of the Thirdworld – A Challenge to Theology', *VJTR*, 46, 1982, p. 122.
130. Since the arrival of Vasco de Gama from Europe in 1498 at Calicut, Kerala, South India.

CHAPTER 4

Liberation Movements: A Comparative Analysis of Black and Dalit Movements

The status of Dalits in India and Blacks[1] in America is characterised by their relative deprivations and disabilities. The Blacks were first imported from Africa into Virginia in 1619 as plantation labour, though they have been stressing for a long time that that they are part and parcel of American society. Initially, Blacks were called 'Negroes', and were enslaved by the whites. By about 1700, the growing demands of the expanding plantation economy of the new world attracted slave traders to bring increasingly large cargoes of Black slaves from Africa. Soon after, slavery was institutionalised in American society. In this system, family members, even wives, husbands and their children could be separated easily.Black children often derived their status from their mothers. Blacks were denied not only socio-economic and political and legal rights, but even minimum civil rights. The Dalits on the other hand are the original inhabitants of India though they have been treated as 'Untouchables' under the fourfold division of the *varna (colour)* system.

A system of slavery and serfdom also existed in India, for instance in the State of Kerala[2] and some other parts of South India, but this was not as severe as in America. In Kerala the Untouchable castes, especially the *Pulayas*, *Cherumans* and

Panas (a tribe), were recruited for agricultural labour. They were considered to be the property of their high caste Hindu masters and were sold and bought like a commodity in the market, but their family members could not be separated from one another as in the case of Blacks in America. Instead, these slaves were assigned to particular farm sites of their masters and were obliged to live there and work for them. They also suffered from social, cultural and religious disabilities and educational, economic and political deprivations. They were not allowed to worship at the Hindu temples nor even to read the sacred Hindu scriptures. They not only suffered from 'touch pollution' but also from the extreme form of 'distance pollution'. Untouchable women were obliged to leave their breastsuncovered and were even sexually exploited. The numerous forms of exploitation, deprivation and disabilities were institutionalised and governed by certain rules and regulations, violation of which was punished in various ways. Thus, both the Indian Dalits and the American Blacks have suffered from cumulative deprivations and inequalities in their respective societies.The authority of castes and the supremacy of ascribed values as determinants of social status are highly typical characteristics of Indian society to which neither individuals nor social groups are exceptions. Dalits as a distinct group in Indian society by virtue of heritage could enjoy only the provision of the lowest rank of social status. As a consequence, they remained socially, economically, politically and culturally backward as compared to any other social category.

However, as a result of consistent efforts in several directions, the widening spread of education and consciousness of rights enshrined in the Indian Constitution, there has been a great change in the position of Dalits. In this Chapter, I intend to deal with the problem of social protest movements with special reference to achievements of Dalits in India and to compare them with those of Blacks in the United States of

America.Comparing caste and race, Coxemphasises that factors influencing the choice of occupation for both the races in the United States (Blacks and Whites) are fundamentally different from those which operate in the caste system in India.[3] The questions asked by caste members in viewing the field of labour are different from those which confront Whites and Blacks. In estimating the possibility of an occupation, the caste-man wants to know primarily the attitude of his caste and the degree of purity of occupation in question for upper mobility. However, in both societies, the domination of the subordinate groups is upheld by a social ideology to which the subordinate groups must seem to subscribe in front stage interaction but which they may reject in backstage discourse among themselves, i.e. both Blacks and Dalits do not subscribe to the racial and caste inequalities, though they may be victims of their respective race and caste ideologies. On this point Berreman[4] is in agreement with other sociologists such as Simpson and Yinger[5] and Cox that in the Western forms of inequality non-egalitarian practice confronts egalitarian ideology.

Sociologists and social anthropologists adopted various theoretical approaches in studying issues related to caste, gender and social movements in India. However, some major theoretical approaches may be grouped as follows: 1. Structural approaches grounded on functional and dialectical models. 2. Historical approach; and 3. Conflict approach.In this chapter I do not intend to review all these but attempt to find common grounds for an intersectional theoretical approach and also to show the biases and limitations from which the different approaches suffer.

An intersectional theoretical approach interlocks various theoretical concepts in order to study a research problem. A series of concepts related to caste, gender and social movements in this approach could be integrated into a viewpoint on the basis of theoretical formulations. It is my endeavour to find out the underlying theoretical and conceptual formulations of various approaches to study the issues of caste, gender and social movements and then unite them into a viewpoint which would achieve a fair degree of conceptual analysis of a particular problem.

A comparison of the given situation of caste, class and gender in India with race, class and gender in the United States of America,[6] suggests that multiracial feminism provides similar integrated concepts in the study of all three. Multiracial feminism provides an analysis of the above intersections and asserts that gender is constructed by a range of interlocking inequalities: what Patricia Hill calls 'a matrix of domination'; the idea of a matrix of several fundamental systems interacting with and through each other. A person's experiences of race, class, gender and sexuality differ depending upon his social location in the structure of race, class, gender and sexuality.[7]Multiracial feminism encapsulates all aspects of the problem under the intersectional theoretical approach.

In the case of caste and gender in India, an individual or group may face a similar situation and it might be very useful to adopt an intersectional approach in order to understand the crux of the issue.What is most important conceptually and analytically in this approach is the articulation of multiple oppressions.[8] The intersectional theoretical approach is quite open to the development of a multidimensional paradigm and articulation of the basic issues from different dimensions. Further emphasising the importance of this approach, Brewer said that as theorists explicate the intersection of race, gender and class our conceptualisation of racial inequality will change. Similarly, the intersectional theoretical understanding of caste and gender in India gives a more specific multidimensional picture of the problem. Understanding race and gender as a relational, interlocking, socially constructed system affects how we strategize for change and also alerts us to sources of inertia and resistance to change.[9] In the case of India, the relationship between caste and gender depends upon the same situation as in the case of race and gender in USA.

For an adequate sociological analysis of these social protest movements for a new social identity based on de-stigmatised caste and racial considerations of their ideologies and their styles of assertion, it is essential to put both the Dalit and Black protest movements together into a common theoretical framework.There have been two types of ideology among the Dalits and Blacks. The first is an *acquiescent* ideology in which one accepts his/her low status or position and avoids any confrontation with others but may request the oppressor to allow access to education, employment etc., in order to serve them better. Such a person is submissive, and the dominant group grants him/her some of the facilities out of generosity. The other popular ideology is protest by the deprived sections of the society who organise themselves to resist innumerable types of exploitation and oppression by the dominant groups.

Both the Dalits and Blacks have organised assertive efforts for their respective societies. Their protest ideology involves resistance, confrontation and conflict with the oppressors. Dalits and Blacks alike have adapted these to achieve their desired goals of social equality, social dignity and de-stigmatised social identity.Retrospectively, it can be seen that the identity achieved with the help of acquiescent ideology was a type of self-mortification since the identifier accepted the status of servitude. A movement based on such ideology could hardly be called a movement to achieve social mobility which might lead to the formation of a new social identity. It was a situation of sponsored mobility where the dominant groups granted access to modern education and employment opportunities out of generosity.Under the rubric of an acquiescent ideology, there was no enhancement of self-image, honour, dignity and esteem, as patronage was received for being obedient, humble and submissive. Sponsored mobility merely buttressed the super-ordinate subordinate relationship[10]. To support his argument, Rao has cited the movement of the *Chammbhars* in Maharashtra[11] who did not challenge the superiority and hegemony of the caste-Hindus, accepting their status as leather-workers, and also following all the religious rituals and rites of caste-Hindus enabling them to get modern education which, however, resulted in individual rather than group mobility.[12]

Booker T. Washington in the US followed the same ideology as his followers and supporters that is to accept their unequal status but to pursue business-oriented education so that they could serve their masters better.[13] Since this meant accepting positions of servitude, this movement did not raise the honour and self-respect of the Blacks. Gunnar Myrdal stressed that 'Washington was an accommodationist leader because he never relinquished full equality as the ultimate goal. Washington's main motive was 'accommodation for price'. He was prepared to give up social and political equality if the Blacks were allowed to work undisturbed with their White friends for education and business.'[14]In contrast, the protest movements of Dalits and Blacks asserted the demand for self-respect, social dignity and equity and gave a new direction to liberation struggles in their respective societies. These movements did not depend on any kind of patronage from the dominant groups; rather they sought confrontation. Basically, the protest ideology of both movements centred on socio-economic-cultural dimensions rather than economic and political disabilities.

Historically speaking, the Brahminical orthodoxy and legitimacy of caste in India were first challenged by Buddhism in the 6th century B.C.E. which preached the equality, justice and the fraternity of all human beings. In the present century, the Untouchables have been drawn towards Buddhism ever since Ambedkar revived it as an emancipatory religion for the oppressed.[15]Some Indian Dalits and Black Americans rejected their parental religions, i.e. Hinduism and Christianity, in order to escape from the trap of degraded social status. They either sought for reform in their parental religion or embraced another religion in protest. In either case, there were organised movements. In India, from the 13th century to the present day, reformist movements like the 'Bhakti (sic) Movements'[16], which attracted Dalits, were led by Kabir, Ravidas, Shivnarayan, Chaitanya,Chokhamela Namdev and others, who attacked the caste system and stressed equality of status. Katti Padma Rao says that:

> The Bhakti movements subscribed to the theory of one God only. The Bhakti poets rejected the practice of worshipping plurality of Gods. They also discarded caste and untouchability. They proposed the ideal of humanism instead.Although, these were essentially reform movements, the ideal of Humanism, which came to the forefront served as an instrument in providing an alternative to the movement of religious orthodoxy.[17]

Oommen has emphasised that:

> All the Bhakti Movements shared the following characteristics: First, they were 'reformist' in that they only attempted to correct some of the evils of Hinduism, particularly the practice of untouchability, without questioning the caste system in general. Second, they were mostly initiated by caste Hindus... Third, once caste with differing ritual rank was associated with the movements, the participants developed a dual identity; a religious ideological identity with fellow participants of the movements, and a socio-cultural identity with social collectives (caste) to which they traced their origin. Fourth, none of the Bhakti Movements had a program of socio-economic status; the equality professed by them remained a mirage.[18]

A new style of protest was established by Swami Vivekananda and Dayananda Saraswati in the middle of the 19th century. Their movements, called Neo-Vedantic movements, upheld the *varna* system as an occupational division of society, though they certainly called for the removal of the practice of untouchability in Hinduism. Thus, these movements are reinterpretationist, talking of equality, self-respect and the dignity of all human beings but within the fold of the religion of their origin, i.e. Hinduism.

A number of backward class movements were launched in the pre-independence period. The backward classes organised themselves against the Brahmanas in particular as they thought that most of the socio-economic advantages were cornered by them depriving the agricultural intermediate castes and communities.Likewise, another important movement emerged in Kerala, stated by Sri. Narayana Guru Swami who established a new social identity for the *Ezahavas*, a former untouchable caste. This was also based on reinterpretation of orthodox Hinduism.These were similar to Jotiba Phule's *Satyashodhak Samaj* movement, with the similar aim of ending oppression by the Brahmanas. The Brahmanas were the first to exploit modern educational and employment opportunities.

The upper non-Brahmana castes failed to get access to these opportunities. The *Sri Narayana Dharma Paripalana* (SNDP) movement, among the *Ezahavas* of Kerala, is an example of conflict between the depressed classes and the upper non-Brahmana castes. The Ezhavas were a caste of toddy-tappers in Kerala. They were like the Nadars of Tamil Nadu and the *Idigas* of Karnataka. The Ezhavas were the largest single caste group constituting 26 per cent of the total population of Kerala. In a developing country like India, movements led by the backward classes speak of their low status, disadvantages, discriminations and deprivations which they suffered for a long time at the hands of the ruling classes and communities.

The SNDP movement is an example of a 'regional' movement. It pertains to the Ezhavas of Kerala who were untouchables. The ideology of the movement was formulated by Sri Narayana Guru Swamy. He formed a programme of action known as the 'SNDP Yogam'. The Yogam took up several issues, including the right of admission to public schools, recruitment to government employment, entry into temples, on roads and political representation.

Most of these objectives were realised. The movement, as a whole, brought about transformative structural changes which included upward social mobility, a shift in the traditional distribution of power and a federation of 'backward castes' into a large conglomeration. Caste reforms and mobility movements were launched in almost all parts of India during the British period.These movements had two objectives:(1) To protest against the hegemony of Brahmins in particular and of other upper castes in general; and(2) To elevate the position of the backward castes in the caste hierarchy by imitating lifestyles of the upper castes, including having higher education and prestigious jobs. These movements invariably created 'ethnic' awareness and politicisation among various caste groups. The*Izahavas* have suffered from educational, religious, economic and political disabilities. Sri Narayana Guru Swami gave them a new religion of one God, one religion and one caste which changed their lifestyle and social outlook. He also established a set of religious institutions, like temples, priests, monks and monasteries which are parallel to that of Brahminical Hinduism and facilitated their protest and challenge against the religious, economic, educational and political supremacy of the upper castes.

The same type of protest ideology of reinterpretation of faith was adopted by Blacks in the USA. For instance, in the second and third decades of the 20th century, Marcus Garvey launched such a movement to establish a new social identity of the Blacks. He created a new religious faith, New Christianity, characterised by Christ as a God of Blacks only, since they considered themselves as oppressed and the oppressed are always blessed with God. Garvey also made a move to prepare a separate Black Bible which contained the pictures of their holy saints and angels. In addition, he established the Black Theology which emerged as the theology of liberation by identifying the Blacks as the oppressed and the Whites as oppressors.[19] According to Rao, the Black Christian theology which ran parallel to white Christian theology, 'gave them a new basis of identity, legitimising their efforts towards self-determination and their efforts to gain honour and prestige'.[20]

Another set of protest movement was launched on the basis of the ideology of rejection. This for both Blacks and the Dalits, meant rejecting their parental religion and embracing another which advocated equality and self-respect and also satisfied their human dignity. As far as Dalit liberation movements are concerned, one has to remember that there are three philosophical preceptors – in North IndiaMahatma Jotiba Phule, B.R. Ambedkar and in South India E.V. Ramaswami Naicker.[21]Though all of them emerged from the impact of Bhakti Movements, they had shaped the abolition of caste as a theoretical weapon for the social revolution.

Phule was a pioneer who came forward not only as the leader of a movement, but as the founder of a new philosophy. Phule was a Sutra, an agricultural community of the same rank as the Marathas. In 1851, he became the first Hindu to run a school for the Dalits. In 1873, in Maharashtra, he organised an anti-Brahmin movement, emphasising the building of a social system free from social inequalities, Brahminical hegemony and orthodoxy and the caste system which eventually led to the foundation of the *Satya Shodak Samaj*[22] 'to redeem the *Sutras* and *Adhisutras* (Untouchables) from the influence of Brahminical scripture..., to teach them their human rights and to liberate them from mental and religious slavery'.[23]

He thus organised the first protest movement among the lower castes. 'His championship of untouchables, his ruthless attack on Brahmin domination, his exposure of the origin of castes, the Aryan doctrine, his demand for complete equality...

his demand for education for the lowest, and his insistence on equality between men and women, constituted a thorough declaration of war on the old hierarchical order. He considered that the main instruments of realising the programme were the spread of education and enlightenment, an anti-caste consciousness and the fight against Brahmin domination and against the upper caste monopoly of advance under the British Raj'.[24]

Dr. Ambedkar, who kindled this fire of 'social revolution' among the Dalits, stated that 'religion must recognise the fundamental tenets of liberty, equality and fraternity. Unless a religion recognises these three fundamental principles of social life, religion will be doomed'.[25] Ambedkar was inspired by Jotiba Phule in his political struggle to ensure rights for the Dalits. Forced entry into the temples, the eradication of untouchability, freedom from the traditional, inferior jobs forced on the untouchables in Indian villages, gaining concessions and special privileges for the untouchables in education and employment and separate electorates for the untouchables were some of the many movements he started. Certainly, Ambedkar was a Hindu till a few months before his death, but he was anguished at the iniquity of the caste system; 'To untouchables' he said, 'Hinduism is a veritable chamber of horrors. The iron law of caste, the heartless law of karma, and senseless law of status by birth are veritable instruments of torture which Hinduism has forged against the untouchable'.[26] Hence in October 1956, as a result of his disillusionment with the Hindu religion, he subsequently rejected Hinduism and embraced Buddhism, which satisfied his conscience and his understanding of the concepts of equality and justice.

Ambedkar's embracing of Buddhism, along with thousands of his followers in 1956 at Nagpur in Maharashtra State, has been popularly known as his religious conversion movement. However, Zelliot has pointed out that 'conversion as a way out of the untouchables' status was not new in India. Islam, and more especially Christianity, drew large numbers of their converts from the lower castes, and Sikhism in the twentieth century actively encouraged untouchables' conversion.[27] Communities of those who are at the lower ebb of the society are always looking for an outlet to break up the chains of oppression and marginalisation; Dalits used to change their religion to come out from oppression. Hinduism to Christianity and Islam or vice versa was the case in various parts of Tamilnadu during 1980s.

In the history of Tamilnadu of the last hundred years, one cannot forget the influence of Periyaar generally known as EVR, in the development of Tamil renaissance and his involvement in the social movement against Brahminical hierarchy. He was born on September 17, 1879 in Erode, Tamilnadu. He could not continue his education with the elementary school. There are many humiliating incidents, which seem to have been the seed of his strong opposition to caste discrimination. The humiliation which he had experienced made him anti-brahministic and drew him into radical social involvement, such as the socio-cultural revolution that changed the caste system.

His views on caste, class, political involvement, women's liberation, religion, economic equality and various other social aspects were very radical and challenging. He went in search of understanding the causes for this discrimination; finally,he came to a conclusion that Hindu religion and Brahmins were the causes of all oppression and bondage. The social life of South Indians was very much based on the religious worldview of predestination. This worldview leads everyone to a passive acceptance of a discriminatory hierarchical caste-ridden society.

Periyaar spent his whole lifetime working for a society based on human dignity, equality and social justice. He took a clear-cut approach to humanity based on humanism. According to him what is assumed to be public welfare can be a cause of personal welfare. He says that 'When I work for public cause I feel extremely happy. Is this not the gratification of my selfishness? Many are benefited by my public service, I feel happy and enjoy gratification. This happiness and gratification are part and parcel of my selfishness. This type of selfishness is quite welcome because it does good to all and not just to one'. Periyaar started his work for the common good of all the people. When India was under colonial power, the Dravidians were also oppressed by the Brahmins. They enjoyed superior status in society in all its dimensions – religious, social, political, cultural and economic. Hence Dravidians were becoming slaves and untouchability was practised in all areas starting from sacred shrines. This made him involve himself in social action for the oppressed people in Tamilnadu.

There was a widespread feeling during EVR's time that the Brahmins were dominating public life and government positions out of all proportion to their numbers and most of the government decision making positions were occupied by Brahmins. One of the reasons behind this was that education was not given to the non-Brahmins. Dalits were treated as slaves and untouchables; they were forbidden to walk through the streets of the high caste people; they were forbidden to wear *dhotis*(long white cloth, tied around men's waists) below their knee; they were not allowed to wear gold ornaments; they were not allowed to fetch water from the common water tank; they had to take water with a mud pot only.Dalit children could not get education. Dalit women could not wear their upper clothes and they could not have their own house.[28] There are a few among these that still exist, but Pericarp eradicated some of them. Pericarp protested against these attitudes through his writings and speeches.

Periyaar found that the causes of some of the social evils were the Hindu religion and Brahmins. The word for caste in the Sanskrit language is *Varna*. It originally meant colour.According to Periyaar, Brahmins were Aryans, who came to India sometime about the middle of the second millennium BC and were originally fair skinned people in contrast to the dark Dravidians, the original inhabitants of the country. The great Hindu epics were written by the Brahmins and portray Dravidians in a negative image. These literatures are mythical stories which were created by Aryans to support their supremacy. Aryans, in order to preserve the purity of their blood and the fairness of their skin, divided the people into four classesthroughout their literature. These were classified and called castes. Among these castes the first group sit on the shoulders of the two later groups, while the middle one feels rather comfortable, by claiming domination and supremacy over the last group with its discriminatory practices. Therefore, according to Periyaar the evil of caste system, reinforced by the Hindu religion, should be eradicated first, if India was to change.He called all the non-Brahmins and the Dalits to come out as a united force to root out the caste system and the Hindu religion.[29]

In 1919,Periyaar joined the Indian National Congress,[30] committed to the cause of national independence and also to the cause of the liberation of the Dravidians and Dalits. As the party's regional president, Pericarp protested against the principles and politics of his party, which never condemned the untouchability practised among the party leaders and members. His demand for the reservation of a fixed quota of seats for the non-Brahmins both in the provincial committee and also in the cabinet was turned down. He slowly became alienated from the conservative Brahmin leadership of the INC and so resigned. However, through other channels he continued to work for social justice and liberation.[31]

The self-respect movement was started by Periyaar in 1925 in order to restore the self-respect of the non-Brahmins. As the founder leader of the *Dravida Kazagam*[32] in South India, he emphasised the creation of a just social order without any caste hierarchy. In the early years the main goal of this movement was to get communal representation in all spheres of public life. This movement functioned as a non-political organisation, which confined its activities to social reform.This movement was also 'an anti-religious, pro-British movement aimed at overthrowing the caste system altogether. It insisted on equality between men and women attracted the lower castes and classes and spread rationalist, egalitarian thinking based on the idea that religion and caste institutions are the core of all evil.'[33]

Periyaar ceaselessly fought for the 'abolition of God', religion and the Brahmins. For him, the roots of evil in society were to be found in religion. In a celebrated saying, he proclaimed: 'God does not at all exist. The inventor of God is a fool; the propagator of God is a scoundrel. The worshipper of God is a barbarian.'[34] According to Periyaar, the aims of this movement were fivefold: 1. God should be eradicated, 2. Religion should be eradicated, 3. Gandhi should be eradicated, 4. Congress should be eradicated, and 5. Brahmins should be eradicated.According to him, Hinduism had been founded by the Brahmins 'for their own power interest; they built on the ignorance, illiteracy and poverty of the people and exploited them. Religion must therefore be abolished; the caste system and domination of the Brahmins must be destroyed'.[35] Periyaar's philosophy on religion was 'Religion suppresses man, it is against reason; on the other hand, rationalism and atheism liberate man'. Here Periyaar's talk of religion and God, referred to Hinduism and its domination. But he said that if any religion supported the people's community life as well as individual moral life, then the Self-Respect Movement, would support that religion.

The contributions of Periyaar and his movement to contemporary Indian society are undeniable. It greatly helped the linguistic and cultural renaissance of Tamilnadu and also it helped to give political and cultural consciousness and identity to the Tamil Dalits. The protest and struggles which are going on at present may not be against the same oppressors, but Periyar started the movement. Some people opposed Periyar for his radical views on Hinduism and caste system but most of the people in Tamilnadu gave political solidarity to Periyaar because of his struggle to achieve equality and justice.Periyaar was known as the liberator for Dalits in the first half of the 20th century. Many Dalits may not accept Periyaar as their liberator, but the fact of the matter is that Periyaar as a non-Dalit revolted against the caste oppression and was involved in the struggles to get equal rights for Dalits. In the context of the early years of the century Periyaar's approach should be appreciated; the oppression of Dalits was from the Brahmins; therefore his anti-Brahmin attitude was suitable.

In that particular context in India one can call Periyaar a liberator of the oppressed.Periyaar rejected all types of myths of the Aryan religion and culture and organised his protest movements again the Sanskritic culture of the Brahmins and self-respect movements among the Dravidians. Periyaar's movement played an important instrumental role in changing the political power map of Tamilnadu while the movements organised by Phule andAmbedkar made a powerful impact towardschanging that social system in North India.[36] They not only rejected the Brahminical supremacy of the Hindu caste system, but also advocated a new social order based on social justice.[37]

As stated above, the ideology of rejection was also adopted by Black Americans in several protest movements launched to evolve a just society and to achieve a dignified social identity. Through such movements, a large number of Black Americans rejected the parental religion and converted to another which preached equality, justice and fraternity to all. Though Christianity advocated brotherhood and equality in principle, the situation was one of utter frustration in which Blacks were given the impression of living in the same religion yet were denied equality and justice. They identified Christianity with Whites, therefore, and embraced Islam, thus protesting against multiple forms of oppression but also against the domination of Whites in American society. The first such Black protest movement was launched by Elijah Mohammad, who rejected Christianity and embraced Islam, and also started the Black Muslim protest movement in the USA.

In the 1960s, the Black movement in the US reasserted itself and the Black protest movement ran parallel to the Civil Rights movement.[38] During this period, the important Black leader was Malcolm X, who was also actively involved in the Black Muslim protest movement. He linked Black Muslim ideology with African nationalism and Black-African civilisation and insisted on rejection of White western civilisation. A new identity formed on the basis of African heritage, was also adopted by Marcus Garvey and Du Bois, both of whom emphasised the superiority of their race and culture. In fact, Garvey's protest movement may be seen as a synthesis of two ideologies of protest (a) a reinterpretation of Christianity, and (b) a rejection of American cultural values.

Both Dalit Indians and Black Americans strove to achieve their desired goals of equality and laid stress on the civil rights of the oppressed as a counter to atrocities perpetrated on them. In Maharashtra, the *Mahar* movement under the leadership of Ambedkar adopted the civil rights ideology while in Agra, a city in Uttar Pradesh, a self-respect movement was launched by *Jatav* Youths. These movements generated a sense of self-respect and an awareness of their basic rights as enshrined in the Constitution of India. From the 'Mahad March in 1927 to the Yeola Conference in 1936' Ambedkar adopted the ideology and means of civil rights to protest against the socio-economic, cultural-religious, and political disabilities and oppression of the Dalits. He not only protested and fought against the practice of untouchability and the tenets of Hinduism but also demanded basic civil rights for Untouchables. However, social awareness among Dalits is being manifested in conflict, especially in rural areas where atrocities on Dalits have increased tremendously in comparison to the past. This indicates that there is a need to generate still more awareness among them of their legal and constitutional rights so that they can protect themselves under the law.

Inspired by Ambedkar's ideology, Ram Vilas Paswan, a Dalit Member of Parliament, also launched a self-respect movement in December 1991. This movement was organised by the '*Dalit Sena*'[39]which he headed from Tsundur, Andhra Pradesh, where 122 Dalits had been massacred by Caste-Hindus. During the course of his movement between 6 December 1991 and 14 April 1992, Paswan highlighted the issues and problems faced by the Dalits and also drew the attention of the whole nation towards the increasing atrocities in Indian society.He not only demanded protection for Dalits from atrocities but also made them aware of their socio-economic, political and legal rights.

In the 1950s, a new chapter in the history of Black protest movements had been added in the USA by Martin Luther King Jr. who adopted the civil rights ideology as a strategy in the Black movement and organised the Southern Christian Conference,[40] and by Du Bois, who established the *National Association for the Advancement of Colored People*.[41] King practised non-violent direct action on the model established by Gandhi during India's independence struggle with Britain. He moved the Black struggle from the courtroom to the street and from the street to the church pew. He also led several economic boycotts, desegregation and voter registration campaigns, always adopting a non-violent ideology of civil rights.

Similarly, Du Bois also organised movements demanding full civil rights, economic opportunities and education for all the Black youth. He was influenced by Marxism and had developed an interest in pan-Americanism though he always maintained that race was stronger than class. Du Bois, 'vacillated between Marxism and a middle class ideology and the latter eventually got the better of the former in him. This was the strategy that he adopted in fighting for basic civil rights'.[42] Thus, both Du Bois and Martin Luther King Jr protested against the Whites' supremacy and the racial segregation which had subjected the Blacks to multiple types of deprivation.A new ideology opened in the history of social protest movements with the formation of the Black Panther Party in the USA, and the Dalit Panther Movement in India. While the immediate cause of the formation of the Black Panther Party was the increasing brutality by the White police, the increasing atrocities perpetrated by the caste-Hindus on the Dalits were responsible for the formation of the Dalit Panthers.

The Black Panther Party was organised in October 1966, at Oakland in California, with the aim of protecting the Blacks from police brutality and other harassment by the Whites. Bobby Seal and Huey P. Newton organised this movement for self-defence by carrying arms. It was an extremist development in the protest movement of Black Americans. The Panthers emphasised revolutionary nationalism rather than cultural nationalism.[43] They were very radical and militant and were able to penetrate into the poor working class of the urban ghettos in the USA.

The Dalit Panthers in India, for their part, were a militant organisation started by Dalit youths, mainly neo-Buddhists in Bombay.[44] The movement was born in Bombay and had been very popular among the ex-untouchables in Maharashtra. They organised themselves to attack the upper-caste Hindu capitalists and those who committed atrocities on Dalits. The anger of the Dalits was beginning to be expressed in the literature produced by young Dalit writers like Baburao Bagul, Narayan Surve, Namdeo Shasal, Raja Dhale and J.V. Pawar. The Dalit Panthers Movement in India officially born on 9 July, 1972and was formed under the leadership of Raja Dhale as president, Namdev Dhasal as defence minister, and J.V. Pavar as its general secretary.[45] To protect their fellow Dalits from violence and atrocities, they were prepared,if necessary, to adopt violent strategies. The name Dalit Panther was obviously inspired by the Black Panthers – the militant Black organisation in the USA, thus, both the Black Panthers and Dalit Panthers accepted the ideology of class-conflict and chose to directly confront the oppressors by adopting radical and violent means. The *modus operandi* of the Dalit Panthers would be to converge in large numbers at a village where injustice was done and protect their people by using force, if necessary. Dalit Panthers came to be known as a new force to be reckoned with. They drew their organisational structure from the Black Panther Party and were also greatly influenced by Black literature.

The Dalit Panthers, embellishing the concept of Dalits' emancipation in their 'Manifesto', emphasised that a complete revolution was needed. 'We do not want a little place in the *Brahmin Alley*. We want the rule of the whole land; we are not looking at persons but systems and change of heart...liberal education etc. will not end our state of exploitation. When we gather a revolutionary mass, rouse the people out of the struggle, the giant mass will become a tidal wave of revolution'.[46] However, the ideologies of Jotiba Phule and Ambedkar had helped the Dalit Pathers to reorganise themselves in Maharastra.

The Dalit Panthers have avoided the mistakes that the Republican Party committed. The Republican Party was, for example, exclusively confined to the Mahar community, or in the latter days to the neo-Buddhist community. Firstly, the Dalit Panthers insisted right from the beginning on involving other oppressed communities. Secondly, they were considerably less vehement than the Republican Party about accepting and practising Buddhism.The Republican Party had been plagued by a personality cult for the party, Ambedkar was a kind of demi-god. The Panthers kept clear of, and were not plagued by, personality cult.Thirdly, the Panthers very severely criticised the corrupt leaders. Fourthly, the Dalit Panthers quickly realised that no political party could start an effective agitation to put an end to untouchability, as most parties had let themselves be caught by the vicious circle of election-politics.The Dalit Panthers, therefore, kept their organisation away from party-political agitation; they decided not to contest elections and to launch an agitation for social reforms. One must admit that, at least, for some time the organisation scrupulously practised these policies. The Dalit Panther Movement, in spite of its limitations, gave much needed confidence and courage to the Dalits who had for generations lived on contempt and at times on pity. Their contribution to Indian political and social life was significant in the sense that their actions stirred India's latent tolerance into the realisation that in a democracy people have to assert their rights.

The Dalit Panther Movement attracted the attention of society towards issues like atrocities and inequity and helped in enlightening society. The Movement also acted as a check on the power politics of Dalit Political parties such as the Republican Party of India by boldly exposing the mendacity of their leaders. The Dalit Panther Movement also helped initiate a debate on the need of an objective analysis of the thoughts and ideology propounded by Ambedkar.The Movement was successful to the extent that it forced the decision-makers to recognise the needs of the Dalits and to commit institutional resources to implement corrective measures. For example, the Panthers compelled the Government to fill the backlog of reserved quota in government and bank services. In the literary field, especially in poetry, the Movement injected a new type of 'revolt literature'.[47]Perhaps, the most noteworthy achievement of the Dalit Panther movement was its contribution to literature. The Dalit literature shook the foundations of Hindu orthodoxy; and shaped the Dalit writers as fighting rebels.[48]Rao also firmly affirms that:

> [T]he fight for liberation of the Dalits gave a new awareness to the Literary Movement of the Dalits as also a new power. The movements for

> liberation and fight began to stimulate each other. The contribution of the Dalit Literary Movement was significant, – in bringing a new outlook in their ideas in the social, economic, and political fields, – especially in reconciling them with the philosophical outlook of Dr. Ambedkar.[49]

The Dalit Panthers created a revolutionary consciousness among the oppressed through literature. Patankar and Omvedt have mentioned that:

> [T]he achievements of the Dalit movements are impressive, and are too often overlooked. They have given birth to a tradition of struggle in many areas, not only on cultural and ritual issues but on breaking feudal bonds. They have mounted powerful pressure on the national movement resulting in constitutional provisions for reservations and laws making untouchability an offence; unsatisfactory as these have been, they have still provided weapons in the hands of low-caste organisers. They have created a deep-seated conviction of equality and self-confidence which is inevitably making itself heard.[50]

The Black protest movements bring out the similarities and differences in the socio-cultural, political and economic aspects of their social life. American racism in many ways parallels Indian casteism and the condition of Dalits in India is very similar to that of Blacks in America. Though untouchability has not been practised against the Blacks in the American social system, the practice of racial segregation has beenvery much there.Historically, most of the Blacks were both psychologically and materially deprived by the presumption that they were racially inferior to the Whites. In a similar fashion, the Dalits were deprived by the caste system in India. They were denied educational, political, economic, religious as well as other civil rights before the period of British rule in India.

Thus, the major cause behind the social protest movements of both Blacks and Dalits was their centuries-old exploitation, oppression and repression in their respective societies. Yet, the socio-cultural differences between India and America are so great that the various types of protest movements tend to be more different than alike. While the Dalits in India have always been inhabitants of the country, the Blacks were migrant labourers in the USA which led to their enslavement by the Whites. Whereas the discriminatory practices against the Blacks are racial, based on the colour of their skin, the Dalits are the victims of religious discrimination based on the theory of *chturvarna* of the Hindu religion and suffer from ritual disabilities.

The caste system has been prevalent for centuries in Indian society while racism in the USA is only 350 years old. The most important difference between the Blacks and Dalits in the structural placement of the respective societies is that the Blacks, though they have several political opinions or factions among them, are not segmentally divided into numerous endogamous groups like Dalits. The Dalits are heterogeneous castes based on different cultural and linguistic divisions, while this is not the case for American Blacks. Moreover, they also do not suffer from ritual disabilities, as do the Dalits.

Class-based divisions among the Dalits are not as sharp as in the case of Blacks. It is only in urban society that a middle-class Dalit group has appeared in increasing numbers and their bourgeoisie is still comparatively radical in its thinking. In contrast to this, Black capitalists have promoted a cultural and national integration approach which is opposed to the revolutionary approach adopted by the lower strata among the Blacks. Another important difference between the Blacks and Dalits is that the latter are a social category which is broad enough to include even the poor and downtrodden of other sections of society while the Blacks maintain a racial category, and can easily be distinguished physically from the Whites and segregated because of their visible racial identity.

Any social movement is an organised effort by an individual, group or community to achieve a particular goal. Essentially, the social movements launched by Blacks and Dalits are based on the ethos of protest which has been directed against their socio-economic, religious-cultural and legal oppression and exploitation.

The status of the Blacks in the USA has changed drastically especially in the last forty years as a positive result of powerful and effective Black protest movements. These movements broke down the barriers of institutionalised racial segregation. For the Blacks, the social, cultural and psychological process that activated and maintained these movements reinforced collective and political personal identities. Politically correct terms used in reference to Blacks today are 'African-Americans' or 'Black Americans', instead of 'Negro' or 'coloured people'. Black Pride is in vogue in addition to the pursuance of the equality of rights and integration. As a result of these protest movements, the government was forced to adopt the policy of affirmative action and other measures which have done much to improve their socio-economic status in American society. The policy has helped in structural changes and in creating a new class of Black bourgeoisie, even though others have remained in the lower class. However, the mass mobilisation of the Blacks has led to the emergence of a new 'Black consciousness' which has helped them to form a special identity which is recognised both by American society and by the rest of the world.

Similarly, the Dalits too, have organised several protest movements and intensified their struggle against socio-economic, religious, cultural and political deprivation and oppression in Indian society. The caste system of today in India is not the same as it was a hundred years ago. These protests movements have brought about various structural and functional changes. And yet, though Dalits have achieved much in their struggle for socio-economic and political rights in the

Indian social system, atrocities against them by caste-Hindus have increased rather than decreased. However, these atrocities may paradoxically be taken as a positive phenomenon in the social life of Dalits, for wherever and whenever they assert their legitimate rights, the result is confrontation and consequently atrocities.

As yet, the Dalits are economically very poor and weak but psychologically and morally they have become very confident and strong to raise their voice against exploitation and oppression at any level. The social consciousness generated by Dalit protest movements have played a significant and important role in making them confident enough to fight against age-old discrimination. This consciousness may be termed as Dalit consciousness, which, as in the case of the Black Americans, reflects the consciousness of a collectivity. It is unfortunate, however, that the policy of protective discrimination or reservation policy, a result of these decades-old social protest movements, has proved to be beneficial only to a limited section of the Dalits. The beneficiaries of this policy are very small in number in comparison to the percentage of their population and form a small segment of the middle class among Dalits which may be termed as Dalit bourgeoisie. The policy needs to be more effective in its implementation and realistic in taking into account the Dalit population and position.

To sum up, it may be stated with full conviction that due to the emergence of Dalit consciousness and Black consciousness, the Dalits have become dignified and the Blacks have become beautiful for their respective communities. But it is essential to note that governmental policies in the USA and India still need to be made more effective in their implementation. In India, for example, the laws need to be made and enforced in order to wipe out the practice of untouchability and caste-based discrimination. Only by such measures can the Dalits and the Blacks be fully integrated within their respective societies in a meaningful way.

Endnotes

1. The term 'Blacks' and 'Negroes' are used here in this research only to identify the 'Suffering Community'; it is not the intention of the researcher to use it as a derogatory word.
2. Kerala isone of the States (provinces) in South India.
3. C.O. Cox, *Caste, Class and Race*, Modern Reader, 1948, pp. 438 - 439.
4. G. Berreman, *Caste and Other Inequalities*, Folklore Institute, 1979.
5. G.E.Simpson & J.M.Yinger, Racial and Cultural Minorities: An Analysis of Prejudice and Discrimination, Harper & Brothers, New York, 1953.
6. Hereafter mentioned USA.
7. Zinn & Dinn, 1996,p. 11.
8. R.M. Brewer 'Theorizing Race, Class and Gender: The New Scholarship of Black Feminist Intellectuals and Black Labour Women', in S.M. James and A.P.A. Buisa (eds.), *Theologizing Black Feminism*, London, Routledge, 1993, p. 13.
9. E.N. Glenn, 'Race and Gender Stratification', *Review of Racial Political Economic*, vol. 38, no. 1, 1992, pp. 35 - 36.
10. M.S.A. Rao, *Social Movements in India*, Vol 2, New Delhi, Manohar Anand Publications, 1984, p. 208.
11. Chammbhars are one of the Untouchable castes in Maharashtra. And Maharashtra is one of theStates (Provinces) in western part of India.
12. Rao, *Social Movements in India.*
13. B.T. Washington, Inferior and Superior Races, *North American Reviews*, April 1915.
14. G. Myrdal, *An American Dilemma: The Negro Problems and Modern Democracy*, New York, Harper Brothers, 1994, p. 210.
15. A. Thumma, *Dalit Liberation Theology: Ambedkarian Perspective*, ISPCK, 2000, pp. 72–74.
16. Bhakti Movements means Devotional Reform Movements emerged from Hindu religion itself.

17. K.P. Rao, *Caste and Alternative Culture*, Gurukul Lutheran Theological College and Research Institute, 1995, p. 105.
18. T.K. Oommen, *Protest and Change: Studies in Social Movements*, New Delhi, Sage Publications, 1990, p. 258.
19. M. Garvey, 'Arms and Objectives for the Evaluation of the Negro Problems', in Broderick Francis (ed.), *The Black Protest Thought in Twentieth Century,* Routledge, 1971, p. 90.
20. M.S.A. Rao, *Social Movements and Social transformation,* Manohar Anand Publications, 1981, pp. 210 -213.
21. He was fondly called EVR or Periyar which means the elderly statesman; forthis research he was mentioned as Periyar.
22. Means 'Truth Seeking Society'.
23. D. Keer, *Mahatma Jyoti Rao Phooley*, Dhanjay Keer Prakashan, 1987, p. 126.
24. Ranadev, p. 344.
25. D.C. Ahir, *The Legacy of Dr. Ambedkar,* Delhi, B.R. Publishing Corporation, 1991, p. 301.
26. Ibid., p. 293.
27. E. Zelliot, 'Buddhism and Politics in Maharashtra', in D.E.Smith (ed.), *South Asian Politics and Religion*, Princeton, PrincetonUniversity Press, 1966, pp. 191 - 212. And also see 'Religion and Legitimation in the Mahar Movement', in B.L. Smith (ed.), *Religion and Legitimation of Power in South Asia*, L.E.J. Brill, 1978, pp. 88 - 105.
28. J. Maliekal, *Caste in India Today*,Bangalore, CSA Publication, 1980, p.57.
29. Ibid.
30. Hereafter mentioned as INC.
31. K.P. Rao,*Caste and Alternative Culture*, The Gurukul Lutheran Theological College & Research Institute, 1995, p. 127.
32. Known as Dravidian Movement.
33. Lieten, p. 322For details on different ideological trends within the Self-Respect Movement see also Ram, p. 30
34. Quoted by Ram, p. 393.

35. M.M. Thomas, p. 128. This was part of Periyar's statement on his 92ndbirthday!

36. K.P. Rao, *Caste & Alternative Culture*, The Gurukul Lutheran Theological College & Research Institute, 1995, pp. 126 - 127.

37. For concrete cases, see L.I. Rudolf & S.H. Rudolf, *The Modernity of Tradition*, New Delhi, 1967; and the study of Rao on the *Yadav Movement, in Social Movement and Social Transformation*, Delhi, Macmillan Company, 1979, pp. 123 - 130.

38. T. Draper,*The Rediscovery of Black Nationalism*, New York, Kegan Paul Ltd, 1979, pp. 544 - 555.

39. 'Dalit Sena' means 'Dalit Army' which is a militant outfit of Dalit Youths in North India. Eventually it has become a political party.

40. Which was known as SCLC.

41. Known as NAACP.

42. M.S.A. Rao, *Social Movements in India*, p. 201.

43. C.E. Jones, The Political Representation of the Black Panther Party, *Journalof Black Studies*, vol. 18, no. 4, June, pp.38 - 45, 416 - 441.

44. Bombay is now called Mumbai. For the sake of clarity, the writer is using the old name Bombay in this research.

- The government must stop giving grants to religious institutions immediately and the wealth of religious places must be used for the benefit of Dalits.

- Religious and casteist literature must be banned.

- The division in the army along caste lines must be ended.

- Blackmarketeers, hoarders, money-lenders and all those exploiting the people economically must be destroyed.

- The price of essential commodities must be reduced.

46. N. Dhasal, 'Itihasachi Chakra Ulti Firvu Naka Nahitarjal', Pamphlet Published by Namdeo Dhasal (in Marati), Bombay, 1974, p. 28.

47. R.K. Padma,*Caste & Alternative Culture*, p. 136.

48. Ibid, p. 137.
49. Ibid, pp. 139 - 140.
50. B. Patankar & G. Omvedt, 'Kanjhawala', *Frontier*, 2 December 1978, p. 423. It is doubtful whether the Congress Party would have abolished untouchability without the Dalit movements... and very unlikely that it would have organised a system of 'protective discrimination'.

CHAPTER 5

Indian Liberation Theology

'Interrogating theology of liberation about its legitimate ancestry is like asking a Mexican Indian or a Colombian coffee planter for the historical truth behind their family tradition' writes Frei Betto in the Festschrift for Gustavo Gutiérrez's sixtieth birthday. Guitierrez is generally acclaimed as the father of Liberation Theology, since that was the title of an article, he wrote in a local paper immediately before the Medellin Conference of the Latin American Bishops, which gave the strongest support to the Theology of Liberation.But Gutierrez himself got the inspiration, according to Betto, from his visit to Brazil in 1969, where basic ecclesial communities and the episcopate were confronting the military dictatorship. But one cannot deny 'the European roots springing from Maritain's integral humanism, Mounier'scommitted personalism, Teilhard de Chardin's progressive evolutionism, de Lubac's social dogmatics, Congar's theology of the laity, Lebret's theology of development, Colombia's theology of revolution or Metz's political theology'.[1]

Liberation Theology has its familiarity among well-educated Indians– journalists, political scientists, socialists, grass root activists, and so on. For many non-Christians in India, and Asia at large, that has been a point of lively interest regarding Christianity at the global level. It has been welcomed so much that a call was given out for a similar Hindu liberation theology.[2] On the other hand, this theology has been found so dangerous and subversive that the government of Singapore ordered the closure of the office of the Christian Conference of Asia (CCA) on its territory. Accusations have been levelled against liberation theology by other Asian countries.[3]In 1987, the Christian Conference of Asia's headquarters in Singapore were closed by the government and it was expelled, accused of supporting 'subversive movements'.It is against this background of welcome and rejection that this chapter analyses the story of the genesis and development of an Indian theology of liberation, the way it is being pursued and the path ahead.[4] This cannot be done without referring to the stimulus from Latin America, even as Indian theology follows its own distinctive path of liberation set in its own specific context.

In a broad sense, the roots of Indian liberation theology go back to the Indian experience of anti-colonial and anti-imperial struggles. The energies released in anticolonial struggles were kept alive even after independence. The backbone of liberation in India was the experiences of the struggles of the marginalised people.[5] More particularly,the many battles waged by the tribals, workers and agricultural labourers, fishermen and others in the effort to free themselves from the oppression to which they were subjugated.[6]

Another important root for the development of an Indian liberation theology goes back to the experiences of the 1960s and the 1970s. It was the time of proliferation and involvement of the so-called grassroots 'action-groups'.[7] These groups consisted of young people hailing mostly from upper and middle class backgrounds. They were deeply moved by the injustices and oppression to which the poor were subjected, renounced their bright prospective careers, and chose to be in solidarity with the marginalised, and struggle for their liberation. A few of them even renounced marriage to be agents of liberation. Thousands of these action groups made up of such dedicated youth spread out all through the country, and took up different issues of the people.[8] The issues depended upon the particular context, but one thing they all shared was to impart nonformal education to the people and lead them to the awareness of their situation of bondage and exploitation. These groups did not belong to any conventional political party. In fact, most of them kept away from political parties, disillusioned as they were with the unfulfilled promise to better the lot of the poor.

This liberative fervour in the country was fanned by the movement initiated in the mid 1970s by Jayaprakash Narayan, a seasoned social revolutionary who challenged the anti-poor political regime under the leadership of Indira Gandhi. His movement is called the Janata movement, which later on became a political party in India. He sowed the seeds of liberation, particularly in the states of Bihar and Uttar Pradesh, and built up from below a strong liberative movement of peasants and other marginalised groups. Against this backdrop, the Indian ecological movement is ultimately connected with the issue of liberation and social justice. The wanton destruction of the environment has serious and life-threatening effects on people who depend upon nature for their survival.[9]

Among the numerous ecological movements, most of which are spearheaded by Indian women, one such movement is called the Chipko Movement. This movement of villagers was a response to those economic vested interests who wanted to commercialise the forests and market the trees. Symbolically it was expressed by village women hugging the trees and not permitting anyone to cut them because trees were an integral part of their village economy and life support system. This unique movement spread in different parts of India like wildfire and it became an important component of the Indian liberation movement. It is the experience of committed Christians involved in such liberation struggles and movements going beyond religious affiliations that was the origin of an Indian theology of liberation. However, to be able to understand the present-day liberation process that sustains an Indian theology of liberation, one needs to ask what the situation of oppression is against which liberative movements are directed.[10]

It is not the intention of this study to attempt even a general picture of the situation of oppression that characterises the lives of millions of the poor and marginalised in India. The complexities are simply overwhelming. Nevertheless, this study highlights three forces which substantially contribute to the continuous oppression of the poor in the country. In India, caste is an oppressive social structure which is very much alive, even more than ever before, with the difference that it has assumed new and different forms of selfexpression. M.N. Srinivas, one of the foremost Indian social scientists called caste the 'Twentieth Century Avatar'.[11] Its face is changing both in rural and urban areas, but its oppressive effects have not disappeared and they are strong, particularly on women.This ancient institution continues to have its hold, availing all the means and instruments of modernity. It is all-pervasive and there is nowhere to which its tentacles do not reach out. It is a fact that the communist party is headed by Brahmins. This is true of many institutions and movements which are manifestly meant for the liberation of the downtrodden but in actuality are under the control of upper castes. Since in India, in practice, there is an overlapping of caste and class, meaning that the higher castes are also those who wield economic power, the continuation and strengthening of caste amounts also to the economic oppression of the poor by the upper and middle castes.

Unlike in China, there has not been any serious land reform and land distribution in India. The traditional bases of discrimination are still very much active, with a wide gulf between the upper castes and poor sections of society. In such a situation, the modern programmes of globalisation and liberalisation of economy mean quite a different thing to what may be the case in the West, or even in China. Liberal economy is the driving force behind so called globalisation.Globalisation, though it appears to have an aura of uniting people more and more closely, is in fact a process of progressive exclusion.[12]

Liberal economy and globalisation strengthen the traditional forces of dominating castes and in this process leave behind millions of the poor to fend for themselves. In this way, the problem is not so much distribution as exclusion.Culture is an important factor; therefore, the forces of oppression seek to control and dominate it.Be it education or media, culture is in the hands of the urban elite, inspired by the liberal economic spirit, who try to make inroads into the rural areas. These urban elite drain rural resources and sacrifice villages at the expense of liberal economy. Their economic policies have turned the villages into the periphery of the cities.

Closely connected with the above two factors is the third important source of oppression. It consists in debarring the poor and the marginalised from having access to natural resources. To illustrate this with examples of everyday life, millions of poor fishermen no longer have access to fishing by which they always lived, since the seas are controlled by the massive fishing enterprises of big companies who with huge trawlers, sweep through the seas. The tribal people in whose lives and cultures the forests are so much an inalienable part, are deprived of access to the very source of their livelihood, since forests and their trees have become objects of exploitation by entrepreneurial interests. Extreme poverty forces the small farmers to part with their land and flee in their thousands to the cities in the hope of being able to survive. But in cities, they are confined to the pavements and to eke out their existence by volunteering to do odd and ill-defined jobs.

The process of liberation in India is as much active as the effort of oppression. The chief protagonists of this liberation are the poor themselves. The liberation process has different traits according to the nature of the oppression at work and it differs from region to region. The self-assertion of the people resulted in a heavy-handed reprisal on the part of the upper castes and classes.

The emergence and flourishing of right-wing forces such

as the '*Hindutva*' is to be explained in context. *Hindutva* is the ideology that tries to identify India and Indian culture with Hinduism. This ideology gave impetus to the revival of Hindu religious fundamentalism. An important part of the maintenance of order is the preservation of the *varnssramadharma* (the fourfold caste order). The preservation of the dominant modern economic order is coupled with the preservation of the traditional casteorder. The roots of Hindu nationalistic ideology can be traced from the emergence of the Indian Renaissance.

In the face of such experiences, the liberation struggle has even taken on a militant form with leftist ideology for example, the Naxalite movement in Bengal which found no other way than open violence to be able to effect land reform. Many landlords with immense land holdings were murdered by the militants. In Andhra Pradesh the 'Peoples' War Group' wanted to represent the interests of the poor and exploited farmers and other marginalised groups. The battle against the oppressive forces is carried on also on the cultural front. The movements challenging the dominant cultural values and patterns play a very important supportive role in the struggle for liberation. Through folk media such as peoples' theatre, popular lyrics based on the experiences ofthe oppressed and other literary activities the intensity of liberative praxis is maintained.[13]

Having reviewed the background of the forces at work in the genesis of liberation theology and its dynamics, it is important to understand what India has learnt from the Latin American theology of liberation. Latin American theology of liberation has brought insights for the development of an Indian theology of liberation and has reinforced and reaffirmed some of India's culturally-based orientations. However, the mainstay of the Indian theology of liberation is the experience in India of the struggle for liberation.

The Latin American theology has powerfully informed the truth that faith is primarily a matter of praxis and a way of life in conformity with the gospels. The holy alliance of gospel and praxis found inroads among the Indian theological circles. This had found an echo among the Indians in whose religious tradition so much importance is given to *anubhava* or experience. Religions are understood as *margas* – the ways. Further, the fresh understanding of theology which came from the Latin American continent is the age-old, Indian perception of theology as God-revelation and self-realisation. Similarly, it responded to the Indian mainstream of religious faith as steadfastness, rootedness in the practice of truth.

This is the realisation that faith has far-reaching social and political implications and that faith is something that relates to history as a transforming force. Latin American theology of liberation has contributed to India on this score. It has also impressed upon Indian Christianity the necessity of socio-political mediation for a relevant and transforming faith-praxis. In this process, Latin Americans have brought theology closer to social sciences. It appears that it is the first time in history that such an attempt of the alliance of these two 'faith and politics' has been made to relate theological reflection arising from praxis with other social sciences and with economics, in such a way that theology acquires rootedness in the reality of the everyday life.

The traditional Christian life and theology were, by and large, marked by strong individualism due to missionary theology. It is in this shape that Christianity was introduced in many Third World countries, including Asian countries. The Latin American theology of liberation, through the rediscovery of the Bible, has brought to the fore the communitarian dimension of Christian faith and its implications for a life of mutual dependence and responsibility. In Latin America, the basic Christian communities, with the poor and the marginalised as the focus have been the privileged locus to experience the communitarian dimension of faith.

This resonated with the strongly communitarian character of Indian ethos which one can find particularly among the marginalised groups and the tribals. Among these various groups, solidarity and bonds of unity are being built up today for the common task of liberation. This is expressively manifested among the Dalits to become liberated from the oppression of upper castes and classes.

Another contribution has been the method employed in re-reading and interpreting the Christian tradition. Particularly significant has been the Latin American attempt to re-read the Bible as the story of God's preferential love for the weak and the powerless. Through solidarity with the poor, God brings about change and transformation in the world. These insights into the biblical message by Gustavo Gutierrez and others have made the living of Christian faith today for millions of people something exciting and challenging.[14] The new hermeneutical approach to the Bible anchored in the option for the poor, has led Indian theologians to explore similar readings of scriptures for other religious traditions.

Much influence has been exercised by highlighting the person of Jesus as liberator. This has brought Jesus closer to the life and suffering of the Indian masses. The image of Jesus, which the Asians received in the past, has been one very much coloured by the cultural and historical conditionings of Western theology. Jesus only sought peoples' allegiance to Him and to His church.But the image rediscovered from the Gospels in the Latin American liberation theology has presented a Jesus who is amidst the poor and the weak and in solidarity with the rejected and the marginalised; a Jesus who suffers and understands deeply human pain and suffering.[15]

Latin American theology has alsoopened up new horizons by bringing the message of the Reign of God as a reality that addresses our life and struggles in history. It brought to general awareness Jesus' central message of the Reign of God as the basis of our Christian life and praxis. This fresh re-centring on the Reign of God is also something very pertinent from the Indian point of view. This is so, not only for its historical and socio-political implications, but also for its consequences for inter-religious dialogue. In fact, this theme of the Reign of God is one which offers a solid foundation for true universality that transcends all kinds of fences, and thus helps Indians to develop fresh expression of relationships with other faiths.[16]

The historical developments in the West, the inherited Christian tradition in Asia has been one very much opposed to certain secular ideologies like socialism. A re-reading of Christian sources by the Latin American theology of liberation had brought the praxis of Christian faith closer to certain social and secular visions and ideals. This faith-perspective has contributed to deepen the dialogue already initiated in India between Christian faith and social and secular ideologies. It has widened the horizons of dialogue and, more importantly, has clarified the possibility, legitimacy and even the need for a closer collaboration with those committed to secular ideologies.

It is the merit of Latin American theology to have brought to the awareness of Christian faith reflection on the systematic evils and dehumanisation inherent in capitalism and its pursuit of money and profit at the cost of human beings.[17] The Latin American theologians have created the general awareness that faith and theology cannot be indifferent to economy and economic systems, that economics is not simply a technical question; it is also a human issue, and therefore related to faith. For that matter, any religious tradition concernedwithhuman beings and their welfare mustcritically relate to economic systems. Through the analysis of the working of economy and other systems, liberation theology has contributed to the development of new perspectives in understanding oppression, poverty and injustice.

Though liberation is the common concern, yet there are quite substantial points which differentiate Indian commitment to liberation praxis and the formulation of a distinct Indian liberation theology with its own foci and features. In this connection one may recall here the words of James Cone who has articulated well the impossibility of fitting Black theology of liberation into other types of liberation agenda.

> The context of Black Theology of liberation is a theme that is derived from black religion's acceptance of the biblical claim that god discloses his presence in the struggle of the poor for freedom. The method which Black Theology uses in its analysis of this liberation is contextual and dialectical. This means our thought about liberation is not derived from Euro-American reflections, whether it be Marx or Marcuse. Black Theology's reflections on liberation are derived from the social context of the black struggle of freedom, as found in our prayers, songs and sermons...[18]

The primary focus of theological reflection should be one's meeting with God in the contemporary historical situation. Starting with praxis gives a meaning to the historical process whereby community transforms itself in transforming its own environment – persons, things and structure.Praxis comprises not merely action but also passion: *passion-from* as openness to the mystery of life, and *passion-for* as striving for values, ideals and goals. It is the world of praxis that mediates the presence and the in-breaking of the divine. The praxis is a form of total response to the challenge of God embedded in history. The Indian praxis of liberation must go hand in hand with the holistic and integral vision. The socio-political struggle for liberation is not simply a matter of the empirical order or of ethical concern; the Indian approach places the empirical and ethical concerns within the frame of the totality of reality, which comprises the divine, cosmic, and human dimensions. Commitment to liberation is commitment to human persons and it calls for profound action.[19]

> The commitment to man, if it is to be real, calls for selfless action, *nishkama-karma*. This in turn demands a deep awareness of oneself, of one's pre-

> conscious drives and needs. It also demands an experience of a greater love which alone can carry us beyond our *ahamkara*, our little ego. This awareness and experience is possible only through contemplation.[20]

Kappen reiterates that contemplation is not just sufficient but the process of becoming is important, i.e., 'what one contemplates and thereby attaining to a richer and fuller mode of being'.[21]

There is a striking difference between the liberation theology as formulated in Latin America and the Indian experience. In India the project of liberation is not confined to the context of Christian reading and reinterpreting Christian sources and traditions. In India, liberation cannot but be an inter-religious project. In the pluralistic Indian society, the poor cut across various religious affiliations. Therefore, any liberative endeavour should be attempted in its very dynamics to this inter-religious character. The multi religious character of the liberation project set the various religious partners in dialogue with one another. Therefore, an ongoing inter-religious dialogue is in the very texture of Indian liberation theology.

This being a substantial issue for Indian liberation theologians, it is clear that one cannot simply transpose into India a liberation theology developed in Latin America, or for that matter anywhere outside. The poor, the oppressed and the marginalised Indians are the active subjects of the process of liberation. It is their experience, their struggles, which give rise to the formulations of any genuine theology of liberation. Now that in Asia the overwhelming majority of the poor and the oppressed belong to other religious traditions, the question is not so much about formulating a Christian theology of liberation out of a faith-praxis as in the case in Latin America. Here the praxis of liberation is by the suffering masses and those in solidarity with them, most of whom do not share the same faith as Christians. As Christians, the question is how to be part of this struggle and be in solidarity with the people who do not share a common faith. How from a Christian faith perspective could one give articulation and meaning to a praxis of liberation that comes from the poor and the marginalised who are mostly non-Christians?In the search for integral liberation, obviously the religious pluralism of India is a great resource to reckon with.[22] These traditions are not simply a world of ideas or a set of doctrines but first and foremost a way of life with a particular world-view and a particular approach to the Divine, society and nature.

As the Asian bishops noted, these religions are 'significant and positive elements in the economy of God's design. In them we recognise and respect profound spiritual and ethical meanings and values. Over many centuries they have been the treasury of the religious experiences of our ancestors, from which our contemporaries do not cease to draw light and strength'.[23] The texture of Indian life in all its aspects is so woven with the fibres of religious experiences and insights that liberation in India is not possible without the resources of religious traditions, in spite of the ambiguous roles they have played in the past. There is a very active ferment of liberative praxis and thought today originating from Buddhism, Hinduism, etc.[24]

Religion can be a formidable resource and force for liberation. But religions also legitimise an oppressive system. Hinduism with its practice of the caste system has also caused the institutionalisation of oppression. No true liberation of the people can therefore take place in India without coming to grips with the enslaving role religions have played and continue to play. Hence, an Indian theology of liberation has to be a critique of the legitimising role of religion in society.[25]While mentioning religions, one should be aware of the fact that the various religious traditions are composed of many strands and streams characterised by historical, geographical, cultural and ethnic differences.[26] It is a fact that within these religions themselves the most stimulating forces of liberation are associated with the religious experiences of the marginalised and neglected peoples. It is in these traditions that the heart and soul of the poor and the oppressed come alive in myriad forms.[27] The religious experience of the oppressed and marginalised form the core values of theological discussion in India.

Latin American liberation theology has as its main point of reference the Christian Scriptures to motivate and interpret the faith-praxis. It refers to the exodus event, the prophets,liberative praxis of Jesus and so on. In an overwhelmingly Christian continent, it is quite understandable that the reinterpreted Christian Scriptures have been an inspiring source for liberation and social transformation. In Asian societies, obviously Indian liberation theologians cannot limit themselves to the Christian Scriptures and their interpretations.One needs to take seriously into account the various ways the scriptures of other faiths have responded to poverty, oppression and injustice. Therefore, even when Christian Scripture is reinterpreted from the perspective of the poor with the objective of liberation, this cannot adequately respond to the liberative project in a country like India. It is important to refer to and take serious account of the sacred writing of other living faiths and their understanding of freedom and liberation.

In the early stages of its development, the Latin American theology impressed upon the rest of the Christian world the crucial importance of the socio-political realities over a one-sided and otherworldly interpretation of salvation. Further clarifications and developments within this theology have moved along the lines of an integral understanding of liberation, which calledfor serious theological efforts to harmoniously interrelate social and historical realities with a fuller understanding of salvation.

In Indian theology, there is another aspect which equally

pertains to the understanding and praxis of integral liberation: it is a matter of inner freedom and interior liberation which a person needs to experience, and this experience needs to be inextricably related to the socio-political realm. Gandhi's praxis and vision of liberation went along with these lines. As the Indian Theological Association noted in its statement while discussing the theology of liberation,

> Though the integral liberation which Gandhi envisaged for India is not realised, the method of liberation which he evolved remains a potent and comprehensive, but unexploited resource. That method is praxis, which first of all recognises the fact of all being locked in a situation of structure of bondage and alienation, *and the need for someone to be liberated in order that the rest may be liberated.* Hence it does not isolate individual liberation from the social.[28]

Ultimately this integral approach is rooted in the Indian worldview in which the inner and the outer worlds mutually interpenetrate.[29]

One of the significant contributions of Latin American theology in the area of spirituality is to have tried to integrate and theologically reconcile the too often dichotomised action and contemplation. This has been so well done by Jon Sobrino.[30]Indian theology of liberation would go further to develop a spirituality of liberation from an integral vision of reality – the divine, the human and nature. An integral liberation can result only from an integral approach to reality.[31] Therefore, the praxis of liberation in India is viewed simultaneously as a process of liberation of the self, society and nature – all organically linked together by common bonds of unity.

Acceptance of diversity and pluralism is a much-needed spiritual attitude and virtue today. The struggle for pluralism is also an important ingredient in the Indian theology of liberation.[32] In fact a major political question in India is the recognition of legitimate regional, ethnic and linguistic diversities, since pluralism is a very central liberation concern to theology in India. The biblical explorations of Latin American theology are very valuable for India's experience. They are, however, inadequate to come to grips with India's pluralistic situation. That is why, in India, one needs to reread the biblical sources from the perspective of pluralism and diversity.

The history of the people should be taken seriously.Their life, aspirations, oppression, struggles, etc. are important. One of the crucial concerns in India is the recovery by the oppressed and subjugated peoples of their authentic selves – the tribals, Dalits, women, and so on. Freedom from poverty and economic exploitation evidently does not define the whole of the liberative process. The alienation of their true selves and the loss of their dignity and identity has been the worst thing that has happened to them. Indian women's experience of subjugation and oppression has a distinctive character which derives from the nation's past history, its religious traditions and the peculiar constellation of various forces – traditional and modern. A call for sharing of their experience of struggle, a questioning of the present social order, challenging the exploiters and acting with the poor for structural change are part and parcel of the Indian liberation theologies' agenda. In all these varied and complex situations, Latin American Theology can neither define India's experience,[33] nor offer solutions. But India shares its concern with Latin American Theologies for liberation and the need to begin as a methodologically important point.

Indian theologians have stated, 'We must be open to any analysis of society that contributes to the deeper understanding of the human condition and provides effective strategies towards liberation'.[34] They are aware of the usefulness and the shortcomings of Marxist analysis. Hence they said: 'We must look for adequate analytical tools. For this, the peoples 'own perception of their situation and struggles for liberation expressed in and through their myths and symbols is to be first sought for and then critically incorporated into theologising'.[35] Various kinds of socio-cultural analysis have revealed that oppression and exploitation are being widened and the wounds of the oppressed are deepened even more and left unhealed.[36]

The nexus between liberation theology and Marxism is one of the hot issues that has been the subject of much controversy. Some of the leading Latin American representatives of liberation theology would maintain that this theology does not owe its origin and growth to Marxism.[37] Nevertheless, it is true that the Latin American objective of interpreting the Christian faith and letting its power work in the concrete history of poverty, oppression and injustice, found in the Marxist social analysis, is a helpful tool. Even though one may not claim that the use of this analysis is indispensable for liberation theology, however, it has been widely made use by the Latin American liberation theologians.

One may not fail to acknowledge certain important points deriving from this analysis. However, viewed from an Indian perspective, this Marxist analysis itself appears to be part of the general Western 'Scientific' approach drawing inspiration from the Enlightenment. In this case, one lays bare through rational analytical tools, so to say, the mechanics of the socio-economic machinery. One might with the faculty of reason dissect society and its functioning, but that does not in any way guarantee that liberative praxis would follow. The awareness that social reality created through the rereading of the present with reference to the living myths and stories among people have a greater energising force in many parts of Asia.This is especially so in South Asia and shows that a cold rational analysis of society has not been able to inflame the minds and hearts of the masses to work out their liberation from oppressive conditions.[38]

Further, the analysis of Asian societies, especially South Asian societies, is very complex. The situation of oppression cannot be analysed simply in terms of class. There are other ethnic, racial, linguistic, cultural, religious and caste factors which are central to any proper understanding of Indian society. It is true that, in India, more and more studies show that there is, to a large extent, an overlapping of class and caste and yet the latter cannot be reduced to the former.[39]Economic analysis in term of class is certainly helpful. However, experiences like caste oppression cannot be adequately accounted for by such an analysis.

One needs to acknowledge that, by bringing the historical and the dialectical dimensions of reality into the understanding of Christian faith, the Latin American theology of liberation has made a remarkable contribution. In this attempt, it is also evident that the representatives of this theology have drawn extensively from the dialectical thought of European philosophical tradition, and particularly from Marx.[40] In India too, the use of this dialectical method and philosophy have partial application and justification. For Indian history also shows significant revolutionary movements of protests and resistance to oppression.[41]

Asian Liberation theologians, particularly EATWOT theologians,include Marxian analysis in their framework. One of the tools that was found useful in this enterprise is the Marxian tool of analysis. Some may question this, because how can Christians use Marxian tools of analysis in theology and then call it Christian theology? Here a careful distinction needs to be made between social analysis and ideology. Can Marxism be used as a tool for social analysis to unravel the operation of new-colonial forces? To some extent that it is useful as claimed by Bastian Wielanga.[42] He asks the question – 'what is unchristian about using Marxian tools to decipher the complex Indian economic and political systems? Christianity, as a religion, has no analytical tools and Marxism is no religion.'[43] Marxian social analysis as a tool is useful, but we cannot own Marxism as an ideology. One of the leading figures identified with the liberation movement, Dom Helder Camara[44] has affirmed the use of Marxist tools of social analysis by the Christian church, while recognising the failures of Marxist rulers.[45]

However, Russel Chandran, the former principal of United Theological College, Bangalore, and the Founder President of EATWOT, pleads for a leftist, socialistic option and points to the role that the socialist bloc plays in checking exploitation and oppression of the Transnational Corporations and Multinational Corporations throughout the capitalistic bloc. He saw, at the same time, the danger of 'doing away with Marxist fundamentalism' in socialist countries including China.[46] He also warns that even Marxist fundamentalism could betray the cause of liberation theology of the oppressed. Absolutisation of any particular forms of communism can betray the cause of the working class. Marxist analysis is inadequate because the situation is too complex and with the almost totalitarian power of the transnational corporations and multinational corporations Marx needs to be reinterpreted.[47]In India, it seems Marxists' attitude towards caste is highly questionable. During the last two decades, some leftists and communists seriously discussed their policies towards caste. They have thus debated their past involvement in caste movements, their interpretation of current caste-class conflicts, and their goals and strategies for the future. All of them emphasised the need for class struggle, some giving it more importance than others. According to Saral K. Chatterjee, a social activist from CISRS, he said:

> The highly differentiated caste structure and slavery could not be conceptualised as part of the typical primitive society; these could only be relevant to later developments according to Marx's analysis. As a result, the idea and ideology of caste as well as its morphological aspects, the nature of oppression and the inherited inequalities

perpetuated by it, and its persistence through the interaction of social, cultural, religious, and economic factors remained neglected in Marxian analysis.[48]

The limitations of Marxist ideology have led many to look for alternative ideologies. Gandhianism with its ideals of *Swaraj* (Self-ruling) and trusteeship, its method of non-violence and *Satyagraha* (seeker of Truth) has been viewed as a possible alternative. Indian theologians reject capitalism and at the same time are not clear about any proper ideology for Indian liberation. They have therefore stated:

> While rejecting capitalism, we are not yet clear on the alternative for India. We need an Indian form of socialism which may have to borrow from Marxism, Gandhianism and other Indian systems. The search for an Indian alternative has to continue.[49]

From the theoretical viewpoint, the Indian Communist Party focused its attention on questions of class analysis and of political strategy and tactics; cultural and religious traditions received much less attention. In fact, communist writings and policy statements did not often speak about the caste system. When they did, they strongly linked the caste struggle with class struggle and emphasised the latter.The 1930 Platform of Action of the Communist Party of India[50] for example declared:

> British rule, the system of landlordism, the reactionary caste system, religious deception and all the slave and serf traditions of the past throttle the Indian people and stand in the way of its emancipation. They have led to the result that in India, in the twenty first century, there are still Dalits who have no right to meet with their fellowmen, drink from common wells, study in common schools, etc... Only the ruthless abolition

> of the caste system in its reformed, Gandhist variety, only the agrarian revolution and violent overthrow of British rule, will lead to the social, economic, cultural and legal emancipation of the working pariahs and slaves...The Communist Party of India (CPI) fights for the complete abolition of slavery, the caste system and the caste inequality in all its forms, social, cultural etc.[51]

The 1968 CPI's (Marxist)[52] *Memorandum on National Integration* thus spoke of atrocities against Depressed Classes: 'This phenomenon ... is a common practice, throughout the country, the legacy of the evil practice of untouchability and social oppression and brutality that persists in our rural areas... The democratic opinion and forces must assert themselves and force the government to give up its present policy of using the state machinery in support of the village oppressors against rural poor, against *Harijans* and backward communities but use it, use its full strength, against the vested interest and bring about radical economic and social transformation in the rural side of our country'.[53]

At the action level, leftist and Communist leaders were certainly not conspicuous in anticaste and anti-untouchability struggles. They concentrated on the organisation of industrial workers, where they often clashed with Dalit leaders. The Communist record in the past has had its moments of achievement and there is no doubt that in many places the Communist parties and other revolutionary forces have built a solid base among the poorest sections of rural toilers, Dalits and Tribals.[54] But experts generally agree that there was a large gulf between the Dalits and leftist movements. Communist parties are the prime beneficiaries of peasant movements and land reform legislation, and the actual tillers of the land; the Dalits were out of the purview of mobilisation even by the Communist parties of India. Reluctance to take up the Dalits' specific demands, fearing that this will drive the rich and middle-class peasants away from the Communist party meant the agrarian proletariat constituted mainly by the Dalits were not the focus of 'peasant' movements in India.

The proliferation of Communist parties and factions, each of them claiming to follow the most appropriate ideology and strategy,has substantially damaged the prospects of a unified movement of the agrarian poor, even in those regions where the potential existed.Communist parties of India both CPI and CPI(M), which are caught in the vortex of electoral politics, have topander to the sentiments of the Dalits to gain electoral support contrary to their doctrine that caste consciousness is 'false' and the only authentic consciousness is 'class' based. In most cases the leaders of the Communist parties are drawn predominantly from high castes, who cannot easily build an empathy with the Dalits.

Liberation in depth is a spiritual process. As all those who know grassroots realities in India will realise, there is nothing like a dichotomy between the spiritual and the social. The struggles for liberation are lived in their material concreteness beneath which one can observe an unfathomable spiritual depth.

In spite of this fact, there is still some controversy in India regarding two orientations: one of them stresses the importance of 'spiritual' motives and isassociated with ashram. Ashram is an environment wherein one tries to free oneself from all kinds of bondage and reach the state of true liberation. This ideal associated with ashram has come under severe critique by those who are involved at the grass roots with the struggles of the people. To them, the ashram ideal would represent an elitist approach to liberation centred on the individual self.[55]

Those actually involved in the struggles emphasise the importance of the collective aspect of liberation and the structural aspects of bondage. Bringing together the *ashram* type of liberation practice and the grassroots praxis of socio-political liberation is an important task. It appears that one needs to begin from the urgent task of socio-political liberation which could be supported by some of the motifs from the traditional Indian spirituality represented by the *ashram* ideal.

According to Gutierrez, Theology is the second step that follows, 'whereas commitment is the first step'.[56] In India, many people at the grassroots are involved for the cause of the liberation of the poor and oppressed. There are many Christian and non-Christian men and women associating themselves with the liberation of the oppressed.This is because, first, liberation is not the monopoly of Christians and second, there is something deep down in the human which does not permit ugliness and godless selfishness to rule. Thirdly, the reality is that one never waits for clarity on all theoretical matters before plunging into committed action. Fourth, what wonderful people are those who dedicate themselves to the liberation of the poor and marginalised. There is nothing that restrains them or holds them back. Through their open encounter with reality they have transcended the prison of selfishness.

In India, the role of the Church could be particularly important for the task of liberation.The influence Christianity can have on society is not so much directly as through certain values and orientations which have become embodied in secular institutions. For example, the equality of all before the law is something of crucial importance. In traditional society, through strong social stratification, rules and regulations were made to apply differently according to one's social status and rank.[57]Then there is the institution of modern democracy which has its roots in the Christian tradition and in some of the fundamental values of the gospel. By bringing to bear these values in social and political vision and practice, the Church can contribute to the democratisation process taking place in society.

The Church can play an important role in the social transformation of India and the liberation of the oppressed by forging a relationship with people of other faiths and working together with them. In India, religion plays an important role in the lives of the people. The various religious traditions undoubtedly contain a lot of moral perspectives. One needs to start with concrete involvement in situations of bondage and on that basis develop deeper inter-religious relationships. But there are very serious difficulties on the part of the Church in effectively playing a liberative role in India. There are many reasons for this; a few are discussed in the following paragraph.

There is a general association of Christianity with colonialism. Closely connected with it is the fact that Christianity is seen in India as a 'foreign' religion,which is not only due to historical reasons, but also because of the current practice of the church in its life, worship, structures, etc. Further, there is the fact of strong institutionalisation of the church which started from the 19th century onwards. What is to be particularly taken note of is that the church is associated with many institutions in the urban areas catering to the upper classes. This is true of all parts of India. This strongly institutionalised image of the church with a lot of economic resources and power and rooted strongly in the urban setting, puts it in no position as truly an agent of liberation for the Indian masses of the poor who are mostly concentrated in Indian villages. Moreover, it is a fact that the church in its practice is very much along the lines of following a simple social welfare or developmentalist approach. This is in marked contrast to the demands of the situation where liberation is very much bound up with political debate.[58]

One should also note that there is a fairly effective role being played by Christians in the task of liberation. This is often done at the grassroots level by committed Christians – laity, clerics and religious workers – who have created a certain impact in some parts of the country. The active participation of such Christians can be seen in organising people, in leading movements of liberation of the Dalits, tribals, child labourers, bonded labourers, construction workers and so on. The involvement of such Christians can also be seen in judicial activism through which they are able to prevail on people to free themselves from their bondage.

The effectiveness of the liberative role of the church in India depends to a great degree on the Western nations which have historically come to be associated with Christianity. However secular one may think it is the West cannot disown its Christian historical roots.It is the experience of many in India that a Christian preaching about equality, human dignity, liberation, etc., is glaringly contradicted by the nations of the West with historical Christian roots. The efforts of Indian Christians to involve themselves at the grassroots for the liberation of the poor and the oppressed tend to be often suspected because of the connection of Christianity with the West.

It has by now become abundantly clear that one cannot transplant the Liberation Theology of Latin America in Indian soil. The Indian situation is radically different from that of Peru, Brazil and other Latin American countries. A theology or even inculturation that is clerically inspired and clerically controlled is not going to affect the life of the people. The truly Indian theology can come only from below, by celebrating faith through the values and concerns expressed in their everyday life. In India, this daily life is inspired by the Indian religions and the poor masses. But Christian theology already liberated from its Western clutches through the experience of the Latin American Liberation theology is today more than ever in a position to plunge completely into Indian culture. Even the ideal of liberation from poverty and oppression has to be expressed in and through the deeper religious experience.

Liberation theology in India is an attempt to overcome the violence on God-given life, help the people regain it and accompany them on their path to fullness and integration. Liberation theology can help to identify and kindle the hope for a transformed world.It would be a falsehood to claim that a developed theology of liberation exists in India.But Indian liberation theology has helped Indian theologians and the people of grassroots praxis to do theology with the Dalits, for the Dalits and by the Dalits.

Endnotes

1. M.H. Ellis and M. Otto (eds.), The Future of Liberation Theology, Essays in Honour of Gustavo Gutiérrez, Maryknoll, 1989, p. 32. The immediate roots of the liberation of theology from its traditional straight jacket should be seen, however, in the shift in theological thinking that occurred between the Dogmatic Constitution on the Church and the Pastoral Constitution on the Church in the modern world by the Pontiff. Through the fourteen drafts of Dogmatic Constitution on the Church, theology was freed from its class-room context and moved into the actual environment of the people today.
2. N. Sahgal, 'Wanted: A Liberation Theology for Hinduism', *Indian Express*, June 8, 1986.
3. G. Evers, *Christianity and Harmony in Asia*, unpublished paper presented at the Theological Advisory commission of the Federation of Asian Bishops' Conference, Hong Kong, 1993.
4. P. Puthanangady (ed.), *Towards an Indian Theology of Liberation*, National Biblical Catechetical and Liturgical Centre, Bangalore, 1986. See also F. Wilfred (ed.), *Leave the Temple: Indian Paths to Human Liberation,* New York, Orbis Books, 1992.
5. In India historiography underwent a significant change since a group of scholars to highlight the role played by the marginalised people in unsettling the colonial power. The earlier history-writing made it appear that the independence of India was the result of some enlightened elites educated in Western ways. The individual case studies have been collected in ten volumes, R. Guha et al. (ed.), *Subaltern Studies,* Oxford University Press, 1982; 'Emergence of the Theology of Liberation in India', *East Asian Pastoral Review*, vol. XXIV, no.1, 1987, pp. 65 - 69; 'Towards of an Indian Theology of Liberation', *Vidyajoti*, vol. L, no.4, 1986, pp. 210 - 220.

6. B. Stein, *Peasant State and Society in Medieval South India,* Oxford University Press, 1980.
7. F. Wilfred, 'Action Group and the Struggle for Justice in India. Ecclesiological Implications', *The Ecumenical Review*, vol. 39, 1987, pp. 291 - 309.
8. W. Fernandes, *Social Activists and Peoples' Movements,* ISI, 1985.
9. *Janata* means ordinary people
10. Chipko means hugging trees to prevent from cutting.
11. M.N. Srinivas, *Caste: Its Twentieth Century Avatar,* Viking, 1996. Y. Ambrose, Sociological Reflection on Indian Liberation Theology. *Theology Digest*, Summer, vol. 35, no. 2, 1988, pp. 112 - 114.
12. J. Sobrino and F. Wilfred (eds.), 'Globalisation and Its Victims', *Concilium*, 2001, p. 5.
13. Naxalite is a Left wing extremist group fighting for social justice and equality and a fair deal of land distribution. They fight with revolutionary ideology.
14. G. Gutiérrez, *A Theology of Liberation*, Orbis Books, 1973; M.H. E.O. Maduro (eds.), *The Future of Liberation Theology*, Orbis Books, 1989; R. Gibellini, *Frontiers of Liberation Theology in Latin America*, Orbis Books, 1979.
15. A.A. Yewangoe, *Theologia Crucis in Asia: Asian Christian Views on Suffering in the Face of Overwhelming Poverty and Multifaceted Religiosity in Asia*, Amsterdam, 1987.
16. F. Wilfred, *Beyond Settled Foundations: The Journey of Indian Theology,* The University of Madras, 1993.
17. F.J. Hinkelammert, *Ideological Weapons of Death: A Theological Critique of Capitalism*, Orbis Books, 1986.
18. J. Cone, 'The Context and Method of Black Theology', *Voices from the Third World*, vol. IX, no.2, 1986, pp. 86 - 99.
19. S. Anand, 'Training Priests for Human Liberation', in K. Kallarackal et al. (eds.), *Human Liberation,* Jnana Deepa Vidyapeeth, 1983, pp. 229–230; Statement of the Indian Theological Association 10th Annual Meeting, 1986, vol. 30; Kuncherai Pathil (ed.), *Socio-Cultural Analysis in Theologising*, ITA, 1987, pp. 1 -11.

20. S. Anand, 'Training Priests for Human Liberation', p. 231.
21. S. Kappen, *Liberation Theology and Marxism,* Ash Kendra, 1986, p. 231; L. Boff, *Passion of Christ, Passion of the World: The Facts, Their Interpretation, and Their Meaning Yesterday and Today,* Maryknoll, Orbis Books, 1987.
22. A. Basu, 'Historical Perspective of Liberation in Hinduism', *Journal of Dharma*, vol. II, no. 1, 1977, pp. 82–98; S. Basu, 'Liberation in Hindu Philosophy', *Indian Philosophical Annual*, vol. 5, 1969, pp. 75–80; S.J. Samartha, Theologies of Religion and Theologies of Liberation: A Search for Relationship, *Journal of Religion*, vol. XXI, no. 2, 1996, pp. 198–203; F. Hrankhuma, *Christianity in India: Search for Liberation and Identity,* ISPCK, 1998.
23. Statement of the First Plenary Assembly of the Federation of Asian Bishop's Conference on Evangelisation in Modern Asia, held in Taipei, Taiwan, April 1974, no. 14. Gaudencio Rosales and C.G. Arevalo (eds.), *For All the Peoples of Asia, Federation of Asian Bishop's Conference's Documents from 1971 - 1991*, Claretian Publications, 1992, p. 14.
24. B. Bhikku, *Dhammic Socialism, Thai-Inter-Relgious Commission for Development*, Bangkok, 1993 R. Boblin, *Revolution from Below: Buddhist and Christian Movements for Justice in Asia, Four Case Studies from Thailand and Sri Lanka*, University Press of America, 1988.
25. See Statement of the EATWOT consultation on Religion and Liberation, 1987, VTW, vol. 11, no, 1, 1988, p. 171.
26. J.T. Appavoo, *Folklore for Change*, TTS Publications, 1986.
27. F. Wilfred (ed.), Folklore and Quest for Justice, *Jeevadhara*, vol. XXIV, no. 139, 1994.
28. P. Puthanangady (ed.), *Towards an Indian Theology of Liberation*, Indian Theological Association, 1986, p. 18.
29. A classic example is the Hindu Scripture of the Bhagavad Gita, which presents a scene of battlefield. To Arjuna who is hesitant to fight and tries to shy away from the heat of the battlefield, the Lord Krishna appearing as the Charioteer exhorts that it is his duty to fight *adharma*– unrighteousness.

Against the backdrop of the battlefield, the Bhagavad Gita unfolds the inner landscape and the struggles and battles going on within. It indicates the various bondage to which one can be enslaved and the ways to liberate oneself from them.

30. J. Sobrino, *Spirituality of Liberation: Towards Political Holiness*, Claretian Publications, 1988.

31. J. Sobrino, 'Towards a Liberating Spirituality', *Voices from the Third World*, vol. XIII, no.1, 1990.

32. A. Pushparajan, *A Challenges to Religious Pluralism, The Commission for Dialogue,* Madurai, 1994. K. Pathil, *Relgious Pluralism: An Indian Christian Perspective*. New Delhi, ISPCK, 1991.

33. In this connection, Jae Sik Koh notes how, for example, the category of 'people' in Latin American theology, devoid as it is of cultural specifications, cannot really correspond to the 'Minjung' (people) as experienced in Korea and which is central to Minjung theology. He observes, 'At the risk of oversimplifications, *minjung* is an emerging, holistic reality, whereas Pueblo (the poor) is the oppressed class. Accordingly, while the former is a more comprehensive, symbolic, cultural concept, the latter is a more exclusive, concrete, socio-economic concept'

– 'Minjung Theology and Liberation Theology',*Voices from the Third World*, vol. XII, no.2, 1989, pp. 132 - 162.

34. Statement of the ITA, no. 24, 1986, p. 9.

35. Ibid.,

36. Statement of the ITA, no. 35, 1986, p. 11.

37. E. Dussel, 'Theology of Liberation and Marxism,' *Mysterium Liberationis: Fundamental Concepts of Liberation Theology*, Orbis Books, 1993, pp. 85–102.

38. P.C. Joshi, *Marxism and Social Revolution in India and Other Essays,* Patriot Publishers, 1996.

39. For detailed scholarly discussion of the inter-relationship of class and caste refer Gail Omvedt, *Dalits and the Democratic Revolution,* Sage Publications, 1994.

40. This is, of course, not to say that Latin American theologians

are only repeating European thinkers as some Western theologians claim. J. Moltmann, 'An Open Letter to Jose Miguez Bonino', in A.T. Hennelly (ed.), *Liberation Theology: A Documentary History,* Orbis Books, 1990, pp. 195–204.

41. F. Wilfred, *From the Dusty Soil, Contextual Reinterpretation of Christianity*, The University of Madras, 1995.

42. Bastian Wielanga is a German theologian living in India for many years. Worked with MMT and P.D.Devanadan, Bangalore and currently heads the Centre of Social Analysis, set up by Tamilnadu Theological Seminary, Arasaradi, Madurai, India as a study and documentation centre for the training of graduate and post-graduate theological students in social analysis. It also simultaneously interacts with social movements and provides documentation regarding their concerns.

43. B. Wielanga, *Marxist Views on India in Historical Perspective,* CISRS, 1976, pp. ix–xi.

44. Auxiliary bishop in Rio de Janeiro in 1952 and then Archbishop of Recife

45. T. Yates, *Christian Mission in the Twentieth Century,* p. 183.

46. J.R. Chandran, *An Understanding of Christian Responsibilities in Development/Liberation,* unpublished manuscript, 1981, p. 11.

47. J.R. Chandran, *Christian Mission,* p. 11. See also J. Mbiti (ed.), *Confessing Christ in Different Cultures,* report of a colloquium held at the Ecumenical Institute, Bossey, 2–8 July 1977, p. 215.

48. S.K. Chatterjee, 'Why Dalit Theology?' in J. Massey (ed.), *Indigenous People: Dalits, Dalit Issues in Today's Theological Debate,* ISPCK, 1994, p. 182.

49. Statements of the ITA, 1985, no. 45, p. 19. The new policy of liberalisation has created a new debate. Although it is in the beginning stage, the outcome from it for the poor and the oppressed is very much in question. See P.T. Kuriokose, 'Liberalisation and Option for the Poor: A Christian Perspective', *IMR,* vol. 19, no.1, 1996, pp. 49 - 57.

50. Hereafter mentioned as CPI.
51. Quoted by Ranadev, p. 339. This Platform of Action was prepared during one of the radical phases of the CPI.
52. Hereafter mentioned as CPI (M).
53. Quoted by Ranadev
54. G. Omvedt, *Frontier*, September 30, 1978, p. 36.
57. G. Gutiérrez, *A Theology of Liberation*, SCM Press, 1974.
58. M. Galanter, *Law and Society in Modern India,* Oxford University Press, 1997.
59. For a detailed analysis of the difficulties and complexes of the Indian Church, see A.M. Varapradasam, The Social Psychology of the Church in India and her Mission Perspectives, in D.S. Amalorpavadass (ed.), *The Indian Church in the Struggle for a New Society*, Bangalore, National Biblical Catechetical and Liturgical Centre, 1981, pp. 175 - 197; A. Raj, *Children of a Lesser God*, Madurai, DCLM Publications, 1992; M. Azariah, *Mission in Christ's Way in India Today*, Madras, CLS, 1999, pp. 64 - 73.

CHAPTER 6

Origin and Development of Dalit Theology

Dalit theology in the modern sense of the term emerged in the middle of the 1980s on the Indian Christian theological scene.[1] Dalit theology becomes explicit as a confessional reality when Dalits confess that the human well-being they have sought down the centuries has its ultimate depth and foundation in God, and risk their lives for this truth. It becomes explicit as a confessional reality when Dalits, through baptism, confess God in Jesus Christ as the ultimate depth and foundation of the truly human, and make sacrifices for this belief. Further critical reflection upon and articulation of Dalit Christian faith and its relationship to the Dalit quest and its seed is also Dalit theology. Dalit theology as understood in the modern sense of the term is articulated from the perspective of the Dalits and by the Dalit Christian community, especially the professional Dalit Christian theologians and those theologians in solidarity with the Dalit cause. This theology is primarily addressed to Dalit Christians and also to the Indian Church and the Universal Church and for the salvation of the Dalits as a priority and the salvation of the Indian and world society.[2]

The intention here is to show that with the mass conversions of Dalits to Christianity during the period 1870–1960, Dalit theology as a confessional reality clearly emerged on the Indian scene. That Dalit theology in the modern sense of the term emerged in the middle of the 1980s will also be established. Furthermore, it will be shown that the theological reflection on the Dalit situation prior to 1970 and the perception of the Dalit situation from 1975-1986 in the light of Christian faith are two of the important factors accounting for the emergence of Dalit Theology. The influence of Latin American Liberation Theology and Black Theology on Indian Christian theologians will be shown as having played a major role in the genesis of Dalit Theology. But, simultaneously, an attempt is made here to show how this theology's emergence was also due to the impact of the Dalit Christian dilemma and the Dalit struggles on the Indian Christian thinkers and that the liberative Dalit critique of missionary theology, traditional Indian Christian Theology and Third World Theology has also contributed to the birth of Dalit Theology.

In 1535–1537, the *Paribas* (fishermen by caste) along the south-eastern coast of India, and, in 1554, the *Mukkuvas* (another fishing caste) on the south-western tip of the Indian coast[3] accepted baptism in large numbers in order to be protected by the Portuguese from their oppressors.[4] During the 17th and 18th centuries the Jesuits baptised probably more than 100, 000 people of low castes and Dalits who were probably in search of a new identity.[5] During the 1860s and the 1870s there were mass conversions of the Dalits to Christianity in widely separate parts of India, especially among the protestant missions.[6] According to the Indian Census figures, while the Indian population as a whole increased by about 71% in the sixty years between 1872 and 1931,[7] the Indian Christian population had increased by nearly 300% in that period.This difference was primarily due to conversions, especially Dalit mass movements.[8]

Many historians, such as Webster, say that the modern Dalit movement was begun in and through the Christian conversion movements.[9] Several opinions are expressed regarding the reasons for Dalit conversion to Christianity. They range from the spiritual to socio-economic. But there is a general consensus among scholars that, 'the underlying motivation was the search for improved social status, for a greater sense of personal dignity and self-respect, for freedom from bondage to oppressive landowners'.[10] A complete break with the past was impossible for Dalit Christians. But it is beyond doubt that Dalit Christians initiated a movement of Dalit power and cultural changes through a conversion movement which included 'alterations in perceptions of self and the world, in life-style, as well as the acquisition of enhanced resources for self-improvement and self-empowerment'.[11]There now appears to be a scholarly consensus that the Dalits took the initiative to convert in large numbers because they were searching for a 'greater sense of personal dignity and self-respect, improved socio-economic status, education for their children, healing from sickness, solidarity in times of suffering and death, protection from oppression and an end to exploitation'.[12]In the light of the above one can argue that, with the mass conversions of Dalits to Christianity during the period 1870–1960, Dalit Theology as a confessional reality emerged in the Indian arena. Dalit Christians continue to do this theology even today through their participation in the Dalit quest for human wellbeing in which they discern and articulate the word and action of God in Jesus Christ.

In the first half of the 20th century, during colonial rule, the Dalits began to organise themselves and demand their civic and political rights. Dr. B.R. Ambedkar played an important and unique role in articulating the political consciousness of the Dalits during the Independence struggle. After Independence, he was the brain behind the affirmative action for the Dalits that is enshrined in the Constitution of India.Closely following the teaching of Ambedkar, the 20th century symbol of Dalit power and protest, the Dalits asserted their separateness from other Hindus and demonstrated vehement opposition to classical Brahminic Hinduism.[13]

According to Webster there were attempts by the Church in India to relate Christian revelation to the Dalit situation prior to the 1970s. The large number of Dalits accepting baptism from 1850–1930 and their aspiration for dignity and liberation challenged the missionaries to articulate the liberative aspects of the gospel long before the emergence of modern Dalit theology. While affirming the universality of the gospel, the missionaries stressed the poor had a priority in it, especially the Dalits in their dire situation and their obvious openness to the gospel. However, the missionaries failed to reflect theologically on the meaning of the gospel for the Dalits in the mass movements. Moreover, their liberation from the oppression of caste was seen as a consequence of salvation in Christ and not as its constituent element.[14]

The theology of the early missionaries was followed by evangelical theology for the Dalits. This theology stressed that God offered the Dalits His love, forgiveness and friendship: a new self-image, as dignified persons created in His image with a present life free from terrible oppression and fear.[15] During the period of the 'Politics of Numbers' 1930–1950, theology for the Dalits continued to focus on God and His action to establish human equality in history. However, now this theology did so in greater detail and with more stress on God's identification with Dalit oppression and dehumanisation. The Indianness of the Church and its key role in becoming a symbol and instrument of the dignity and unity of humankind as a whole was highlighted. This meant a real conversion on the part of the Church to give up casteism and overcome divisions. Society was to be transformed through social reform and mobility.[16]

Webster argues that the above-mentioned efforts at theological reflection *for* and *about* the Dalits can be regarded as an ignored but important tradition of Dalit theology. I do see its importance. I also see that as theology *for* and *about* the Dalits it is close to modern Dalit Theology. However, there are also major differences between the two theologies, which Webster himself acknowledges.

This earlier traditional theology did not focus on the following: 1. Dalit Christians, other Dalits and other sections of the oppressed as the instruments of God's salvation realised through socio-political action, 2. Dalit theologians supported by non-Dalit Christians as playing a major role in the articulation of Dalit theology, 3. Dalit Christians as the primary audience of this Theology and Dalit liberation as God's priority, 4. Dalit anger in its real psychological depth, Dalit identity and solidarity and 5. Dialogue between Dalits of different religious traditions. Since the differences outweigh the closeness between this traditional 'Dalit Christian Theology' and modern Dalit Theology[17]one would not regard the former as a part of the latter, but as a significant step leading to it and as one important source, which should not be ignored.[18]

Dalits in post-independent India sought new avenues of liberation. One of the best examples of this new wave of Dalit emancipatory movement was the Dalit Panther Movement in Maharashtra which popularised the term Dalit.The Dalit Panthers saw caste as the major source by which their 'humanity' was being virtually reduced to a state of 'being no-people'.[19] Further there was a surge in Dalit literature in the 1970s. This literary tradition had a distinct anti-caste message. It embodied the Dalit search for a culture of their own and developed a counterculture parallel to the 'Great tradition' without being co-opted into the Sanskrit tradition. This literary movement created Dalit folklore with the assertion that they have had a culture of their own and one which is not in any way inferior to any other traditions of India.[20] Dalit literary movements were considerably influenced by Black American Literature and there were direct references, although in passing, to the Blacks' situation in America in these writings.

> The words '*a peculiar institution*' describe the untouchability created by the caste system. The Negro should not change the colour of his hide nor the Untouchable his caste. There is no difference

> between the place of the Negro in America and the step or level of the Untouchable in India. And so, for a long time, both were caught in whirlwind of self-denigration and self-hatred. Both were confined in the prison of fatalism. To prolong this imprisonment, the whites found authority in the Bible's myths and symbols, and the clean castes in the Vedas and Manusmriti![21]

From the 1970s onwards, their social, political and cultural awareness has been forcefully expressed by the Dalits in the country in the form of Dalit literature, Dalit organisation, and Dalit political parties. This awareness positively influenced the Christian Dalits to organise themselves into various grass root movements and to struggle against discrimination within the Churches and against the Government that denied their constitutional rights on the basis of religion. In the last three decades the Dalit consciousness has been accelerated by various historical factors, and this awareness is growing rapidly within the country and in the Churches. Dalit Theology is one of the expressions of this emerging Dalit consciousness.

Dalit historian Franklyn J. Balasundaram quotes Christopher Shelke's opinion, that 'the important event that created a psychological atmosphere for the birth of Dalit theology and gave impetus to the development of the Dalit Christian movement was the protest against the planned 'Freedom of Religion Bill' in 1979. This Bill was introduced in the Indian parliament as a Private Member's Bill by Mr. O.P. Tyagi, hoping that conversion could be controlled. After the first discussion on the Bill the Christians of all denominations came together in almost all the States and publicly demonstrated against the introduction of such a bill, which was actually curtailing the freedom of religion and its proclamation.The introduction of this Bill would go against the fundamental rights which the constitution had granted to every individual'.[22]A very important perception in this period was that Christian leadership was mostly in the hands of non-Dalit Christians, who were uncommitted to the problems of their fellow Dalit brothers and sisters. This awareness led to another important understanding that leadership by Dalits could be more effective in organising the people.

In June 1978, leaders of Roman Catholic and Protestant Churches numbering about two hundred met at Bangalore, South India, for the first National Consultation on the theme 'Christians of Scheduled Caste Origin'.These leaders constituted the vast majority in the Indian church. Their deplorable condition and the discrimination against them by the dominant caste Christians and hierarchical leadership were discussed. The Statement of the Consultation began a process of discussion and debate on these issues in the Indian Church.[23]M.E. Prabhakar, one of the main proponents of Dalit Theology, summarises several other factors which pushed forward perceptions regarding Dalit Theology particularly in the 1980s.[24] According to him the factors are:

1. The spate of group reconversions of Christian Dalits to Islam during the first of half of the 1980s, particularly in Southern districts of Tamilnadu, as a protest against inequality and injustice in Churches.
2. The much publicised and often much exaggerated mass reconversions of Christian Dalits to Hinduism, under socio-economic influences.
3. The precarious situation of Christian Dalits, particularly the urban and rural poor, who adopt a dual identity, as *Harijans* and as Christians, in an attempt to meet their economic and religious needs.
4. The rising consciousness and increasing struggles of all Dalits, against dehumanisation and deprivation.
5. The intensification of atrocities against Dalits and also the increasing communal violence involving religious minorities.

6. The formation of commissions on caste-issues by Church Councils, at the national and /or synod levels, even if they are at the moment more symbolic than action-oriented.
7. The study - action programmes of the Christian Institute for the Study of Religion and Society,[25] under the rubric of caste-class studies, which reveal that both in the dominant Christian and non-Christian traditions there is a bias in favour of the privileged sections, and
8. The formation of the Christian Dalit Liberation Movement[26] as an all-India forum for promoting Dalit struggles against casteism both within and outside the Churches.

As Prabhakar suggests, it is the Christian Dalit dilemma that has thrown up the need for a Dalit Theology, but it is equally true that it is the concern for the totality of the Dalits' struggles, of which the Christian Dalit situations are an integral part, that is the rationale for Dalit Theology.[27]

Theology will fulfil its task only if it is for people – for people who strive for justice and humanity.That is, the primary task of theology is to aid human life and give it a certain direction and goal. After all, the primary datum for doing theology is human life. Only then can theology be a living option.In the India in which Christianity finds itself as a minority religion, it is necessary that theology strives to aid all the people who struggle for justice, dignity of life and humanity. In this process many movements and institutions played major roles in shaping Dalit Theology in India. In the process of doing Dalit Theology from a Dalit perspective, many movements and institutions played a significant role.[28]

On the 8th December 1984 the Christian Dalit Liberation Movement emerged in Madras influenced by the ideas of Wilson. Its aim was holistic liberation especially from casteism. Hence, it stressed the transformation of oppressive social, economic, political and cultural structures and the establishment of human dignity and justice in the wider society and in the Church.[29] The CDLM brought out important documents at various meetings. The First National Convention in New Delhi, 25–27 March 1985, reflected on the theme *In the Struggle of the Least of my Brothers and Sisters.* The participants attempted to reinterpret the meaning of Dalit Christian identity in relation to Dalit solidarity in the liberative struggle.[30] The First National Consultation was on the theme *Struggles and Aspirations of Christian Dalits Today.* The Second National Convention on the theme *Ideology and Vision for the Movement* was held in Bangalore in March 1986. Both these meetings tried to develop a Dalit ideology for liberative action and critiqued traditional missionary and classical Indian Christian theology.[31] They also highlighted the need for an authentic Indian Christian spirituality and theology rooted in the reality of Dalit oppression and liberation.[32]

In the light of the emergence of the CDLM and the documents it produced; M.E. Prabhakar held that 'Dalit Theology'[33] as a specific term was first used in those documents in 1985–86.He also held that Dalit theology as an idea and practice had emerged during the late 1970s and early 1980s.[34] However, 1986 was the year when the term Dalit theology and the basic elements of the concept were first articulated by him in a paper titled: *A working paper on the Indian Christian Dalits.*[35]

Moreover, M.E. Prabhakar does not clarify the name used for Dalit theology prior to 1985 and the circles wherein it had emerged. He also does not make clear whether in using a new name, i.e. Dalit theology, any new element was also added to the concept and practice. Later, in the same article, Prabhakar mentions that in the late 1970s, People's theology in relation to the oppressed, i.e. Dalits, Tribals and women, was being practised by the CISRS-WCSRC[36] circles of which he was a member. Hence, the theology was described as the *Theology of the People.*[37]

In 1979 Dalit Theology emerged in the circles of the CISRS as a result of its involvement from 1977 in Dalit, Dalit Christian and Tribal issues. The involvement of the CISRS was due to the formation of the Caste-class Joint Programme of the CISRS and the WCSRC, on the recommendation of an important national level consultation. It was held at Calcutta in 1974 and was organised by the WCSRC and CISRS to discuss the theme *Caste and Class in the Context of Struggles of People in India for Justice*.[38]

A study of the content and practice of theological reflection and the idea of people's theology shows that the theology aimed to articulate the direct relationship between Jesus Christ the Redeemer and the life experiences, perceptions, hopes, aspirations and self-understanding of people as expressed in their collective efforts, struggles and movements. These struggles are Indian expressions of human dignity, freedom, identity, equality and a better life. Special attention was given by people's theology to the Scheduled Castes and the Tribals, in their concrete specific divisions in a society oppressed by the caste-class nexus.[39]However, to examine the idea of people's theology is to neglect the important role of the Dalit Christians as professional theologians and as a community supported by non-Dalit theologians in solidarity with them in the articulation of a Dalit Christian theology. People's theology also has not used the phrase Dalit theology or Dalit Christian theology, and the term Dalit in a narrow sense to sharply articulate from a Dalit perspective the meaning of oppression, liberation and theology.[40] Hence, people's theology cannot be regarded as Dalit Christian theology, but is an important step towards it.

Webster understands that modern Dalit Christian theology is done consciously by Dalit Christian theologians *about* and *for* Dalits. In a paper entitled *From Indian Church to Indian Christian Theology: An Attempt at Theological Construction*, he argued for the need to develop theologies that would relate the good news to the Dalits to transform them inwardly.[41] The

Dalit Liberation Education Trust[42] later published the paper with the same title in 1992 in Madras. Webster does not find his concept of Dalit Christian theology alive in his own theological writing related to Dalits prior to 1986.[43] For the same reason he does not regard Azariah'stheological writing related to Dalits prior to 1986 as Dalit Christian theology.[44] Azariah has questioned the whole Indian Church, especially its leadership, due to its response to the predicament of Christians of Scheduled Caste origin. Azariah argued on the basis of the Bible that God in Jesus Christ had specially opted for the poor and the victims of injustice to establish justice, righteousness and equality in society and in the Church. He has challenged the Church to continue God's action today by fighting casteism in its midst, in the state and in society and by building up a Dalit Christian leadership.[45]

According to Webster's understanding of Dalit Christian theology prior to 1986 Azariah had spelt out a theology about the Dalits and for the Indian Church as a whole. For the same reason Webster is right when he does not regard the theology written by the Christian Institute of Sikh Studies[46] and CISRS prior to 1986 as Dalit Christian Theology. In March 1975, consultation on *The Gospel for the Punjab* was organised by the CISS. Its focus was the improvement of the low self-image of the Scheduled Castes through personal acceptance of Jesus Christ and His values and the rejection of worldly values.

The consultation failed to focus on the transformation of unjust social structures responsible for the low self-image of the Dalits.[47] Webster critique S. Chatterjee's article entitled *Some Ingredients of a Theology of the People*. In this article Chatterjee had reflected on the CISRS's consultation on the *Theology of the People*. Webster says that this article did not use the experiences of Dalit Christians as a key theological source yet helped stimulate the emergence of Dalit Christian Theology. I agree with Webster's conclusion because of the common elements and differences found between Chatterjee's idea of people's theology and that of Dalit Christian Theology. Chatterjee's theological insights in the article were based on the experiences and struggles of the Dalits and Tribals and also activists involved with them.[48]Prior to 1986, Samuel Rayan[49] had articulated a theology[50] about the Dalits and for the whole Indian church. He challenged the Indian church to make a preferential option to identify with and join the Dalit struggle for a new human history of dignity, equality and liberation. He further argued that the God of the Bible had established this history through the incarnation, ministry, death and resurrection of Jesus Christ who chose to become a Dalit. The theological articulations mentioned in earlier paragraphs and the following are important steps towards the concept and practice of Dalit Christian Theology.

Now, Dalits have become the authentic subjects of theology with their dreams and longings for an egalitarian, just and loving society. Therefore, their history, their oppression, their struggles, their sacrifices and success should be deeply probed into in doing theology.

In April 1981, Arvind P. Nirmal, a Dalit theologian, gave the Carey Society valedictory address on the topic: *Towards a Shudra Theology*[51] at the UnitedTheologicalCollege, Bangalore.[52] Nirmal's Shudra theology was close to Dalit Christian theology being a theology of, by and for the Shudras, a section of whom were regarded as untouchables while the others were lower backward castes. However, as regards his Shudra theology, Nirmal himself had admitted the following: 1. He has not used the phrase Dalit theology, 2. the Dalits in the audience resented the term Shudra which had been imposed upon them and preferred the term Dalit which they had chosen and 3. His study of the Dalit Panther and Dalit *Sahitya* movements after his presentation on Shudra theology gave a new direction to his theology which resulted in his articulation of a Dalit Christian theology.[53] Thus Nirmal's Shudra theology has not been able to articulate the specificity of Dalit Christian theology and so cannot be regarded as one of its articulations. However, for the reasons I have mentioned earlier and the following, Nirmal's Shudra theology is also an important step towards the concept and practice of Dalit Christian theology. But Sathianathan Clarke[54]here strongly argues that Nirmal inaugurated the movement that is now called 'Dalit theology' with his lecture entitled 'Towards a Shudra Theology'. Clarke recalled Nirmal's address:

> I was mesmerized by the passionate creativity with which he tentatively carved out a trail for an authentic, resourceful, and imaginative expression of Indian theology. I was also nervous about the stridently confrontational nature of his talk in which he subtly, though forcefully, countered the dominating castes... I was convinced that the contextual core of liberation theology in India had to do with the emancipation of the Dalits. I was also convinced that Dalit theology ought to constantly and continuously reinterpret and reimagine the Dalitcommunity in the midst of insidious caste assertions of the dominating Caste communities. Indian Christian theology was never the same for me after that evening.[55]

According to Webster, more than any other theologian Wilson clearly shifted and clarified the direction of Indian Christian theology in the line of Dalit Christian theology. Wilson urged Dalit Christians to reinterpret scripture and the theological tradition of the Church in the light of their problems, aspirations and struggles and concentrate on articulating the divine salvific dimension of Dalit liberative action. However, he did not actually construct a Dalit theology, but concentrated more on the critique of the salvation theology of the missionaries and classical Indian Christian theology, from a Dalit liberative perspective.[56] However, Webster failed to clearly point out that while Wilson had spelt out the idea of

Dalit Christian theology, he has not used it to explain his idea of authentic theology. He had also excluded non-Dalit theologians as its agents and has not clearly articulated its universality.

Webster was aware of the CDLM conferences in 1985–86 prior to December 1986 wherein the basic constitutive elements of Dalit theology were spelt out, and of the CISRS-CDLM conference in Madras in December 1986 on the theme *Towards a Dalit Theology*which highlighted the need of such theology.[57] His study of the papers presented at the December conference shows that their idea and practice of Dalit Christian Theology were in accordance with his own understanding of it.[58]Hence, according to him Dalit Christian theology emerged in the middle of the 1980s.[59] While agreeing with Webster, I would also add that in 1986 prior to December, the CDLM and CISRS, which formally supported the movement, jointly organised a Workshop on Dalit Theology at Guntur, Andhra Pradesh.[60] At the December conference, for the first time, a hundred and twenty-five participants consisting of social activists, scholars, pastors, college and theology teachers from all over India attempted to clarify and articulate the meaning and direction of *Dalit Theology*.[61] The results were published in 1988 as a book with the same title, clearly marking the emergence of Dalit Christian theology as an idea and practice in the Indian Christian theological arena.[62]Dalit Christian theology was also articulated and developed by the DLET at Chennai in April 1985[63]also by TTS in Madurai, Tamilnadu,[64] and the GLTC & RI.[65]The latter was the first theological college in India to start, in November 1987, a department of Dalit Theology and offer it as an optional subject recognised at the B.D. and M.Th. level by the Senate of Serampore College, in India.[66]

In the South Indian Churches, from the 17th century till today, the upper caste Christians have discriminated against Dalit Christians.[67] Hence, some groups of them in Tamilnadu left Christianity during the years 1980–85 to protest against this casteism, and embraced Islam.[68] The Constitution Order (Scheduled Castes) of 1950 of the President of India, which was amended in 1956 and 1990, does not recognise Dalit Christians as Scheduled Castes entitled to the economic and political benefits of the state reservation Policy.[69] Hence, some Dalit Christians adopted a dual identity as *Harijans* and as Christians in order to avail themselves of the benefits from the State and the Churches. Others also embraced Hinduism under socio-political pressures.[70] Like other Dalits in the wider society, Dalit Christians suffer from caste oppression.[71]In addition, when they seek benefits from State and Church, other Dalits feel deprived of their share of the State benefits and turn hostile towards Dalit Christians.[72] Matters are further aggravated when Dalit Christians look down upon other Dalits.[73] Dalit Christians are also disunited because they belong to different sub-castes, regions and language groups.[74]

Dalits have also grown in the consciousness of their human dignity as Dalits, which they have expressed through struggles and movements such as the Dalit movement from about 1850 or 1860 till the present,[75] the Dalit Sahitya[76] and Dalit Panther Movements in Maharashtra during the 1960s and 1970s,[77] and the CDLM. These struggles challenged Indian theologians and the churches to establish commissions at the national and local levels and through them to study, reflect upon and respond to the dilemma, aspirations and demands of the Dalit Christians and the struggles of all Dalits.[78] The struggles led the upper castes to retaliate by increasing the number and ferocity of attacks against the Dalits.[79]

Saral K. Chatterjee, in one of his interviews on the 28th March 1995, acknowledged that his understanding of people's theology in his article *Some Ingredients of a theology of the People* was inspired by American Liberation theology. It spread in India in the 1970s and gave impetus to a Third World Theology.[80] Liberation theology influenced Dalit theology to regard the discernment and articulation of the movement of the Spirit in Dalit struggles for liberation as its focus[81] and insisted on involved action in Dalit liberative struggles as the basis for its theologising.[82] J. Webster pointed out that all the essays in the book *Towards a Dalit Theology* show the influence of Latin American liberation theology, thus confirming its role in the emergence of Dalit theology.[83]

M.E.Prabhakar clearly states that Black theology, which emerged in 1968 in the context of the Black struggle for liberation, had inspired Indian Christian thinkers to pioneer and spell out a Dalit theology.[84] With James Cone's article *The Social Context of Theology*, Prabhakar realised that people interpret the universal and eternal revelation of God in the light of their human experiences which are deeply related to their social being, and Christian Dalit theology should emerge through the articulation of the liberative action of God in a society that denies the human dignity of the Dalits.[85] In his article *A Synopsis of Syllabus for a Course on Dalit Theology,*Nirmal sees the context as defining theology[86] and Dalit theology as helping the Dalits in their liberation by relating their forces to Jesus Christ who is the essence of the gospel.[87] These ideas of Nirmal are greatly influenced by the Black theology of James Cone. Webster also sees the relevance of Cone's identification of God with the goals of the Black struggle[88] for the construction of a Dalit theology.[89]

According to K.Wilson the Brahminic ideology had engendered in the Dalits a feeling of inferiority, a psychological dependence and a sense of powerlessness, helplessness and passivity in the face of their oppressive situation. Dalit theologians felt the need to reflect consciously upon the oppressive situation of Dalits in India.

These weaknesses of the Dalit Christians were further deepened when the missionaries stressed the helplessness of the Dalits and their need for the messianic intervention of Jesus Christ to overcome the sin within them which was the root of their suffering. Traditional missionary theology alienated the

Dalit Christians from their fellow Dalits by narrowly interpreting the Christian identity, over emphasising an otherworldly salvation and failing to identify the sinful social structures as the cause of Dalit suffering. This theology also failed to challenge the Dalit Christians to become subjects of their history and articulate, through an interpretation of the Bible, the saving power of God in them, enabling and directing Dalit liberative humanising action.[90]

Indian Christian theology emerged and developed out of a quest for the indigenisation of Christian faith and life.[91] According to the proponents of Dalit Christian theology, till the 1970s most of the Indian theologians used the Brahminic religio-cultural tradition and its thought forms to express their theology. One of the Dalit theologians, Arvind P. Nirmal, appreciated the pioneering work in Indian Christian theology in the following words: 'To speak in terms of the traditional Indian categories Indian Christian Theology, following the Brahminic tradition, has trodden the *jnana marga*(Way of Wisdom), the *bhakti marga* (Way of Devotion) and the *karma marga* (Way of Service). In Brahmabandhab Upadhyaya, we have a brilliant theologian who attempted a synthesis of Sanakara's *Advaita Vedanta* and Christian theology. In Bishop A.J. Appasamy, we had a *bhakti margi* theologian who tried to synthesise Ramanuja's *Vishistadvaita* with Christian theology. In M.M. Thomas we have a theologian who has contributed to theological anthropology at the international level and who laid the foundation for a more active theological involvement in India – the *karma marga*. In Chenchiah, we find an attempt to synthesise Christian theology with Sr. Aurabindo's 'Integral Yoga'.[92]

Nevertheless, Nirmal critically raised the question whether this kind of Indian Christian theology will ever have a mass appeal. In his words: 'Broadly speaking, Indian Christian theology in the past has tried to work out its theological systems in terms of either *Advaita Vedanta* or *Vishista Advaita*. Most of the contributions to Indian Christian theology in the past came from upper caste converts to Christianity. The result has been that Indian Christian Theology has perpetuated within itself what I prefer to call the 'Brahminic' tradition. This tradition has further perpetuated an intuition-interiority oriented approach to the theological task in India. One wonders whether this kind of Indian Christian theology will ever have a mass appeal.'[93]

These theologians intended to synthesise the Christian and Hindu traditions, interpret Christ for the Hindu mind and engage in inter-faith dialogue.[94] However, they did not make any critique of the Brahminic ideology, which had destroyed the wellbeing of the Dalits.[95]In Nirmal's opinion, from the early days of India's ecumenical involvement (involvement with other religions), it has concerned itself with the 'problem' of other faiths. Out of this ecumenical involvement emerged the concern for a dialogue with other faiths and this concern continues to be taken seriously. But this concern has again contributed to 'Indian Christian theology's obsession with the Brahminic traditions'.[96]

This obsession is based on the presupposition that Indian culture is the Brahminical Hindu culture and neglects popular religion and culture. The Brahminical culture has been the dominant culture that marginalised the cultures of the Dalits and the indigenous peoples. Moreover, the intuition-interiority method of this approach failed to pay attention to the unjust, social, economic, political and patriarchal structures that oppress the vast majority of the lower castes and women. Besides, it had no time or inclination to reflect theologically on the sufferings and struggles of the Dalit converts who formed the vast majority of the Indian Church.

Theologians like Nirmal and Saral K. Chatterjee critiqued the use of the Marxist analysis by ThirdWorld theology or the theology of the poor and its presuppositions. These theologians did so despite the relevance to this theology of the question of economic injustice and massive poverty to the vast majority of the Indian people. The study of Indian history by thinkers articulating Dalit Christian theology had shown that the interaction, interdependence, interconnectedness, mutual autonomy and strengthening of several factors, such as the economic, political, social and religio-cultural, rather than one factor, whether it be class or caste, adequately explained the genesis and perpetuation of the system of cumulative domination and oppression in India. This approach analyses Indian history on the basis of the caste-class nexus or framework. It also holds good for Indian society today.[97] This framework considers the caste system and its ideology to be the most important factor. Caste system has its roots in the Brahminic religion, especially the *shastras,* and their hold over the minds of the Hindus and Dalits.[98] The finer points of the caste-class nexus mentioned above have been denied by classical Marxism which has overemphasised economic relations as the cause determining history and the superstructure of political, social and religio-cultural factors.[99]

By refusing to face the concreteness of caste oppression and Dalit slavery of early Indian society because it did not correspond to its own concept of primitive society, and by indulging in abstraction, the Marxist analysis failed to explain very important aspects of Indian history. These are the persistence of the notion and ideology of caste and is further strengthening through the growth of industrialisation and capitalism, the direct positive correlation between caste and class as regards the holders of power, the caste-class aspects of the struggles of the oppressed for liberation, and the atrocities against them especially from the 1970s to the present.[100] The determinism of the Marxist analysis had also failed to make room for the freedom of the oppressed to use the elements of the superstructure as a power to humanizse the economic infrastructure.[101]

In the 1970s Indian theologians began to take the question

of socio-economic justice more seriously and the Indian theological scene thus changed considerably and there emerged 'Third World theology'. The proponents of the Third World theology were held together by their adherence to 'Liberation Theology'. Its chief attraction was the liberation motifs and it seemed entirely relevant in the Indian context where the majority of the Indian people faced the problem of poverty. But the liberation motifs in India were of a different nature since the Indian context is different, and we have to search for liberation motifs that are authentically Indian. The Latin American Liberation theology, in its early stages at least, used Marxist analysis of socio-economic realities.

However, the socio-economic realities in India are so particular that a traditional doctrinaire Marxist analysis is inadequate to unearth them. It neglects the caste factor which adds to the complexity of Indian socio-economic realities.[102] The advocates of Dalit Christian theology hold that Third World theology's basic assumption that the poor in India are a homogeneous group and an economic class[103] is not true. The poor do not see themselves as members of a class but of a caste and as socially outcast or low caste.[104] Moreover, the Indian advocates of Third World theology, in Nirmal's view, also ignored the incidents of violence against Dalits in the seventies. For example, there were several caste struggles at Belchi, Bihar State in 1977, in the urban areas of Northern India (Agra) and in the South (Villupuram) in May 1978, and in Kanjhawala, near the heart of the country's capital New Delhi. All these places witnessed organised violence against the Dalits by caste Hindus.[105] This real-life context was overlooked by Indian as well as Third World theologians as they continued to engage in the Latin American Liberation rhetoric.

These history of caste wars, especially the atrocities against Dalits and the division between the Dalits and the lower backward castes, who regard the former as polluted and outcast, reveals the lack of solidarity among the poor.[106] Furthermore, because of the specificity of their oppression, Dalits have a consciousness distinct from other sections of the oppressed. And so the poor classes in India are 'fixed, enduring, hereditary, heterogeneous, fatalistic and humiliated castes.'[107] The Dalit *Sahitya*Movement (Dalit Literary Movement) and the Dalit Panther Movement were making headway in Maharashtra. But somehow Indian theologians failed to see in these Dalit movements and struggles a potential for theological reflection.

Thus, despite the fact that the Dalits constitute the vast majority, i.e., 50%–80% of the Indian Church and a major section of the Indian population, our theologies failed to articulate the theological dimension of the Dalit reality.[108] Thus Nirmal points out that whether it is the traditional Indian Christian theology or the more recent Third World theology, they failed to see in the struggle of Indian Dalits for liberation a subject matter appropriate for doing theology in India. One wonders how the theologians could have neglected the problems of the Christian Dalits who form the vast majority of the Indian Church.[109]Hence, the need was felt for a Dalit Christian theology to do the following:

1. Spell out the specificity of the nature of Dalit oppression and comprehensively articulate the complexity of its genesis and perpetuation in terms of the caste-class nexus.[110]
2. Critique and challenge in the name of God the caste system and its ethos founded and legitimised by the Brahminic ideology.[111]
3. Strengthen the identity of the Dalits by giving it a theological foundation and by articulating the depth of their concerns, aspirations, struggles and movements for liberation and human dignity.[112]
4. Enable Dalit Christians to find the strength which motivates them to engage in cooperative liberative action with other sections of the oppressed and all people of goodwill.[113]

5. Articulate from the Dalit perspective the comprehensive meaning of God's salvation offered to the human community in Jesus Christ.[114]
6. Help non-Dalits, both within and outside the Church, realise that they dehumanise themselves and the Dalits whom they oppress, and challenge the Indian Church to become more aware of the plight of the Dalits and become involved in their liberative struggles.[115]

Now a days, Dalits and all those in solidarity with them continue to affirm human well being against the caste-class nexus through their struggles and protests. In this process many have become martyrs. These struggles manifest the presence and action of the Holy Spirit in the aspirations, ideas, decisions and actions of the Dalits and all those working with them. This Holy Spirit has been given to the human community in and through the life, death and resurrection of Jesus Christ. Thus, the struggling Dalit community continues to make progress in affirming a theology, which articulates creativity and commitment.

Endnotes

1. J.C. Webster, *The Dalit Christians: A History,* ISPCK, 1994, p. 4, 365ff.
2. D.S.J. Rasquinha, 'A Critical Reflection on the Meaning of Dalit Christian Theology', *VJTR*, April 2002, pp. 251 - 269.
3. Between Goa to Cape Comrin coastal belt in South and South-Western part of India
4. J.C. Webster, *The Dalit Christians,* p. 26; W. Fernandes, *Caste and Conversion Movements in India,*Indian Social Institute, 1981, pp. 13 -15.
5. Fernandes.W *Caste and Coversion Movements in India Delhi*: ISI 1981,pp.16 - 21; J.C. Webster, *The Dalit Christians,* p. 26; D. Forrester, *Caste and Christianity: Attitudes and Policies*

on *Caste of Anglo-Saxon Protestant Missions in India,* Curzon Press Ltd, 1980, p. 15.

6. D. Forrester, 'The Depressed Classes and Conversions to Christianity, 1860–1960', in G.A. Oddie (ed.), *Religion in South Asia*, Manohar, 1977, p. 35.

7. *The Census of India* for 1921 gives us the absolute figures from which I have calculated the relevant percentage. According to the Census the Indian population had during the years 1872–1921 and 1881 - 1921 increased by 54.7% and 25.62%, respectively. See Census of India 1921: India Part II-tables, Volume 1, pp. 6–7. For the period 1881 - 1921 the increase in Indian Christian population was estimated at 385.98%. See J.C. Webster, *The Dalit Christians,* pp. 46 - 47.

8. Ibid., p. 46. According to the Census of India for 1981 the increase in the general population of India during the years 1901–1911, 1911–1921 and 1921–1931 was 5.75%, "0.31% and 11%, respectively; Census of India 1981 se-1 India: Key population Statistics Based On 5 Per Cent Sample Data. 4. According to the Census of India for 1921, pp. 6–7 the increase in the general population during the years 1872 - 1881, 1881 - 1991, 1891 - 1901, 1901 - 1911 and 1911 - 1921 was 23.15%, 13.16%, 2.45%, 7.06% and 1.20%, respectively.

9. J.C. Webster, *The Dalit Christians*, 33ff.

10. Ibid., p. 57, See also G.A. Oddie (ed.), *Religion in South Asia: Religious Conversion and Revival Movement in South Asia in Medieval and Modern Times*, Manohar, 1991; G. Oommen, *The Struggle of Pulaya Christians for Social Improvement*, unpublished PhD thesis, University of Sydney, 1993.

11. Ibid.,*The Dalit Christians,* p. 70.

12. Ibid., pp. 40 - 41, 45; Fernandes, *Caste,* p. 26; J. Boel, *Christian Mission in India: A Sociological Analysis,* Academische Pers, 1975, a dissertation submitted to and accepted by the Free University of Amsterdam for the Degree of Doctor of Social Sciences, 30, pp. 37 - 40.

13. See for details E. Zelliot, *From Untouchable to Dalit, Essays on the Ambedkar Movement,* Manohar, 1996, pp. 53 - 179.

14. J.C. Webster, *The Dalit Christians,* pp. 202 - 206; also see

Webster, *Towards Dalit Liberation*: *From Indian Church to Indian Theology: An Attempt at Theological Reconstruction,* Dalit Liberation Education Trust, 1992, pp. 21 - 25.

15. J.C. Webster, *The Dalit Christians*, pp. 207–212; also see *Towards Dalit Liberation*: *From Indian Church to Indian Theology*, p. 24.
16. Ibid., pp. 213–225, 227–228; also see *From Indian*, pp. 26 - 28.
17. Ibid.
18. J.C. Webster, *The Dalit Christians,* pp. 225 - 227, 241 - 243.
19. J. Massey, *Downtrodden,The Struggle of India's Dalits for Identity, Solidarity and Liberation,* WCC Publications, 1997, p. 2.
20. E. Zelliot, *From Untouchable to Dalit,* pp. 267–333. See also A. Dangle (ed.), *Poisoned Bread*, Longman, 1992.
21. Ibid.,p. 281.
22. F.J. Balasundaram, *Dalit History and Dalit Theology,* unpublished paper, UTC, 1997. And also see C. Shelke, 'Dalit Theology: Emergence and Emergency', *Neue Zeitschrift fur Missionwissenchaft*, vol. 41, 1994, p. 263.
23. M. Azariah; *A Pastor Search for Dalit Theology,* ISPCK, 2000, p. 177.
24. M.E. Prabhakar, 'The Search for a Dalit Theology', in James Massey (ed.), *Indigenous People: Dalits, Dalit issues in Today's Theological Debate,* ISPCK, p. 202.
25. Hereafter mentioned as CISRS
26. Hereafter mentioned as CDLM
27. M.E. Prabhakar, *The Search for a Dalit Theology,* p. 202.
28. Though many movement and institutions played significant roles only a few select ones were analysed in later part of this chapter.
29. M.E. Prabhakar, preface to the 'In the Struggle of the least of my Brothers and Sisters: Proceedings to the first National Conference', New Delhi, 25 - 27 March 1985, p. iii; Beginning and Growth of Dalit Studies in the CISRS and its Joint

Programmes, *Religion and Society*, vol. XL, no. 1 & 2 (March – June), p. 117; 'The Search for a Dalit Theology', in J. Massey (ed.), *Indigenous People: Dalits,* ISPCK, 1994, p. 202; 'Dalit Theology: Emergence of a Contextual Theology', in J. Massey (ed.), *Contextual Theological Education,* ISPCK, 1993, p. 38; J.C. Webster, *The Dalit,* pp. 191 - 192, 236.

30. K. Wilson, 'The Twice Alienated Predicament of the Dalit Christians', in *The Struggle of the Least of My Brothers and Sisters,* pp. 44 - 51; M.E. Prabhakar, preface to *Struggles and Hopes of Christian Dalits in India: Perspectives for Ideology and Vision,* Vellore, 1986; J.C. Webster, *The Dalit Christians,* pp. 191 -192.
31. Refer to the ff. of the article.
32. M.E. Prabhakar, Preface 'A Working paper on the Indian Christian Dalits', *Struggles and Hopes of Christians Dalits in India,* pp. 54 -55; Webster, *The Dalit,* pp. 191 -192, 236.
33. What Prabhakar has termed as Dalit Theology, I have called as Dalit Christian theology.
34. M.E. Prabhakar, *The Dalit*, pp. 37, 40.
35. M.E. Prabhakar, 'A working paper on the Indian Christian Dalits', pp. 54 - 55.
36. CISRS & WCSRC (William Carey Study and Research Centre) is based in Kolkata (Calcutta), India.
37. M.E. Prabhakar, *The Dalit*, p. 37; 'The Search for a Dalit Theology', in M.E. Prabhakar (ed.), *Towards a Dalit Theology,* ISPCK, 1989, p. 41.
38. M.E. Prabhakar, *Beginning*, pp. 98–99, 108–112; S. Chatterjee, 'Emerging Perspectives of the Network', *Religion and Society*, vol. XI, no. 1 & 2, 1993, pp. 10-2; Dalit Theology Project (Director's Report), The Biennium of CISRS and Joint programmes 1988– 1989, Bangalore. Change of perspective within the CISRS. *Religion and Society,* vol. XL, no. 1&2, 1993, pp. 77 -78; M.E. Prabhakar (ed.), 'The Search', *Towards,* p. 41.
39. A. Ayrookuzhiel, 'Religion, Spirituality and Aspirations of the People', *Religion and Society*, vol. XXV, no. 1, 1978, pp. 20 - 29.

40. The term Dalit in a narrow sense means a people with a sense of positive striving for liberation and wholeness from a broken human condition as Scheduled Caste oppressed by the caste-class nexus. Refer to D. Rasquinha, 'A Critical Reflection on the Meaning of the Dalit Christian Theology', *VJTR*66, 2002, pp. 251 - 269.

41. J.C. Webster presented this paper in 1981 at the faculty seminar of the UnitedTheologicalCollege, Bangalore.

42. Hereafter mentioned as DLET.

43. J.C. Webster, *The Dalit Christians*, pp. 232 - 233.

44. M. Azariah is a Dalit Christian leader, was born in 1934, an ordained presbyter of the Church of South India, Madras Diocese. He served the Indian Church in various capacities, such as Chaplain to the Bishop Leslie Newbigin, associated Director of the Community Service Centre (an ecumenical lay training centre); Educational Secretary of the National Christian Council of India; Auxiliary Secretary of the Tamilnadu Branch Bible Society; as the General Secretary of the Church of south India Synod and finally retired as the first Dalit Bishop of Madras Diocese. He wrote many books on Dalit Theology, an ardent writer, speaker and an activist.

45. J.C. Webster, *The Dalit Christians,* p. 189; M. Azariah, 'Injustice and Discrimination against Christians of Scheduled Caste Origin', *Madras Diocesan News and Notes,*August 1978, pp. 29 - 37; Biblical Basis for Church's Concern for the Christians of Scheduled Caste Origin, *South India Churchman*, February 1979, pp. 4 - 5.

46. Hereafter mentioned as CISS.

47. J.C. Webster, *The Dalit Christians,* pp. 230-231; 'The Gospel for the Punjab', *Bulletin of the Christian Institute of Sikh Studies*, July 1975, p. 14; C. McMullen, 'The Self-Image of the Christian in the Punjab', *Bulletin of the Christian Institute of Sikh Studies*, January 1977, p. 21.

48. J.C. Webster, *The Dalit Christians*, p. 232; S.K. Chatterjee, 'Some', pp. 3-5, 9, 14-16, 22 - 23, 27-28.

49. Roman Catholic Indian Liberation Theologian.

50. S. Rayan, 'The Churches and Justice to Christians of Scheduled Caste Origin' *Word & Worship*, vol. XI, no. 6, 1978, pp. 227-239; 'Outside the Gate', *Jeevadhara,* vol. 63, 1981, pp. 216 -228; J.C. Webster has not dealt with Samuel Rayan's theology.
51. J.C. Webster has not dealt with Arvind P. Nirmal's Shudra theology.
52. A.P. Nirmal, 'A Dialogue with Dalit Literature', in M.E. Prabhakar (ed.), *Towards a Dalit Theology,* ISPCK, 1989, pp. 65–66; 'Introduction to', in A. Nirmal (ed.), *A Reader in Dalit Theology,* Gurukul Lutheran Theological College & Research Institute, 1991.
53. A.P. Nirmal, *A Dialogue*, p. 66.
54. Sathianathan Clarke was a former student and faculty of United Theological College, Bangalore, now working at Harvard University as the professor of World Christianity and Religion
55. S. Clarke, *Subaltern Culture as Resource for people's Liberation: A Critical Inquiry into Dalit Culture Theory,* an unpublished paper, UTC, Bangalore, 1998.
56. K. Wilson, *The Twice Alienated: Culture of Dalit Christians,* 1982, pp. 79-93; J.C. Webster, *The Dalit Christians*, pp. 230-236.
57. J.C. Webster, *The Dalit,* p. 192. We also find the following reference to the December conference: M.E.Prabhakar, Dalit, in *The Search for a Dalit Theology*, p. 38; J. Massey (ed.), *Indigenous People*, p. 201; M.E. Prabhakar (ed.),'Introduction ', *Towards a Dalit Theology,*p. 1.
58. J.C. Webster, *The Dalit Chrisitans*, pp. 192–193, 236–241.
59. Ibid, p. 230.
60. M.E. Prabhakar, *Dalit,* p. 38.
61. M.E. Prabhakar, *The Search*, p. 201; M.E. Prabhakar (ed.), 'Introduction', *Towards a Dalit Theology*, p. 1.
62. C. Shelke, 'Dalit Theology: Emergence and Emergency', *New Zeitschrift fur Missionwissenschaft,* vol. 50/4, 1994, p. 257; M.E. Prabhakar, *Dalit*, p. 38; M.E. Prabhakar, *Beginning*, p. 119;'Introduction', *Towards a Dalit Theology*, p. 1.

63. Dalit Liberation Education Trust, Madras
64. Tamilnadu Theological Seminary, Arasardi, Madurai
65. Gurukul Lutheran Theological College & Research Institute, Madras.
66. A.P. Nirmal (ed.), *A Reader in Dalit Theology*; also J.C.Webster, *The Dalit Christians,* p. 236.
67. S.K. Chatterjee, 'Emerging', p. 45;'Why', pp. 27-28; Nirmal, *Towards*, p. 63; J. Gladstone, *Christian Missionaries and Caste in Kerala*; M.E. Prabhakar (ed.), *Towards a Dalit Theology*, pp. 105-110.
68. M.E. Prabhakar, 'The Search for a Dalit Theology', in J. Massey (ed.), *Indigenous,* p. 202; Indian, p.94.
69. Ibid., 'The Search for a Dalit Theology', in J. Massey (ed.), *Indigenous,*p. 205; 'Indian', pp. 92-93; 'Caste', p. 46; Nirmal, 'Towards', p. 63; Chatterjee, Emerging, p. 28.
70. M.E. Prabhakar, 'The Search for a Dalit Theology', in J. Massey (ed.), *Indigenous,* p. 202; 'Caste', p. 48; 'Indian', p. 96.
71. M.E. Prabhakar, 'The Search', in J. Massey (ed.), *Indigenous*, p. 205; S.K. Chatterjee, 'Why', p. 29; Emerging, p. 28; S. Manickam, 'Origin and History of the Christian Dalits in Kerala and Tamilnadu', *Religion and Society*, vol. XXXIV, no. 3, 1987, pp. 21-24; K. Wilson, 'Towards a Humane Culture', in A.P. Nirmal (ed.), *A Reader in Dalit Theology*, p. 163.
72. M.E. Prabhakar, 'The Search for A Dalit Theology', in J. Massey (ed.), *Indigenous,* p. 206.
73. K. Wilson, 'Towards', p. 163.
74. M.E. Prabhakar, 'The Search', in J. Massey (ed.), *Indigenous,* p. 206; 'Beginning', pp. 114-145; 'Caste', pp. 35–36.
75. J.C. Webster, *From Indian*, pp. 6-20; 'The Dalit Christians', pp. x–xi, 5-198; Nirmal, *Towards*; Nirmal (ed.), A *Reader in Dalit Theology*, pp. 56-58.
76. Means Dalit Literatures & Dalit Publications
77. A.P. Nirmal, *Towards*, p. 217.

78. M.E. Prabhakar, 'The Search'; J. Massey (ed.), *Indigenous,* p. 202; 'Beginning', p. 118; 'Dalit', p. 37.

79. Ibid., 'The Search', in J. Massey (ed.), *Indigenous*, p.202; 'Beginning', pp. 114-115; 'Indian', pp. 98-99; A.P. Nirmal, *Towards*, p. 56; S.K. Chatterjee, 'Emerging', p. 50.

80. A.P. Nirmal, *Towards*, p. 216.

81. S.K. Chatterjee, 'Why', pp. 37, 39. This idea has been strongly articulated by G. Gutierrez in *A Theology of Liberation,* SCM Press, 1979, p. 177.

82. S.K. Chatterjee, *Emerging*, p. 54.

83. J.C. Webster, *The Dalit Christians,* p. 236.

84. M.E. Prabhakar, 'The Search', in J. Massey (ed.), *Indigenous*, p. 201.

85. M.E. Prabhakar, 'Indian', pp. 98 - 100; 'The Search', in J. Massey (ed.), *Indigenous,* p. 11; Dalit, p. 45.

86. A.P. Nirmal, 'A Synopsis of Syllabus for a Course in Dalit Theology', *NCCR*, vol. CVIII, Jan. 1988, pp. 88–89. He quotes from page xiii of the Preface of the 1986 edition of J. Cone, *A Black Theology of Liberation*, Orbis Books, 1986.

87. A.P. Nirmal, 'A Synopsis of Syllabus for a Course in Dalit Theology', *NCCR*, vol. CVIII, Jan. 1988, pp. 89–90. Arvind P. Nirmal quotes extensively from James Cone, *A Black Theology of Liberation*, pp. 1, 4.

88. J. Cone, *A Black Theology of Liberation,* pp. 12, 17.

89. J.C. Webster, *From Indian,* pp. 39-41.

90. K. Wilson, *Towards*, p. 151; 'An Approach to Christian Dalit Theology', in M.E. Prabhakar (ed.), *Towards*, pp. 53–54; *The Twice Alienated*, pp. 44-51; Webster, *The Dalit,* pp. 234–235.

91. M.M. Thomas, 'Towards an Indigenous Theology', in G. Anderson (ed.), *Asian Voices in Christian Theology*, Orbis Books, 1976, p. 14.

92. A.P. Nirmal, 'Towards a Christian Dalit Theology', in A.P. Nirmal (ed.), *A Reader in Dalit Theology*, Gurukul, 1991, pp. 4-55. Here he only refers to the Protestant theologians. There are also Catholic theologians who followed this trend. Fr. P. Johanns and the Calcutta School, Swami Prama Arubi

Anandam, Swami Abhishiktananda, Swami Dayananda. For more details refer F. Wilfred, *Beyond Settled Foundations: The Journey of Indian Theology*, pp. 37-61.

93. A.P. Nirmal, 'Towards A Christian Dalit Theology', in A.P. Nirmal (ed.), *A Reader in Dalit Theology*, Gurukul, 1991, pp. 54-55.

94. Ibid, pp. 54-56; 'A Dialogue', pp. 65-76; M. James, 'Ingredients', p. 58; A. Ayrookuzhiel, 'Dalit Theology: A Movement of Counter-Culture', in M.E. Prabhakar (ed.), *Towards a Dalit Theology*, p. 266.

95. Ibid, pp. 250-251, 266.

96. A.P. Nirmal, 'Towards a Christian Dalit Theology', in A.P. Nirmal (ed.), *A Reader in Dalit Theology*, Gurukul, 1991, p. 55.

97. A. Ayrookuzhiel, 'Dalit Struggle and Religious Renaissance in India', in P. Puthanangady (ed.), *Towards and Indian Theology of Liberation*, Indian Theological Association, NBCLC, 1986, pp. 178–179.

98. A. Ayrookuzhiel, 'Dalit Liberation', pp. 49–50; 'Religion and Culture', pp. 33-35, 37-38, 43; S.K. Chatterjee, 'Why', pp. 26, 29, 31.

99. S.K. Chatterjee, 'Why', pp. 24-25.

100. Ibid, pp. 25-26.

101. Ibid, p. 25.

102. Ibid, p. 26. Saral points out that 'the idea and ideology of caste as well as its morphological aspects, the nature of oppression and the inherited inequalities perpetuated by it, and its persistence though the interaction of social, cultural, religious and economic factors remained neglected in Marxist analysis'.

103. A class is an association of free individuals who come together because they perceive that they have the same economic interest or suffer the same exploitation. See Chatterjee, 'Some', p. 2.

104. S.K. Chatterjee, 'Why', pp. 23-24; M.E. Prabhakar, 'The Search', in J. Massey (ed.), *Indigenous*, p. 204.

105. A.P. Nirmal, 'Towards a Christian Dalit Theology', p. 56.
106. S.K. Chatterjee, 'Why', pp. 23-24; A.P. Nirmal, 'Towards', p. 56.
107. D. Rasquinha, 'A Critical Reflection on the Meaning of Dalit Christian Theology', *VJTR,* April 2002, pp. 251-269.
108. A.P. Nirmal, 'Towards a Christian Dalit Theology', pp. 55–57; Chatterjee, 'Why', pp. 23, 37.
109. A.P. Nirmal, 'Towards A Christian Dalit Theology', p. 57.
110. S.K. Chatterjee, 'Why', pp. 23–26, 29–32; M.E. Prabhakar, 'The Search', in J. Massey (ed.), *Indigenous,* p. 203.
111. M.E. Prabhakar, 'The Search', in J. Massey (ed.), *Indigenous*, p. 203.
112. S.K. Chatterjee, 'Why', p. 37; Nirmal, 'Towards a Christian Dalit Theology', pp. 57-58; K. Wilson, 'Towards', pp. 156-157, 162.
113. M.E. Prabhakar, 'The Search', p. 41; Wilson, 'Towards', pp. 160-162, 164-166; M. Azariah, *A Pastor's Search*, p. 180.
114. J. Massey, *Down Trodden: The Struggle of India's Dalits for Identity, Solidarity and Liberation*, WCC Publications, 1997, p. 64.
115. Ibid.

CHAPTER 7

Nature of Dalit Theology

A series of attempts and initiatives began in the early 1980s to systematically articulate Christian faith in the context of the newly emerging Dalit aspiration for liberation. Apart from Nirmal, James Massey, M.E. Prabhakar, M. Azariah, K. Wilson, V. Devasahayam and Franklin J. Balasundaram are some of the prominent people who figure in this theological movement. Considering that theology was perceived by the marginalised people as serving the interests of the elite sections of society, and in the process, side lining the faith of the ordinary people, Dalit theology manifested itself as a counter-theology movement.While paying tribute to Arvind Nirmal, the first Head of the Dalit Theology Department at Gurukul, Russell Chandran remembers that it was during his period at Gurukul that Nirmal contributed most of his creative writings, which included several publications on Dalit Theology.[1]

The rich contributions of Dalit Theology during the last three decades to theologising in India have been significant. There has been a growing sensitivity in the theological world on understanding theology from the people's perspective. Where do we go from here? This chapter argues that while Dalit Theology over the last quarter century has provided a virtual paradigm shift in theologising in India, today we can go ahead only by grappling meaningfully with the rapid changes taking place around us and struggling with the need to provide a theological articulation of the challenges they throw to the oppressed communities everywhere, more specifically to the Dalits. What are the challenges around us? The devastating effects of modernisation have left crucial questions for oppressed and marginalised communities the world over. In India, the forces of communalism and fundamentalism have also made serious inroads into the Dalit movement. The situation calls for an urgent and radical review of paradigms of theologising today. And the historic role played by Gurukul Theological College and institution in pioneering studies on subaltern topics puts on the institution the task of re-interpreting the challenges in the current period from a contextually relevant theological perspective.

This chapter is in four parts. The first part, the theological – Biblical basis of the oppressed and marginalised is outlined within a historical sketch of the last three decades of Dalit Theology. In the second, some of the factors responsible for a paradigm shift in theology are discussed. In the third part, a reference is made to some voices from within which critically look at the course of the Dalit theological movement in relation to direction and focus. In the last section, a few challenges are mentioned facing Dalit Theology today.This chapter is aimed at focussing attention on some of the challenges faced by Dalit theologians today. The discussions at Gurukul Theological College during the last two decades, both within the Dalit Theology Department as well as the wider discussions in the College for 'a bold theological vision', are specifically reviewed here. It is only in the context of such an ongoing discussion that we come to terms with relevant theologising in India today.

Dalits, who constitute almost 20% of the Indian population (over 250 million), were considered untouchables as a result of the Hindu understanding of 'ritual pollution and purity'. James Massey captures the wide usage of the term Dalit as follows:

> Dalit is thus not a mere descriptive name or title, but an expression of hope for the recovery of

> their past identity. The struggle of these 'outcastes' has given the term Dalit a positive meaning. The very realisation of themselves as Dalit, the very acceptance of the state of 'dalitness,' is the first step on the way towards their transformation into full and liberated human beings.[2]

The term 'Dalit' thus does not mean the poor or the outcast, it really denotes the state to which a certain section of the people has been reduced through religion and culture andwho now are forced to continue to live in that predicament. They are outcast and poor, because they, according to the architects of the system, are not fit to be included in the fourfold graded caste structure of traditional Hindu society. On the basis of this status, they were made to bear extreme kinds of disabilities in the form of oppression for centuries, which made them almost lose their humanity and finally they reached the state of being a 'no-people'.[3]

History and a critical analysis of history are fundamental to the Dalit theological task. History in this sense is not abstract or illusionary as Christian classical theology or Hindu metaphysical philosophies are. History is fundamental in the sense that realisation of Dalits as the 'subjects' of history is essential towards the recovery and recapture of their lost dignity. At the outset, it should be noted that the emergence of Dalit Christian Theology in India is intrinsically linked to significant developments within the Dalit Movement in that country. Historically, Dalit protest and resistance movements went through several phases. *Bhakti* movements within Hinduism between the 14th and 16th centuries symbolised the low castes' aspiration for an egalitarian society and religion. These movements were eventually either suppressed or co-opted into the mainstream by the dominant castes or by British colonialism.[4] The first significant attempt at conscientising and mobilising the subaltern sections in the colonial period was the *Satya Shodak Samaj* led by Jotirao Phule (1827–1890), the social reform leader of Maharashtra.

Closely linked to the history of the Dalit movement in India is a historical appraisal of the missionary movement in India. Though St. Thomas, one of the apostles of Jesus, is believed to have brought the gospel to India as early as the first century AD, Christianity spread to most parts of the country due to the work of the missionaries, both Catholic and Protestant. Missionaries were quick to perceive that Indian society is caste based and that its peoples are hierarchically arranged. They had a practical interest in understanding caste and adjusting their mission strategy accordingly, because caste was perceived as a hindrance (and in some cases as an aid) for evangelism. Consequently, the missionaries adopted a mission strategy which was not only in favour of upper caste people but also biased against the low castes and Dalits because it was feared that their entry into the church would lead to 'baptised heathenism' and become a deterrent to upper caste people embracing Christian faith.[5] History, however, is full of surprises! While the dominant caste sections, which were the primary targets of missionary work, did not enthusiastically welcome the gospel and become Christians in large numbers, Dalits joined the church in hundreds and thousands in mass movements. Devasahayam says:

> It was the Dalits (not missionaries) who took the initiative in mass movements and the missionaries were forced to respond to this Dalit initiative. There was a dramatic increase in the membership of the church. Due to mass movements, the nature of Christian church was transformed from a tiny, urban, educated community of mixed social origins to a predominantly poor, rural, illiterate Dalit community. A permanent Dalit stamp was marked on the church and it is this church that has come to stay.[6]

History however has also shown that the 'permanent Dalit stamp' on the Church remained largely as a social reality while the power structures in the Church continued to be controlled by the urban educated communities, often from the dominant castes. That also goes to show that though religious conversion often emerged from the urge to escape oppression and enslavement, the result is not always liberation and fuller humanity.[7]

Dalit theology can be considered as one of the attempts to do theology taking seriously the context of the struggle of the people who are marginalised and oppressed. Like any such local theology it also rejects the assumption that a theology that had been formulated in Europe or America has universal significance and is relevant for all places and all times. Instead it starts from the experiences of the struggles of the people against different structures of domination and oppression. So, the methodology adopted for Dalit theology is quite different from the traditional theology but similar to that of liberation theology and people's theology.Dalit theology observes a methodological Exclusivism in relation to other theologies. It must be made clear that such a methodological Exclusivism does not imply a community Exclusivism. As a community Dalits are open to other communities and other peoples. They are also willing to receive help from all possible sources. Dalit theology also promotes all horizontal community relations.

Dalit theology comes from the Dalit's struggle for humanisation. It is a liberation struggle for their human dignity, i.e. to live as people in the image of God. This has a liberation motif that makes it authentically Indian. This liberation motif emerges from their pathos. A Christian Dalit theology, therefore, is a story of afflictions, bondage, harsh treatment, the toil and the tears of the Dalits. It also anticipates their liberation.

From a Dalit perspective, theological concepts and meaning are reinterpreted. Accordingly, theology may also mean an intellectual explication and self-critical analysis

of the word of God, and the faith of the Church. The centrality of biblical tradition in general and of the gospel of Jesus, in particular, is the humanisation of man. The process of humanisation involves the revelation of one's true self, revolution in one's life situation and re-evaluation of values.

What is the rationale for Dalit Theology in the midst of 'mainline' Indian Christian theology? Dalit Theology emerges from the conviction that traditional Indian Christian theology was largely based on Brahminic traditions and consequently did not represent the life situations of the marginalised communities such as the Dalits. This non-representative character of traditional theology raised serious questions about the credibility of the Christian faith when the Indian Church itself became predominantly Dalit in membership. There were non-Brahminic traditions in Indian history such as the pre-Aryan civilisations and, from orthodox systems of philosophy, there were the *Lokayata* or the *Charvaka*[8] traditions. Classical Indian Christian theology had ignored this dimension of the Indian heritage.[9] One of the tasks of Dalit Theology, therefore, has been to develop an Indian theology that is truly indigenous in nature. 'The task of indigenous theology is one of theological creative interpretation of Indian history and of discovering or capturing 'our story of salvation'.[10]

While rejecting traditional Indian Christian theology which was largely dependent on the Brahminic tradition, as well as the classical confessional theology which was based on formulated doctrines applicable supposedly for all times, Dalit Theology represents a paradigm shift in our understanding of God-human relations. Finality, in this sense, is in the revelation of God and this revelation has a dynamic aspect to it that takes a fresh meaning in each new context. Arvind Nirmal therefore believed that theology always has a heuristic dimension, an enquiry of truth. He wrote, 'Although theology is in pursuit of the Transcendent Truth, its conceptual and heuristic tools have to be derived from empiric and imminent realities. All theological discourse is based on models and metaphors drawn from this world'.[11] He further elaborated this point thus:

> Whether it is the traditional Indian Christian theology or the more recent third-world theology, our theologians failed to see the struggle of Indian Dalits for liberation, as a subject matter appropriate for doing theology in India. What is amazing is the fact that Indian theologians ignore the reality of the Indian Church. While estimates vary, between 50 and 80 percent of all the Christians in India today are of scheduled caste origin. This is the most important commonality cutting across the various diversities of the Indian Church that would have provided an authentic liberation motif for Indian Christian theology. If our theologians failed to see this in the past, there is all the more reason for our waking up to this reality today and for applying ourselves seriously to the 'task of doing theology'.[12]

Dalit Theology emerged out of the conviction that theology should be rooted in the context and, in the Indian situation, as a conscious reflection of the oppressive situation of the Dalits. In this sense, the Dalit theological movement was a corrective to the institutionalisation of inequality and inaccessibility within the Indian Church. One of the major sources when doing Dalit theology is the Dalit experience of suffering and pain. The narration of the story of their pathos and protest has a primary place in this. In their Biblical reflections, the Dalits identify the depth of their suffering with the Cross of Christ which is central to the Christian faith and practice. The Dalits realised that the traditional interpretations of the Cross needed to be revisited in order that they could have a vision of the Cross that can both shatter caste prejudices and strengthen society's resolve to fight them. The Dalits affirm that they need to reexamine the Cross, recognising Jesus as the representative of the oppressed collective.[13] Under Jesus' overarching commitment to humanity, the Cross should be understood as a human choice. Reflections on Dalit theological methods are often offered on the basis of Biblical texts. Devasahayam affirms the centrality of the Bible in the lives of the Dalits:

> In most Dalit homes in the villages, the only valuable thing they have is the Bible, which they cherish and value greatly. They are familiar with the narrative sections of the Bible. It has been our experience that given this devotion to the Bible, theologising through Bible studies will facilitate understanding and acceptance of even new ideas... The Bible, as the point which provides the Christian identity and continuity with our Christian tradition, needs to be brought back to the centre stage of theological reflection.[14]

Dalits must know who they are. An identity obscured by the supposedly divine cultural forces of India must be revealed. Such a revelation is possible only if the Dalits expose themselves to a culture which can reveal their self-hood. This is a new understanding of revelation by Dalit where revelation has to do with the human's self-knowledge and not God's self-disclosure. That means a transformation in understanding God and fellow human nature is revealed to oneself. For the Dalit theologians, God is clearly a Dalit God. The God, who reveals God self, both through the prophets and through Jesus Christ, is a God of the Dalits. This God, who is revealed in the Old Testament and Jesus, who sided with the Dalits of the world, is the liberative paradigm for the doing of theology. It not only helps the Dalits to come to terms with their historical consciousness, which is submerged in pathos and protest, but it also helps them to comprehend a God who in Jesus restores 'humanness' to the despised and the dispossessed.[15]

The Exodus liberation paradigm, which had tremendous

implications for liberation theologies in Latin America, has extensively influenced the thinking and articulation of Dalit theology in India. Arvind P. Nirmal particularly depended on the Deuteronomic account of the affliction, toil and oppression of the forefathers of the Israelites to expound the movement of Dalits from a 'no-people' to 'God's people'. Using the Deuteronomic Creed as a model, Dalit Theology constructs the historical Dalit consciousness which has to do with their roots, identities and struggle for human dignity and 'for the right to live as free people created in the image of God'. Nirmal strongly argues that Dalits can understand only a God who is a servant. Prophets project a God who serves. The servant God, a God who identifies with the servant-hood of Dalits, is perceived by Dalit theologians as a Dalit God. The servant role that the ex-untouchable played in India was indeed a participation in this 'servant-God's ministries.' Thus, Nirmal says, 'to speak of a Servant-God, therefore, is to recognise and identify him as a truly Dalit deity'.[16]

The Christological implications of Dalit Theology lead to a new vision of Christ. The Servant God – a God who identifies with the servant-hood of the Dalits – is central to the Biblical understanding of a Dalit God as a servant God, who does not make others do servile work, but does work himself/herself. Servitude is innate in the God of the Dalits. The servant role that the Dalits played in India was indeed a participation in this 'servant-God's ministries'. Nirmal thus says: 'To speak of a Servant-God, therefore, is to recognise and identify him as a truly Dalit deity. For the Dalit theologians, Jesus is the ultimate Dalit, the servant God whom God reveals. Gospel writers identified Jesus with the suffering servant Isaiah. Since service of others has been the privilege of the Dalit communities in India, the Christology of a suffering servant is very much relevant in Dalit Christology'.[17]

Jesus Christ and his followers were the Dalits of their society.Here one can see a Christ who proclaimed liberation to the Dalits. He is a person who constantly associated Himself with the people who were on the fringes of society. Jesus Christ's identification with the Dalits and the option for the Dalits is interpreted uniquely in an Indian context. Jesus invalidates all systems of purity and declares that the only source of pollution is the uncompassionate heart that generates 'evil thoughts'., that is, harmful intentions that lead to injurious action.

There were certain theological and historical developments, worldwide and in India, that shaped the course of Dalit Theology. This section seeks to identify some of them in the context of their continuing relevance for theologising in the subaltern context.

At the outset, there is the need to ask the right questions about the direction and priorities of the church. K. Rajaratnam asks some pertinent questions: 'Where then is the church? Before we answer that question, we should ask who and what is the Church? What is the agenda of such churches? Indeed, what is the place of the Gospel, of the Good News to the poor in that church or those churches? What is the understanding or theology of such churches? Are history and tradition our only strength? Do we listen to the Holy Spirit? Is there such a spiritual force in the life of the Church? What is the strength of such churches? What are the priorities required in response to the constantly changing challenges – macro-challenges and micro-challenges in the society – local, national and global?'[18] It is in the context of addressing such questions with regard to the church that we discern the contemporary role of the Church.

Historically speaking, it can be argued that the Church in India is shaped greatly by a Euro-centric perspective that we took from our colonial masters and Western missionaries. Our theologies, liturgies, hymns and church structures thus originated in contexts far removed from our own. Indigenous forms of ministry, mostly in the form of inculturation and contextualisation, were attempted in the past by both Western as well as Indian theologians; however, such attempts at indigenisation sought to shape the Indian church in tune with the hegemonic forms of Indian culture and tradition.

It was in the 1960s that a paradigm shift was attempted when Pope John XXIII, addressing the Second Vatican Council, spoke of the 'Church of the poor.' In his inaugural address to the Council, he said: '(The Council) ought to contribute to the diffusion of the social and communitarian content which is inherent in authentic Christianity in its entirety: only in this manner can the Church present herself as the Church of all peoples (universal) and above all, as the Church of the Poor'.[19] Liberation Theology, as the formulated faith of the Church of the Poor, has swept Latin America, and several parts of the Third World, since the 60s.

When Gustavo Gutiérrez spoke of the 'irruption of the poor', he was speaking of the people becoming subjects of their own history; however, in a country like India where Christianity has the public image of a rich institution located in a poor society, how can the Church in effect become the church of the poor? While the majority of the members of the Indian Church are poor Dalits, the Church itself is a rich institution endowed with power and prestige.What should be the mission of the Church in the Indian context?

Deenabandhu Manchala, in his doctoral study, 'Re-visioning Ecclesia in the light of the Dalit Experience', argues that it is precisely the 'Dalitness' of the Indian Church that should give it a missiological direction. The Church should not only be a community that provides a sense of warmth in interpersonal relations, and a sense of belonging but also one that motivates constructive action, keeps public conscience and presents itself as an alternative community. The Dalit identity therefore should be the liberating identity for the Indian Church. As Deenabandhu puts it:

> By opting for the Dalit identity... the Church has the opportunity to be an ally of the victims of

> injustice who through their struggles and yearning are trying to give birth to a new Indian society... However... such an option involves entering into the Dalit predicament – a presence with a despised social identity, and a vulnerable existence. It implies giving up all the privileges and powers, which the Indian Church has enjoyed through its institutional presence, and repatterning the Church's internal life by removing from within all practices and structures of exclusion, domination and deprivation. It points to a Church without institutional power, rigid organisational procedures and denominational identity but in the form of a community of the excluded and with the force of a movement.[20]

Dalit Theology is an essential part of the 'irruption of the poor' within the Indian Church.The Church of the Poor demands not merely an economic and political change, but also a perspectival one. Those who seek to make the Church fully Indian, fully relevant and fully missional, should be prepared to struggle against the forces that perpetuate the Christendom model of the Church. Those who join this struggle must be ready to pay the ultimate price.

Following B. R. Ambedkar's birth centenary in 1991, there was a renewed interest in the relevance of this champion of the downtrodden people for theologising in India. Gurukul itself organised a seminar in which it was affirmed that 'any version of Christian Dalit Theology has to come to grips with his (Ambedkar's) thinking and face its challenges and appropriate its insights.'[21] In a brilliant exposition of the significance of Ambedkar for theologising in India, P. Arockiadoss outlined, at the Gurukul Summer Institute in 1996, the relevance of Ambedkar's words and deeds in doing Christian theology in India today.[22] It was affirmed that from Ambedkar we learn that it is imperative to adopt the Dalit perspective and reject the elite perspective in order to do theology in India. Ambedkar has given concrete as well as valid principles required to make a liberating religion which should be 'earthy, historical and political to make the earth resemble the heaven in which we believe'. Through his mission and message, Ambedkar's life project became one with God's own historical project. God's liberating actions became present in Ambedkar's liberative praxis. Therefore, 'though Ambedkar has not spoken about theology or engaged himself in glorious eulogisation on God', his life and mission are more than mere source materials for theologising; they in themselves have a deep theological significance.[23]

Arockiadoss's affirmation that Ambedkar's life project became 'one with God's own historical project' is likely to generate a serious debate in theological circles on the validity of Ambedkar's method for theologising. Samuel Thambusamy, while agreeing that Ambedkar has great significance for theologising in India – particularly theologising from a Dalit perspective – feels that liberation alone does not warrant the task of theologising. Using the Tillichian criterion for a theological system,[24] he contests Arockiadoss's position that Ambedkar's life and message are more than source material for theologising in India. According to Thambusamy:

> A serious limitation of this (Arockiadoss's) view is that it is tilted towards speaking to the 'context' and does not relate it to the Gospel 'message'. It is true that Ambedkar's theoanthropic praxis cannot be ignored, and his concerns and agenda are valid for the theological task in India. But, this needs to be unified with the 'eternal truth' of the gospel in order to balance the two poles. Fr. Arockiadoss's contention seems untenable if we apply Tillich's criteria for a theological system.[25]

Whether as source material for theologising or as the base

for a new theological methodology itself, it is undisputed that Ambedkar cannot be ignored in the faith-reflection of Indian Christian theology.

A discussion of Ambedkar's relevance would invariably include the question of religious conversion as a tool for liberation of the Dalits. In modern India, religious conversion has been a weapon of the oppressed communities. Even before Ambedkar came on the scene, at mass conversion programmes, Dalits in large numbers joined Christianity. Ambedkar's life-long study of the inseparable link between Brahminical Hinduism and casteism led him to make the famous statement: 'Even though I was born as a Hindu I will not die as a Hindu'. And his last political act was the embracing of Neo-Buddhism along with six hundred and fifty thousand Dalits in 1956, just weeks before he passed away. Conversion continues to be an attractive option for the oppressed sections of India.[26]

What, however, is the continuing relevance of conversion, especially in the present Indian context in which religious fundamentalism and Communalism, with their professed hostility towards conversion to the minority communities, are playing a centre-stage role in public life? In a significant debate between Swami Agnivesh and M. M. Thomas on the question of inter-religious conversion in the aftermath of the demolition of the Babri Masjid, V. Devasahayam forcefully argued for a 'Dalit perspective on Conversion'.[27] According to Devasahayam, the whole discussion on conversion, or the attempt to understand conversion, has been taking place from the perspective of the elite or the so-called upper caste, who were trying to dominate, rather than see it from the perspective of the subjects of conversion. 'For the Dalits, conversion was not child's play as Ambedkar would say, but it is concerned with how to make humans, how to make life, purposeful. It was a search for human dignity, and self-affirmation. It meant a new religion which also meant a new community and a new identity for the Dalits'.[28]

The Dalit perspective is different from ecclesiastical as well as theological thinking on the question of baptism, the visible sign of the new identity of the converts,aswell as conversion. The church's mainline doctrine of the indispensability of baptism has been questioned in modern times by nationalist and ecumenical theologians. M. M. Thomas, in his article, 'The Church – the Fellowship of the Baptised and the Unbaptised?'[29]It states that in India baptism often amounts to the cutting off of one's ties with one community and the embracing of another community, a fact which has kept several Hindus who have accepted Christ as Lord and Saviour from being baptised. In view of the ambiguity of the meaning of baptism in the Indian inter-religious and political context and in reference to the positions taken by several leading theologians,[30] Thomas states that the question of giving a sense of full belonging to the spiritual fellowship of the Church, including participation in the sacrament of the Lord's supper,to the unbaptised *Christ-bhaktas*(Christ devotees) in other religious communities needs exploration.[31]

Dalit theologians, too, agree with others that a society divided on narrow communal and sectarian lines and Christianity cannot go together, but they prefer to describe the Indian society as primarily 'castiest'. The question therefore is whether we can meaningfully talk of participating in the castiest society which is anti-Christian. 'The sin of the church is not that it has isolated itself from the social and cultural community but more precisely that it has failed to isolate itself to come out of this cultural and social community and it has failed to evolve a new social order'.[32]Ram Manohar Lohia and others have pointed out that the struggle against caste and patriarchal structures should go alongside the efforts to build up tolerance towards Muslims and other minorities. In other words, challenging the demonic forces of caste is essential for the protection of the secular fabric of the Indian society as well.

It is undisputed that over the past three decades Dalit

Theology has emerged perhaps as, systematically, the most developed form of subaltern theologies in India. Dalit Theology has enriched substantially a contextual understanding of Indian Christian theology. Questions however remain as to the direction Dalit Theology should take, especially in the context of religious fundamentalism and communalism in India, a force that has made deep inroads into all sections of society including the Dalits. What is the meaning of Dalit Theology in India today? Is it an Indian version of liberation theology? A growing interest in Dalit theology, within India as well as outside in recent years, has raised a number of related issues. The question is often being asked: Is not Christian theology common for all Christians irrespective of caste, colour, and the different historical contexts in which Christians find themselves? Are we not in danger of creating divisions and encouraging polarisations, thereby endangering Christian unity by speaking about Dalit theology? In the context of Dalits giving shape to Dalit Theology, would we encourage non-Dalits to develop a non-Dalit theology?[33]

Questions about the future and continuing relevance of Dalit Theology are also being raised. The point has been made that over the last three decades of Dalit Theology, the marginalised communities have gained critical space to realise their virtual absence from that which was being projected in the name of Indian theology. This counter-theology has also given the dominated communities creative space to inquire into what their religious resources are which would represent their subjectivity; expressions of their own particular theological collective experience. There is therefore a justification now for a shift from the dialectical method that has characterised Indian liberation thinking, primarily through the emergence of Dalit Theology, to a more dialogical theological approach. This shift is essential for movement forward, as 'the dialectical method adopted by Dalit theology had its roots in a quasi-Marxian western philosophical orientation.'[34]

It is of course debatable whether the marginalised sections of society have gained the critical space to participate fully in the life of society and the church or even whether the dominant communities have been given the creative space to contribute meaningfully to this process. These assumptions need to be probed into further. The criticism about the Marxism – Liberation Theology – Dalit Theology relationship has, however, been raised by others too. Samuel Jayakumar argues that the Dalit consciousness that has emerged from the articulation of Dalit liberation theologians is not primarily the consciousness of Indian people who are poor and oppressed. 'It is a construct consisting of components from ideologies such as Black theologies, Ambedkarism, Marxism and liberation theology, rather than drawing from the historical experiences of the poor and the oppressed Dalit Christians'.[35] Jayakumar also seeks to 'analyse the missionary contribution to the formation of Dalit consciousness and uplift of Dalit Christian communities, and then to critique Dalit liberation theology in the light of historical evidence'.

These criticisms raise a number of issues that necessitate continued discussion within the Dalit Theology movement as well as at the larger theological – ideological levels. Two issues that emerge here, however, need to be probed into a little further at this juncture: The questions are -What has been the response of Indian Marxists to issues such as caste, patriarchy and liberation theology? And what has been the approach of Dalit Theologians to Marxism and liberation theology?[36]

The response to these questions are at the ideological level at which the Marxists interact with the Christians. Kerala is perhaps the only place in India where the Marxists and the Christians share a common social platform. What has been the relation between the two? Till the first half of the twentieth century, it can safely be argued that they had an antagonistic relationship, with the church and Marxism playing a confrontationist role with regard to each other's beliefs and values. Since the 1960s, however, a vocal section of the church (led by the Catholics) was attracted to Liberation Theology and started using Marxian tools to analyse oppressive structures such as caste, patriarchy and capitalist growth. There were sections within the Left that were sympathetic to the efforts of liberation theologians and others to raise issues of caste and patriarchy; there was also some dialogue in the 1980s between the 'Neo-Marxists' and the Liberal-Liberation theologians on identifying a common ground for action and reflection.

However, the official stream of the Communist parties of India was wary of admitting any factors other than 'class contradictions' as the basis for social analysis.The official position of the Party was, and continues to be, that with the resolution of class contradiction, the other 'contradictions' will 'wither away.' Therefore, it is not necessary to specifically focus on these issues. There were a few discussions, in the 1980s, between the Marxists and the Christians in Kerala, but they could not be sustained. The unofficial nature of the dialogues and the dominant sentiment within both the camps being suspicion and hostility to each other, however, made any sustainable relationship rather difficult. The present ideological tension within the Kerala unit of the Communist Party of India (Marxist), between the 'dogmatic Marxists' and the 'neo-Marxists', is indicative of the difficulties that will exist in any viable Christian – Marxist relations in the future.

The criticism that the ideological moorings of Dalit Theology are Marxian stem perhaps from the rather blurred lines that divide Dalit Theology, Liberation Theology and Marxism. In the sense that both Dalit Theology and Liberation Theology represent the spiritual quest of the oppressed and the marginalised sections of society for their fuller humanity and liberation, they share several common aspects of faith and ideology. It can further be argued that Marxism, as the ideological framework for the struggles of the oppressed in an exploitative world, provides valuable tools for the social analysis of such subaltern theologies. The pioneers of Dalit Theology, however, while acknowledging these parallels, affirmed that the path of Dalit Theology is different from both Liberation theology and Marxism. With regard to Marxism, Arvind Nirmal mentioned:

> It was in the seventies that Indian theologians began to take the questions of socio-economic justice more seriously. The Indian theological scene thus changed considerably and there emerged what is known as 'Third world theology'. The advocates of the Third World Theology were held together by their allegiance to 'Liberation Theology'. It was yet another imported theology. Its chief attraction was the liberation motif, which seemed entirely relevant in the Indian situation, where the majority of the Indian people face the problem of poverty. But somehow I felt that liberation motifs in India were of a different nature, the Indian situation was different and that we had to search for liberation motifs that were authentically Indian. The Latin American Liberation Theology in its early stages at least used Marxist analysis of socio-economic realities – the haves and the have-nots. The socio-economic realities in India however are of a different nature and the traditional doctrinaire Marxist analysis of these realities is inadequate in India. It neglects the caste factor which adds to the complexity of Indian socio-economic realities.[37]

The position of Nirmal has been echoed by several other leading Dalit Theologians of India. The Latin American Liberation Theology, according to Franklyn J. Balasundaram, is 'an imported theology. Marxian tools of analysis are used to make this theology and the liberation that it seeks, primarily, economic liberation. In other words, its traditional doctrinaire Marxist analysis is inadequate in the context of the socio-economic realities of India.'[38] The efforts of the Dalit Theologians of India, over the past two decades, was to search for 'liberation motifs that were authentically Indian.' Apart from the caste factor, they also recognised that the multi-religious and multi-cultural context of India is vastly different from Latin America and therefore calls for a theological system that takes seriously the complexities of the Indian situation.In the context of the shift taking place in Latin America from Liberation Theology to Pentecostalism and other charismatic movements, Richard Blise asked the pertinent question: 'In Latin America, for example, many Roman Catholics have declared their solidarity for the poor for over forty years in order to bring about social change. But now the poor are declaring their solidarity with the renewal movements. Why?'[39]

The ideological and theological insights of Liberation Theology have provided significant insights and methodology for the struggles of the oppressed communities of Latin America, India and elsewhere. Globally too, Liberation Theology has also played the crucial role of the networking of the people's theologies and movements.At local levels, however, liberation movements should take seriously the complexities of each context and, in their struggles, depend heavily on the spiritual and cultural resources of the region. Abraham Ayrookhuziel never tired of emphasising the need to undertake the study of Dalit religious heritage, both in its folk form and in its historical form, for the 250 million Dalits in India to regain their religious status.[40]

Parattai J. Theophilus Appavoo recently extended the scope of Dalit struggles to the need to explore relevant forms of technology as well.Unlike the present day Material Developing Technology (MDTech) which 'deskilled' the people, he maintained that the indigenous communities in most parts of the world, including the Dalits and the Sudras in India, went for Human Developing Technology (HDTech). The logic and rationale of MDTech is unsustainable whereas HDTech, while yet underdeveloped, can be developed for the benefit of oppressed groups such as Dalits.[41]

In response to Samuel Jayakumar's criticisms that Dalit Theology does not reflect the consciousness of the poor and the oppressed in India but is a construct consisting of components from various ideologies and that the missionary contribution to the formation of Dalit consciousness and raising up of Dalit Christian communities should be taken more seriously, John Webster asks: 'Is not discontinuity with the missionary era as important a historical reality as continuity? Is not a conflict model of both empirical churches and Indian society in general more realistic (especially for Dalits) than the equilibrium or organic model used by Jayakumar?'[42] The question remains; can one ignore the role of identity and power within the church and outside?

Endnotes

1. R.J. Chandran, 'Rev. A. P. Nirmal: A Tribute', *NCCI Review*, January 1997, p. 27.
2. J. Massey, Down Trodden: The Struggle of India's Dalits for Identity, Solidarity and Liberation, WCC, 1997, p. 3.
3. K.P. Kuruvilla, Dalit Theology: An Indian Christian Attempt to Give Voice to the Voiceless (unpublished paper).
4. G. Oommen,. 'The Emerging Dalit Theology: A Historical Appraisal', *Indian Church History Review*, vol. XXXIV, no. 1, June 2000, p. 19.
5. V. Devasahayam, *Outside the Camp: Bible Studies in Dalit Perspective*, Gurukul, 1992, p. 37.
6. Ibid, p. 30.
7. A critical appraisal of religious conversion is done in the concluding section of this chapter.
8. Philosophy of Worldliness and Pleasure.
9. J.R. Chandran, 'A. P. Nirmal: A Tribute', p. 30.
10. A. P. Nirmal, *Heuristic Explorations*, CLS, 1990, pp. 172–173.

11. Ibid., p.7.
12. A.P. Nirmal, 'Towards a Christian Dalit Theology', in R.S. Sugirtharajah (ed.), *Frontiers in Asian Christian Theology: Emerging Trends*, Maryknoll, Orbis, 1994, p. 30.
13. Ibid, p. 54.
14. V. Devasahayam, *Doing Dalit Theology in Biblical Key*, Delhi/ Madras: ISPCK/Gurukul, 1997, p. 4.
15. G. Oommen, 'Emerging Dalit Theology', p. 20.
16. A.P. Nirmal, ed, *A Reader in Dalit Theology*
17. *An Indian Christian Attempt*, p. 45.
18. K. Rajaratnam, *Sent Into the World!,*unpublished paper, keynote address delivered at the Assembly of the Kerala Council of Churches, Kottayam, 25 May 2004.
19. D. de Sousa, *What Happened to the Church of the Poor*?, unpublished paper.
20. D. Manchala, *Re-visioning Ecclesia in the light of the Dalit Experience*, unpublished doctoral thesis.
21. A.P. Nirmal and V. Devasahayam (eds), *Dr. B. R. Ambedkar: a Centenary Tribute*, Madras, Gurukul, 1991, p. i.
22. Fr. Arockiadoss lists ten areas where Dr. Ambedkar's life and message are relevant for theologising in India today: 1. Ambedkar's Life Project is a Theological Project, 2. From Ambedkar we learn the Right Perspective for Theologising, 3.Ambedkar provides us with the Right Option for Theology, 4. He Provides a Paradigm for Identifying and Interpreting the Signs of the times, 5. Ambedkar helps us to Identify the Messianic People of India, 6. From Ambedkar we learn that the Dalits, and their Likes, are the Real Subjects of Theologising in India, 7. From him we also learn that the Language of Dalit Theology will be Angry and Conflictual, 8. Ambedkar Gives the Basic Norms for Critiquing Religions and Entering into Inter-Religious Dialogue, 9. Ambedkar Provides the Right Yardstick to Evaluate the Church in India and its Various Missionary Efforts, 10. He also supplies a Critique for Judging the Erstwhile Indian Theologies and Inculturations. (Refer: V. Devasahayam (ed.), *Frontiers of*

Dalit Theology, Delhi, ISPCK & Gurukul, 1997, pp. 290–313.)

23. V. Devasahayam (ed.), *Frontiers of Dalit Theology*, Delhi, ISPCK & Gurukul, 1997, p. 291.

24. 'According to Paul Tillich, any theological system must satisfy two basic needs: the statement of the truth of the Christian message and the interpretation of this truth for every generation' (Source: P. Tillich, *Systematic Theology*, vol. I.3) Quoted: S. Thambusamy,*The Significance of Ambedkar for Theologising in India*, unpublished paper.

25. S. Thambusamy, *The Significance of Ambedkar for Theologising in India*, unpublished paper.

26. *The Hindu*, 15 October 2004 (Chennai Edition) reported that hundreds of Dalits from the southern States had, on14 October 2004, embraced Buddhism in the presence of monks from the Nagpur Monastery, in Perambalur district. 'Renouncing' Hinduism and Hindu Gods were among the oaths administered at the ceremony, organised by the Dr. Ambedkar Youth Front and the International Buddhist Youth Organisation (IBYO).

27. Broadly speaking, the debate was between the positions: 'I personally refuse to be converted' (Swami Agnivesh), 'I believe in conversion... there is a necessity for decommunalising conversion' (M. M. Thomas) and, 'We need to have a new perspective and a new viewpoint which should be the perspective of the oppressed Dalits and the backward class' (V. Devasahayam). For details see, J. John and J. Athyal (eds), *Religion, State and Communalism: A Post-Ayodhya Reflection*, Hong Kong, CCA, 1995, pp. 95-131.

28. J. John and J. Athyal (eds), *Religion, State and Communalism: A Post-Ayodhya Reflection*, Hong Kong, CCA, 1995, pp. 110-111.

29. P. Kumari,(ed.), *Liberating Witness*, Dr. K. Rajaratnam's Platinum Jubilee Commemoration Volume I, Gurukul Theological College, Madras, 1995, pp. 8-16.

30. In this context, Dr. M. M. Thomas refers to several studies. Two of them are: 1. The NCCI Consultation in the 1960s on 'Renewal in Mission' where it was argued that 'in the perspective of the Bible, conversion is turning from idols to serve a living and true God' and not moving from one culture

to another and from one community to another as it is understood in the communal sense in India today' and further that so long as baptism remains a transference of cultural and communal allegiance, 'we cannot judge those who while confessing faith in Jesus are unwilling to be baptized' (Renewal in Mission, NCCI. 220).2. The studies of the GurukulCollege in this area – notably, the survey conducted in the city of Chennai where it was revealed that many persons in the city who had accepted Jesus Christ as their personal Saviour had chosen to continue in their own religious cultural and caste communities without conversion to the Christian community. Refer also to the Gurukul publication, *The Debate on Mission – Issues from the Indian Context* (edited by Herbert E. Hoefer, 1979).

31. P. Kumari, *Liberating Witness*, 1995, pp. 13-14.
32. *Religion, State and Communalism*, p. 112.
33. K.P. Kuruvilla, *An Indian Attempt to Give Voice to the Voiceless*, unpublished paper.
34. S. Clarke, *Theory of Atonement: An Indian Cross-Cultural Theology of the Cross*, unpublished paper presented at the CTI-UTC Study Project on 'Interrogating Mission', UTC, Bangalore, January 2003, pp. 16-19.
35. S. Jayakumar, *Dalit Consciousness and Christian Conversion: Historical Resources for a Contemporary Debate*, Oxford, Regnum International & Delhi, ISPCK, 1999, p. 46.
36. S. Jeyakuamar, *Dalit Consciousness and Christian Conversion*, 1999, p. xix.
37. A.P. Nirmal (ed.), *A Reader in Dalit Theology*, Madras, Gurukul, p. 56.
38. V. Devasahayam (ed.), *Frontiers of Dalit Theology*, Delhi, ISPCK/Gurukul, 1997, p. 25.
39. R.H. Blise, *The New Missiology: A Call to Freedom*, paper presented at the Consultation on Contemporary Reflections on Global Oppressed Communities: A Multi-Faith Approach, Gurukul, Chennai, February 2003, pp. 23-26.

40. G. Robinson (ed.), *Religions of the Marginalised: Towards a Phenomenology and the Methodology of Study*, UTC, Bangalore & ISPCK, Delhi, 1998, p. 17.

41. P.J.T. Appavoo, *A Dalit's Reflection on Technology*, an address delivered at the Sixteenth Convocation of the Academy of Ecumenical Indian Theology and Church Administration, Chennai, 20 August 2004, unpublished paper.

42. J.C.B. Webster, *Book Review*, Dalit Consciousness…, Dharma Deepika, January 2000, p. 76.

CHAPTER 8

An Analysis of Dalit Theology

In the previous chapter, the origin and development of Dalit Theology was analysed from historical and theological perspectives. In this chapter, Dalit theology will be analysed critically to see whether the scope and method employed by the Dalit theologians has any relevance to the liberation of Dalits in India or whether it is merely a fashionable theology articulated by seasoned Indian liberation theologians.

Dalit theology is considered as the greatest achievement of Indian theology, seen especially from the socio-political angle. It is undisputed that over the past two decades Dalit Theology has emerged perhaps as the most developed form of subaltern theologies in India. Dalit Theology has enriched substantially a contextual understanding of Indian Christian Theology. It has made a significant impact in the way theology is to be pursued in India, and has also attained international attention. While, in many other areas of theology, the gulf between theory and reality is great, this is not the case as far as Dalit theology is concerned. In the first place Dalit theology has shaken the traditional way of pursuing theology by drawing our attention to the experience of the most oppressed and marginalised groups in Indian society. *Immediacy, concreteness and a certain urgency* characterises the Dalit theology and has spared it to some extent from futile theoretical discussions and theological narcissism.

The realism of Dalit theology derives from its contact with

the earth and the experience of hard physical labour and sweat. The experience of negativity by the Dalits has created an atmosphere conducive to the projection of alternatives to compliance with the system or following the trodden path. For example, to a given reality the depth of suffering, material deprivation, psychological wounds, dependency and social humiliation, has triggered the Dalit imagination for new theological trajectories mirroring their experience more closely. Further, the nature of Dalit experience is such that it has led also to radicalism in thought. It is counter-culture in spirit. The millennia of suffering and oppression has created in the Dalit people an anti-establishment and anti-hegemonic urge, which can be seen reflected in their theology.The radicalism of Dalit theology can be seen also in the way it unmasks the traditional social constructs of purity and pollution, high and low, and its restlessness regarding ideological justifications: be it in society or within the Christian communities. It is to the credit of Dalit theology and subaltern theological orientation to have challenged the development of Indian theology along traditional Sanskrit and Brahminical lines and the exclusive use of so-called classical texts.

Dalit Theology has its seminal roots in the autochthonous tradition of the Dalits. The first thing one should remember about this autochthonous Dalit tradition is that it is a living tradition surviving from ancient times though dependent and powerless. It appears in the form of myths, proverbs, songs, festivals and rituals telling the story of Dalit origins and their enslavement under religious symbolism. Protest and the search for justice and equality are often explicitly expressed in songs, rituals and festivals.As a direct result, Indian theology was awakened to the plurality of socio-political and cultural experiences in the country. Within the Christian communities themselves, Dalit Theology has led, at least, to a greater awareness of the issue. The success of Dalit Theology is due in great part to its co-operation with Dalit movements, from which it has derived a lot of inspiration, tools of analysis, and it has for its own part also animated Dalit movements, especially among the Christian communities. There has also been a very concrete hermeneutic on the part of Dalit theology, and Biblical studies are beginning to emerge which offer many fresh and innovative insights.

There is yet another important contribution that has come about in India that has come through the Dalit movement and Dalit Theology. It is the affirmation of the earthliness of human life and the fulfilment of the material needs of life as bound up with salvation, salvation itself being understood as total well-being. Dalit Theology also functions as an important check on theology, guarding it from taking recourse in abstract and abstruse discourses.

In this chapter, attempts have been made to raise a few questions: To what extent does Dalit Theology have the right to claim to be contextual theology? To what extent it is inclusive? Will this theology lead to liberative action? Is it the protest of just a small elite from the Dalit Community? India has a population of 1 billion, of which 25% are Dalits and 2.5% are Christians. Around 20 million people are Christian Dalits and the rest belong to indigenous faiths, Buddhism and Hinduism. What is wrong with Dalit Theology today? What can we do to remedy it?

In the first part of the discussion the main deficiencies of present-day Dalit Theology are analysed. Critical attention is given to the scope and methods of Dalit Theology which are even now widely used by Dalit Theologians. Questions however remain as to the direction Dalit Theology should take, especially in the context of growing religious fundamentalism and communalism in India, a force that has had a deep impact on all sections of society including the Dalits.

What is the meaning of Dalit Theology today? Is it an Indian version of liberation theology? A growing interest in Dalit Theology, within India as well as outside in recent years, has raised a number of related issues. The question is often being asked: Is not Christian theology common for all Christians irrespective of caste, colour, and the different historical contexts in which Christians find themselves? Are we not in danger of creating divisions and encouraging polarizations, thereby endangering Christian unity by speaking about Dalit Theology? In the context of Dalits giving shape to DalitTheology, would we encourage Non-Dalits to develop a Non-Dalit Theology?[1] Questions about the future and continuing relevance are also being raised.

When we analyse a particular theological construction, we have to see the relevance of the particular theology with reference to historical data as well as the present reality of the 'subjects' of the theology. This involves the socio-political analysis of the human context in which the theology is at work. Then we also have to see the method which has been used and the scope it has provided for doing theology.The liberative motif of Dalit theology as a theological construction needs a critical appraisal to see whether it has the relevance and theological grounding to lead Dalits into liberative praxis.

Theologising is not at all a popular enterprise in the Church in India today. A lot of people, including some bishops and religious leaders, look suspiciously on the theologians. They are firmly convinced that theologians are trouble-makers and that they are responsible for all that is going wrong in the Church. Besides, many priests and Church leaders maintain that the theology they were taught in the seminaries has been of no use to them. It has in no way helped them in their priestly ministry. Is it any wonder, then, that many young people take a dislike to theology and that they are unwilling to invest time and energy in this unpopular, not to say risky business of theologising?

Apathy is strong among Church leaders, most of whom are of from the so-called 'upper' caste background. I see the role of Dalit Christian theology as challenging the primary casteist structures of the status quo, both inside and as well as outside the Church. That is its prophetic function based on what we believe the Church should be: unveiling the structures of power that feign neutrality to hide the operation of caste within the Church while still using the power of caste in ways that are unjust.

Another important role of Dalit theology is to empower Dalit communities to reclaim their position in a way that could lead them to bring out their own experiences and express them in their own symbolic modes. This would add strength to their struggle for empowerment and for a more equal distribution of power and resources. And this is actually happening today through networking with the many resistive forces, of which Dalit Christian theology is but one. This is part of the general awakening of the broader Dalit community.

Most of the theologising in India is done in seminaries and theological colleges which are quite cut off from the real life of Dalit people. The professors and students of Dalit Theology have little living contact with local Dalit communities. As a result, they do not reflect on the faith experience of the Dalit community, nor do they engage in a fruitful dialogue with other faith communities. It is not surprising, then, that our ghetto theology is largely irrelevant to the lives, problems and needs of the local community.

Dalit theology has also become too identified with theological institutions at the expense of its identification with the Church. There is a gap between Dalit theologians and the Dalit pastors and the communities that they serve and minister. Generally speaking, in some cases Dalit Theologians are uprooted academics who have undergone a Western orientation and a thoroughly alienating intellectual formation through their higher education in foreign countries. They often feel out of place anywhere, at home or abroad, tending to be split-personalities, who think like Europeans but feel like Indians. This lack of self-integration and disorientation from their cultural context deeply affects their theology. Dalit theology has failed to impact the Church largely because Dalit theology is too far removed from the Churches, even those that are predominantly comprised of Dalit members. For greater impact, we need to find ways to bridge or perhaps close this gap.

By and large Dalit theology tends to be abstract and theoretical without any vital link with action and involvement in the world. Even when professors and students engage in social, cultural or religious activities, such activities are not reflected upon and integrated into their theology. As long as classroom study and involvement in the external world are kept as discrete water-tight compartments, we shall have to put up with sterile speculation on the one hand and un-reflected activity on the other. Only the fusion of action and reflection can lead to the development of a living theology. And it is possible that this lack of social praxis as an integral element of our theological education is responsible for the absence of genuine commitment on the part of many professors and students. A purely theoretical education never leads to deep personal commitment.

If theology is the reflection on one's faith-experience in the context of today's world, then it presupposes the existence of genuine faith. And there can be no faith without a firm commitment to God. But because of the predominance of the academic approach to Dalit theology, the prevalence of a purely secularist outlook on life, the shattering impact of modern Biblical research and the unsettling effects of historical studies, there has been a slow and steady erosion of the faith of many professors and students alike. Today it is not unusual to find many uncommitted people in seminaries.There are some who have reduced their Christian faith to a convenient ideology for social action or humanitarian service. There are others who tenaciously defend doctrinal orthodoxy without showing any commitment to God or to the service of the Gospel. There are yet others who tend to absolutize things that are of minor importance in the Christian scheme of things.

Even today insufficient attention is given to the harmful effects of the use of foreign language in Dalit Theology. Language is still looked upon as an innocent expression of thought and a useful means of communication. But it is much more than that. Language is the form of our thought. It deeply affects the way we experience and understand reality. It is the vehicle of a culture. Hence the language we use determines the shape of our theology. If much of our theology is still imported from the West, it does not really fit into the cultural landscape of India.Similarly, in Dalit Theology too, Dalit theologians continue to use strange vocabularies which alienate both the Dalit community and the Dalit theologians.

The point has been made that over the last two decades of Dalit Theology, the marginalized communities have gained critical space to realize their virtual absence from that which was being projected in the name of Indian theology. This counter-theology has also given the dominated communities creative space to inquire into what their religious resources are which would represent thesubjectivity and expressions of their own particular theological collective experience. There is, therefore, a justification now for a shift from the dialectical method that has characterized Indian liberation thinking, primarily through the emergence of Dalit Theology, to a more dialogical theological approach. This shift is essential for movement forward, as 'the dialectical method adopted by Dalit Theology had its roots in a quasi-Marxian Western philosophical orientation'.[2]

Three areas that need further study as possible future directions for the Dalit Theological movement will be discussed briefly. These are: a call to repentance on the part of the Church as well as the Dalit Christian communities, the continuing relevance of poor religious conversions in the present day and the need for our theological discourse to take seriously the changing social contexts of the Dalits.

The practice of exploitation and discrimination of the Dalits has been officially proclaimed as illegal in free India, but every day we hear reports of atrocities directed against Dalits from several parts of the country. Fifty years of independence and five hundred years of Christianity among the marginalized sections have not built up a just and inclusive community in India. Though the Indian Church is proud of its tradition and heritage, the Church has been preoccupied with its institutional image and is reluctant to make radical changes towards the Dalitisation of the Church even in a situation where the Dalits constitute the majority of the membership of the Church. As M.E. Prabhakar has said:

> The emergence of the Christian Dalit Movement and its commitment to fight against casteism within churches and society, and to promote along with the Churches, the Christian Dalit struggles for civil economic rights, are not fully recognized or appreciated by the Church. Indian Christianity has not yet accepted the emergence of Dalit Theology which can initiate a counter-culture within the Church.[3]

Firstly, the primary task of the Church in such a context is to admit its mistakes of the past, repent and resolve to side with truth and justice. In the face of continuing violence and oppression of the Dalits and the Church's reluctance to rise to its prophetic mission, the Church is called upon to renew and radically redefine its mission. There is another aspect of repentance: a self-critical appraisal of the course Dalit Theology has taken. Introspection is also part of reflection. While focusing on a faith-affirmation of the marginalised and the dispossessed it is important to ask whether Dalit Theology side lined or marginalised certain areas. In this context, two areas that call for renewed attention can be mentioned here.Dalit women speak of the 'twice-alienated' or of the 'Dalits among the Dalits' – the condition resulting from ostracism by society at large because they are Dalits and their powerlessness within the Dalit community itself because they are women. For them, the past was not only conditioned by the Hindu caste structure but also by the patriarchal system.[4]Women often bear the brunt of caste atrocities. If the course of Dalit Theology over the past three decades has not been sufficiently receptive to a womanist reading of the Dalit movement, there is room for introspection and repentance there.

Secondly what is the message of Dalit Theology for the Dalit Christians? The question would sound rather preposterous; the primary task of Dalit Theology is to provide hope and strength to the victims of centuries of oppression and exploitation. It is however necessary to ask if there is room for self-criticism and correction among the Dalit Christians too. Ambedkar, when he decided to leave the grip of Hinduism, considered Christianity too as a possible faith to embrace with his followers.A study of the Dalits who had embraced the Christian faith, however, led him to raise several harsh criticisms, especially about their 'selfishness and self-centeredness' and their general apathy towards other outcasts. In Ambedkar's own words: 'They don't care a snap of their finger what becomes of their former caste associates so long as they and their families, or they and the little group who have become Christians, get ahead. Indeed, their chief concern with reference to their old caste associates is to hide the fact that they were in the same community. I don't want to add to the number of such Christians'.[5]

Dalit theology needs reflection; a reflection not only of the 'selfishness and self-centeredness' of the Dalit Christians alone but observations that raise basic questions on the relationship of the Church to other Dalit communities. In the context of the sustained demand of Indian churches to include Dalit Christians in the government category of reservation and the continued opposition of the non-Christian Dalit movements to such a move, the need to re-define the theological tasks as those of building bridges and cutting across the religious divide among the oppressed communities becomes imperative.

The Dalits' conversion to Christianity led to not only a numerical increase in the membership of the Church, but also to an inner transformation of the oppressed communities. Dalit mass movements have come to be seen as liberation movements in which the power of the dispossessed to challenge the Hindu social order was affirmed. Later, Ambedkar used religious conversion as a means of social liberation from the caste system.[6] As was pointed out earlier, the unfortunate thing about conversion was that although Christianity is an egalitarian religion, the caste system found its way into it in India. Dalit Christians within the Church were discriminated against and were denied power within the ecclesiastical structure. Although Dalit Christians constituted approximately 70% of the Indian Christian population, they were marginalized and ignored until recently.

The Dalits who joined the Church in large numbers realized bitterly that the caste system is not only a reality within Hinduism but is practised in the church as well. In the context of this realization, there is a need to take a fresh look at the continuing relevance of the missionary strategy of conversion in India. Russell Chandran states that Aravind Nirmal had a radically relevant approach to conversion:

> Nirmal's theology does challenge us to abandon the traditional missionary policy and call upon people of all faiths to believe in Jesus Christ and become disciples of Jesus, telling them that when they believe in Christ they are not required to renounce their religious beliefs and practices unless they are contrary to the mind of Christ, such as idolatry, superstitions, caste discrimination, corrupt practices etc. Christ came to fulfil, not to destroy; to enrich, not to impoverish. We certainly have the responsibility of helping the people of

> other faiths to know Jesus Christ and become his disciples and to discern which practices are against Christ.[7]

The need to raise questions about the continuing focus on conversion with the Indian Churches, especially the evangelical movement, raises several issues of importance. On the one hand, the messages presented at evangelistic campaigns and crusades, though often directed at the poor and the marginalized sections of society, gloss over their socio-economic situations and instead present the Gospel as a means to salvation in effect, as escape from the miseries of this world.

A related development is the effort by some Hindutva(Hindu religious revival/reform movements) to try to absorb Dalits into a monolithic Hindu fundamentalist culture.[8] Their systematic propaganda concentrates on the message that Dalits had been truly a part of 'Hindu' religio-cultural structures and several Hindu organisations are involved in re-conversion efforts to drive home this ideology. Although it is a clear historical distortion, Dalits are caught up in a dilemma as to whether to declare their solidarity with Hindus or with Dalits. In fact, Dalits are caught between Hinduisation and Dalitisation.[9]

One serious criticism often levelled against Dalit theology is that it still operates largely within the traditional caste framework of India and, consequently, does not take sufficiently seriously the rapid changes which are at work.There is no doubt that rural India is the heartland of casteism and the primary context of the dehumanization that Dalits experience. This continues to be the situation and Dalit Theology has rightly been shaped around the caste atrocities in rural areas. However, today there is also the need to take seriously the rapid changes affecting all sections of society, especially the Dalits. The traditional social location of the Dalits was the religiously governed social structures of rural India. The 'outcast' social and economic roles of the Dalits such as menial and 'unclean' work, though considered as polluting, was essential for society to function. Not only the ideology and theology of the oppressive structures but even subaltern currents like Dalit theology operate within this framework.

While the process of modernisation set in motion by the architects of independent India initiated the de-villagisation of India, it is only during the last two decades that rapid urbanization has taken place in India. This has thrown up enormous challenges for the subaltern movements of the country. The traditional paradigms of oppression and exploitation are breaking down, partly as a result of the socio-economic and political policies of modern India, but more so because of the great exodus that has begun from the villages to the towns and cities. According to U.N. population studies, by 2030, two thirds of Indians will be living in the urban areas. Yet another factor is the process of liberalisation and privatisation initiated by the Indian government during the last two decades and the challenges they pose to the Dalits and other marginalized sections, both in urban and rural areas.

Due to the new economic policy of liberalisation and privatisation, there has been an increase in mass poverty. In the villages traditional agricultural patterns are being rapidly replaced by monoculture plantations, aqua culture and floriculture, and by production not only for the consumption of the local community but for export. Land alienation, loss of jobs, rising prices and decreasing government funding for basic amenities in health and education are all factors contributing once more to a rise in mass poverty. While the new economic policies pose a serious threat for most sections of the population, it is undoubtedly the Dalits who are most affected. It has been shown that most Dalits feel that they have much to lose by liberalisation. According to a study done recently in the *Economic and Political Weekly*, 'States like Andhra Pradesh have experienced what is known as the 'casteisation' of liberalization…'.[10]

The implications of these rapidly changing developments for the Dalits and other subaltern communities are that while the location changes, the realities remain the same, with little variation. As the Dalits move from rural to urban areas, they are able to overcome, to a certain extent, the shackles that bound them in a seemingly immutable and eternally caste-based social structure. That is a welcome development. The new situation, however, gives rise to new challenges. The migrating Dalits adding to the number of the urban poor located in the slums and pavements of the cities, the polarization of slum dwellers in major cities on caste-region-language lines, the lack of employment opportunities for Dalits due to their inadequate educational background and the resultant new forms of exploitation and exclusion, are all factors yet to be explored fully by social scientists and theologians.

In the ultimate analysis, the task of Dalit Theology, in rural or urban contexts, can be defined as the need to keep hope alive. Dwight Hopkins recently affirmed that the task of subaltern movements such as Black Theology and Dalit Theology is the need to heed the little traditions that tell the dominant powers 'we beg to differ'. According to him, the fear of moving forward is real, but it is the courage, conviction and persistence of the 'minorities' to follow through till the end that prods them forward.[11] That is the hope, faith and agenda of Dalit Theology – the conviction that 'Another World is Possible'.

Dalit theology has already made its impact on the theological scene in India but it has a long way to go. In this section we may venture to identify some future tasks. It is obvious that the emergence of Dalit theology is closely related to or even rooted in the emergence of Dalit consciousness. Without an awareness of the injustice committed to Dalits by Indian society and the organised struggle against Dalits, we cannot talk about a Dalit theology.Dalit consciousness was severely criticized by many non-Dalit Evangelical Christian leaders in India. According to Selvaraj:

> By creating a Dalit-consciousness Dalit theology has only benefited those who have become Dalit Bishops or Dalit Christian leaders, or Dalit pastors. This has resulted in the creation of a spiritual vacuum and material corruption in the Church that is perhaps worse than the pre-Reformation Roman Catholic Church. There is nepotism and unlawfulness and forging of political alliances in order to strengthen their leadership positions. The so-called Dalit Bishops and leaders do not participate in the agony and pains of Dalits but enjoy a good life at the expense of Dalitism.[12]

The situation of Dalits in general and Dalit Christians in particular continues to be oppressive, and a large majority have never gained a heightened social awareness. It was horrifying to know that caste discrimination and caste atrocities occur in all situations. Even now, there are cities, towns and villages in India where the local tea-shop still does not allow Dalits to enter inside, and that they are served tea outside in separate cups.No organized struggle has been attempted against such practices because the landlords are too powerful to be resisted. If this is the reality in India, how can one speak of Dalit consciousness? To gain a new awareness of oppressive structures, there should be organised movements and struggle. For Marxists, economic injustice becomes the focal point of their struggle; it is their strategy. It is still important, but we know that the oppressive structures are not merely economic, they are social and cultural. In fact, a revolution in consciousness has taken place through literature, art and other cultural media in many a place.

Dalit theology should also be committed to developing strategies that are necessary for creating awareness among all Dalits about the oppressive structures that dehumanize them. Dalit Christians have recently been mobilised to fight for reservations. Up to a point it is beneficial to the community but in the long run it will not serve the purpose of consciousness-raising. Forces of discrimination are deeply entrenched; economics can only reinforce the values and structures of the status quo.

Nirmal has repeatedly affirmed that Dalit theology should be seen in the context of the struggle for Dalit identity. Suppressed groups everywhere are conscious of their lost identities. Their culture, religion and, in some cases, even languages were destroyed by elite aggression. Only by destroying them can they be enslaved by the dominant castes and classes. Serious research and study is necessary. Dalit stories, myths and symbols provide a basic source for our research in this area.They have to be collected and analysed and as some of the historians remind us, there are 'hostile resources' in the materials produced by the dominant groups. But they have to be critically analysed and interpreted. The picture of the early history of Dalits is still not clear. Some attempts are being made, but they need to be deepened.

The discussion about identity should also take into consideration the solidarity of Christian Dalits with the Dalits in other religions. There are many common concerns and traditions. They are now divided; each group has developed its particular form of sub-culture. But without suppressing such individual identities, how can we build a common front? Here theology faces a special problem;a Dalit theology is based on Christian symbols and language. How do we evolve a common language? Are there insights from other traditions which we must integrate into our theological formulations? Is there a Dalit hermeneutics that can be commonly applied to different Dalit traditions?

The vision of Dalit theologians is to evolve a pluriform community thatallows different identities to flourish. How can we keep this vision as Dalits continue their struggle for identity and justice? Without this common vision our individual identities, when affirmed as mutually exclusive, will destroy human communality. Perhaps this aspect should receive further attention by Dalit theology and all contextual theologies. While we reject a universalizing tendency in sectarian theologies, especially those that come out of dominant groups, we need to keep the dialogue open in such a way that there is scope for learning from others. This is an inescapable demand of being faithful to the one Gospel.

Theology is not theoretical formulations; it results in action.Dalit Theologians are concerned not so much to think correctly about Christian faith (orthodoxy) as to live Christian faith in practice (orthopraxis). How people are to live as Christians is the primary question. It can be answered only in terms of values, relationships and structures that nurture one's life. A Dalit community that is qualitatively different from the dominant groups is also the most credible witness to its theology. Do Dalit theologians see any signs of the emergence of this new community? Dalit theology has to struggle against the issue of Untouchability and the Caste system and liberate the Dalits, irrespective of their religious identity. If Dalit Theology fails to take this role then it alienates itself not only from its context but also from people's suffering.

The identity of religion also prevents the Dalits from coming together to struggle against the oppressive system. The indigenous faith of the Dalit community was destroyed by Brahminical Hinduism and other imperial religions like Christianity and Islam. These religious identities were used by the ruling forces to divide and rule. Even the principles of these religions negate each other. So naturally the Dalits are in different camps. Even the Indian Constitution provides positive discrimination to the Dalits who belong to Hinduism and Buddhism. If the Dalits embrace any other religion they stand to lose these constitutional provisions. So there is a need for Dalit Theology either to transcend these religious identities or to make every religious identity an inclusive one.

The Indian Church, by and large, is a Dalit Church. More than 75% of the members of the Church in India are Dalits. Does Dalit Theology have any responsibility for the remaining 25% who belong to other identities like the Upper Caste and Tribals? Can Christian Dalits do theology for the non-Dalits as for non-Christian Dalits? Out of the 250 million Dalit population of India, only 20 million are Dalit Christians. Will the proposed Christian Dalit Theology take into consideration the 200 million Dalits? To what extent does the Dalit community in general accept the 'Christian' contribution as its own in its struggle? Will the Dalit Theology take into consideration the liberation of the dominant caste, or the oppressors?

Dalit Theology needs to identify what is 'Christian 'within the entire Christian tradition and what this means. The adjective 'Christian' is preferred by all the Indian Christian theologians, so we have to think seriously how to characterise the word 'Christian' in the light of the plurality of Dalit faith and cultural identity. Without critiquing missionary movements and the theology, paternalism and confessionalism of traditional Christian theology, we will not be successful in formulating a truly Christian theology in India.

Unless Dalit Theology takes plurality into serious consideration it cannot claim to be a contextual theology of India. It will be making the same mistake as other Indian Christian theologians. India's richness is revealed in its cultural, religious, racial, ideological and environmental diversities. Such a rich plurality gives birth to pluralism. Pluralism therefore challenges the very roots of the current theological endeavour which demands unity. This Dalit Christian Theology has certain limitations;that is to say, non-Christian Dalits are also involved in doing theology or life reflections in the form of ideology. One may argue that that is also theology, a theology which reflects on human experiences of suffering and uses human words. This then raises the issue of the dividing line between theology and ideology.Therefore, the question raised by M.E. Prabhakar seems to be valid: Can we speak of Dalitology, including both Dalit Theology and Dalit Ideology?[13] Dalit liberation has to become an endeavour for establishing a coherent, dynamic thought and action/action-reflection. Is there a need to move forwards this theology/ideology continuum?

Further, expressions such as 'Christian' 'theology' etc. can be misunderstood by Dalits who are not Christians. In a predominantly non-Christian society, using the term 'theology' with its 'Christian' connotations, both in concept and practice, may become a source of suspicion and prejudice, blocking shared praxis. In a pluralistic context, therefore, it will be more meaningful and fruitful to explore the content of spirituality and religiosity that emphasises universal human values. Thus, Dalit Liberation Theology cannot be merely Christian. It has to be inter-religious, inter-ethnic, inter-cultural and even inter-communal, given the fact that in India religious communities are the basic social segments that engage in dialogue and action.

Dalit Theology is not and cannot be exclusive. A theology that is exclusive cannot be Christian. Dalit theology is pursued for others' liberation as well. The goal of Dalit theology is Dalit liberation, their empowerment, i.e. strengthening Dalits, providing comfort to them, encouraging them and sharing the good news with them, the good news that God is with them in their own God given identity and that they are people with worth and dignity, and that human dignity is more important than the question of economic emancipation. At the same time, it speaks about the gospel of forgiveness of the oppressors. The oppressors can share life with the Dalits' quest of inclusive community where all will have and share life. But do the Dalits have life now to share with others? Does life treat them well? Fullness of life is the first priority for Dalits and others can share life with them after the Dalits have attained life and health. In other words, Dalit theology must be informed by a social vision which is liberative in character. Such a transforming social vision ought to be based on the principles of liberty, equality and fraternity. In other words, the common Dalit experience of Christian Dalits along with other Dalits should shape a Christian Dalit theology.At this point of history and historical juncture, Dalit theology and theologians will have to seriously consider how to go beyond the narrow confines of doing theology within a constituency that is exclusively Christian.

It is in this context that the commonalities of all Dalits (Christian Dalits and other Dalits), such as historical consciousness, pathos and misery, become the prerequisites or preconditions for doing theology.Dalit theology will have to be a unifying force (secular and sacred) vis-à-vis Godand will have to search for common characteristics and features that are found in God who became incarnate in Jesus Christ. This is because a perspective for Dalit theology at this juncture of history is to move towards secularisation. How to move from a theology exclusively for Dalit Christians to an inclusive and accommodative project must be explored.

Dietrich Bonhoeffer described secularisation as a movement 'towards autonomy of a human being who discovers the laws by which the world lives and deals with itself in science, social and political matters, art, ethics and religion'.[14]Secularisation is a process. It is not an end product. For Bonhoeffer, Christ confronts the world not in its weakness and dependency on religious or other world views, but at the level of human well-being and responsible action. It is not religious acting that makes a Christian but participation in the suffering of God in the secular life. Bonhoeffer is clear that a sinful, godless world must still be brought to repentance and new life in Christ, but the sin of which it must repent first of all are those of its use of power; and vigour amid its responsibilities for how human problems are faced and dealt with. Christ the ultimate reality of the world takes form in the world in order that the world, in its penultimate secularity, may move towards its ultimate redemption in him.

Some of the vital components that constitute Dalit theology –Dalit identity, Dalit affirmation and Dalit history –ought to be lifted up and articulated as a theology with vigour and vitality. What ought to be done is to integrate all these constitutive elements and situate them within a framework of 'equality', since equality is the regulative principle of justice and a principle of criticism under which every scheme of justice stands.Equal justice is the best approximation of 'brotherhood'. Equal justice is therefore 'the most rational possible social good'. The rule of equality includes both concerns for process and also for equality as a substantive goal. What is important now is to expose the overt and covert forms of social inequality.

The strength of the Dalit Jesus is that He embraces the Dalits in their brokenness, in their suffering; they are able to see themselves in Jesus. This very strength, however, is also a weakness. Dalitness must involve more than just being a particular caste or identity with a particular cultural and historical experience. It must also include as well an ethical concern and commitment to the well-being and freedom of all Dalit people. By calling Christ 'Dalit', Dalit theologians clearly have responded to the need to identify Christ as one who opposes casteism. The Dalit Christ condemns caste oppression. The problem is that it does not go beyond that; it does not portray the complexity of caste oppression. Specifically, it does not address the fact that Dalits oppress each other and that casteism is not the only barrier to Dalit freedom.

Dalit Theology does not confront the reality of oppression within the Dalit community. The Dalit Jesus does not point to the reality of Dalit against Dalit oppression; for Dalits are victimised by each other. The Dalit community and the Church are often divided against themselves over different issues. For instance, the 'haves' in the Dalit community – the middle class – often look down upon the 'have-nots' – the poor. They harbour a sense of resentment toward themselves. A spirit of 'each to his or her own' prevails over a desire to help those who remain trapped in the vicious circle of poverty. The Dalits, therefore, are left divided among themselves.What does the Dalit Christ say to those from the Dalit communities who are to some extent integrated into the caste, political and economic structures of Indian society and who diligently and vigilantly protect their positions within those structures, even at the expense of other Dalits? How does the Dalit Christ challenge those from that same community who look down on those Dalits who have not been successful? What does the Dalit Christ have to say to those who hold on to their caste identity only in order to reap the benefits of affirmative action to the reservation policy and who, therefore, will not publicly acknowledge Jesus Christ as their Lord and Saviour: those who by availing themselves of these benefits deprive those who really need them?

Thus far, Dalit Theology has focused its attention on liberation from caste oppression. However, there is also the question of gender liberation which must find a place in a more inclusive understanding of liberation. Dalit Feminist theologians strongly believe that despite the strong emphasis on suffering and identification with the brokenness of the individual, Dalit theology has failed to acknowledge adequately the Dalit woman and the uniqueness of her experience in the analysis. Neither the presence nor the role of Dalit women in the community's struggle for dignity and freedom is acknowledged and despite the pivotal roles played by Dalit women, they are never accorded the same treatment or respect as their male counterparts. N.G. Prasuna strongly argues that:

> The Dalit women lost the image of God according to the Patriarchal society. It has been lost under various forms of oppression. They have lost the ability to speak. The have lost true laughter. They have lost their health. They have lost their human dignity.They have lost their due place in church. They have to clean the church benches, altar, communion utensils, etc. But they are not

> allowed to sit along with high castes. They are treated still as untouchables, slaves in the church.[15]

Further she advocates that 'at this juncture in our theologizing, Dalit women's experience is the essential component. This experience challenges and contradicts the present concept of God, which is based on power'. Prasuna quotes Elizabeth Schussler Fiorenza to bring out the need for a new renaming of God and its use in the scriptures. Fiorenza reiterates that 'such a process of naming transforms our metaphor of Scripture as tablets of stone, on which the unchanging word of God is carved for all time into the image of Bread that nurtures, sustains and energizes women as the People of God, in our struggle against injustice and oppression'.[16]

A Dalit Christ is inadequate for understanding the meaning of Jesus Christ for a community besieged by more than just casteism and classism. Dalit theologians have probed the structural links between casteism and economic exploitation. A more adequate social analysis of the roots of human oppression also requires attention to the interconnectedness between casteism, sexism and economic and political domination, a task that is especially urgent. No authentic theology of liberation can arise out of these communities without specifically addressing the liberation of women in the above spheres, both within the Church and in society. Dalit women, there, need to continue to name their experience of oppression to keep the issue of sexism before the community and the Church and as an element of Dalit theology until it has been eliminated. Monica Melanchthon argues that:

> Emphasis on the suffering Jesus as a model for Dalit women causes much discomfort for me personally because such a glorification of suffering is a tool often used to keep women in their place and to hinder them from breaking out of the structures that oppress them, thus preventing them

> from experiencing liberation in the here and now. While it is important to acknowledge that the Dalit Christ is present wherever people are engaged in struggle for a community's wholeness and that the face of Christ is seen in the poorest of Dalit women, the emphasis needs to be given to the empowering Christ who through His resurrection proved victorious over all life-denying forces.[17]

Dalit theology is part of the postcolonial struggle of different communities for their distinct identity and space. In a largely homogenizing trend influenced by two processes namely globalization and Hinduisation, Dalits and Dalit Christians are still struggling for a Dalit identity of their own. Intra-Dalit conflicts and Dalit sub-groups still continue despite the striving for a common Dalit identity and solidarity. Therefore, the challenge for Dalit theology is to strike a creative balance.

Hindutva revival/reform movements are trying to absorb Dalits into a monolithic Hindu fundamentalist culture. Their systematic propaganda concentrates on the message that Dalits had been truly part of the 'Hindu' religio-cultural structures. Several Hindu organizations are involved in re-conversion efforts to drive home this ideology. Although it is a clear historical distortion, Dalits are caught up in a dilemma whether to declare their solidarity with Hindus or with Dalits. In fact, Dalits are caught between Hinduisation and Dalitisation. This historic dilemma appears to have had its impact upon Dalit Christians and the Dalit theological movement too. This may be the reason why this new strand of theology appears to be at a standstill right now.

The almost total dependence on Biblical thought for theological construction needs further reconsideration in the light of the historical experience of Dalits.Pre-existing/Christian egalitarian thought and struggle for equality and justice were evident in Dalit history and memory. But the early Dalits had their own ways of protest and resistance. This is ignored by

Dalit theologians.Dalit theologians also need to widen the definition of 'texts', given the oral emphasis in Dalit tradition. By probing into Dalit folklore and songs they are likely to unearth extra-textual sources for doing Dalit theology. This could also help create new hermeneutical principles unique to the Dalit theological movements.

Ancestral worship and female deities appear prominently in Dalit myths and songs. Dalit theologians could explore how the pre-existing religio-cultural ideas might have shaped their journey into Christianity and how they dealt with such questions in their everyday life. All these could function as a rich source of theologising and Dalit faith articulation in India.While pathos, suffering and pain have found a place in Dalit theology, the rich Dalit traditions of celebrating life in the context of communitarian values seem to have been completely forgotten by Dalit theologians, with few exceptions. The rich culture of the Dalits has many egalitarian ideas. This needs to be further explored by Dalit theologians.The 'dialogue' and 'accommodation' that take shape at the popular level of both Hinduism and Christianity need systematic consideration by Dalit theology. It appears that in a silent way people at the village level are moulding meaningful 'systems' of interaction in a pluralistic socio-religious setting like that of India. If the reality of the religion of a people can be studied only through the empirical enquiry into the meaning appropriated by them as persons and community of persons in their life situations,then Dalit theology needs to look carefully into the popular level of Hindu-Christian religious encounter. Luke and Camion's study reveals that religious boundaries at the level of belief systems and rituals are not so marked in the minds of the people in villages. In the popular worship context, there is mutual sharing of practices, symbols and values without so much fuss.These marginalised spaces deserve systematic attention.

So, any contextual theology becomes meaningless if it is not dealing with the issues really affecting the most marginalised section in society. Western academic Theology, Indian Christian Theology, the Third World Theology, have so far ignored the primary problems of the vast majority of grassroots population; hence they are not able to get the recognition of the vast majority. Only upper caste and upper class elites, who are in the hierarchy of the churches and the society, still use those theologies to justify their position and power. But the emergence of Dalit Theology is really shaking the foundations of all the other theologies. At the same time,one must recognize and acknowledge the fact that Dalit theology is facing some serious threats. Hence a need has arisen to deconstruct Dalit theology in the light of new developments.

Endnotes

1. K.P. Kuruvilla, *Dalit Theology:An Indian Christian Attempt to Give Voice to the Voiceless,* unpublished paper.
2. S. Clarke, *Theory of Atonement: An Indian Cross-Cultural Theology of the Cross,* unpublished paper, UTC, Bangalore, 2003.
3. A.P. Nirmal and V. Devasahayam (eds), *Dr.B.R.Ambedkar: A Centenary Tribute*, Gurukul, 1991, p. 91.
4. A. Ganadason, 'Dalit Women – The Dalit of the Dalit', *A Reader in Dalit Theology,* p. 133.
5. T.S. Wilkinson and M.M. Thomas (eds), *Ambedkar and the Neo-Buddhist Movement*, Madras, CLS, 1972, pp. 60-61.
6. V. Devasahayam, *Outside the Camp*, p. 41.
7. R.J. Chandran,p. 33.
8. Indian Political parties with their ideological basis on Hindu fundamentalism and communalism.
9. O. George, 'The Emerging Dalit Theology: A Historical Appraisal', *Indian Church History Review*, vol. XXXIV, no. 1, June 2000, pp. 17-37.
10. P.B. Mehta, 'Affirmation without Reservation', *Economic and Political Weekly*, July 3, 2004, pp. 29-51.

11. Sermon delivered by Prof. Dwight L. Hopkins (University of Chicago Divinity School) at the reformation Sunday worship, Gurukul, Chennai on 31st October 2004.
12. A. Selvaraj, *Christianity and Social Transformation: The Kerala Story*, Trivandrum, ICRO, 2002, p. 149.
13. *A Note on the Evolving Direction for Dalit Theology/Ideology*, CISRS, Bangalore.
14. D. Bonhoeffer, *A Letter from Prison*, 1944.
15. N.G. Prasuna, 'The Dalit Women', in V. Devasahayam (ed.), *Frontiers of Dalit Theology*, Gurukul Lutheran Theological College and Research institute, ISPCK, 1997, p. 115.
16. Ibid., p. 114.
17. M. Melanthon, 'A Dalit Women's Perspective', unpublished paper, Gurukul Lutheran Theological College & Research Centre, Chennai.

CHAPTER 9

Towards A Theology of Dalitism: A Proposal

This final chapter focuses on whether there was any methodology which the Dalit theologians followed when they entered into the process of doing theology from the Dalit perspective. At that early stage not many of the Dalit theologians, probably, thought about methodology.

Among the early contributors to Dalit theology, the great majority were Dalits themselves and the rest were those committed to the Dalit cause. Those who were Dalits expressed in their essays and writings their feelings of pain and pathos. In the writings by non- Dalits, one meets with a kind of experience born of the collaborative efforts made to free society and the Dalits from caste-based oppression. So, the point here is that the pain and pathos experienced by the Dalits is the starting point of Dalit theology. The prefix 'Dalit' to 'theology' also indicates the same truth.The expression 'Dalit' refers to the 'state' in which Dalits are living. That 'state' is oppressive in nature and from which they need liberation. The earliest pioneer of Dalit theology, the late Nirmal, summed up this point in his vision of Dalit theology as follows: 'It will be based on their own Dalit experience, their own sufferings, their own aspirations and their own hope. It will narrate the story of their sufferings and their pains. It will anticipate liberation which is meaningful to them'.[1]

The earliest contributors to 'Towards a Dalit Theology,' there were theology professors, activists or those involved in Church-related work, but all of them fall within the category of 'organic intellectuals'. The earliest contributors toDalit Theology became part of the process of doing theology from the Dalit perspectivebecause either they were Dalit themselves or because of their commitment to the Dalit cause, not because their concern was to work on a research project either to fulfil their academic career or to work for a degree for which they would have to follow a certain definite method. The issue of methodology was not their concern. When James Massey wrote his first essay 'Ingredients for a Dalit Theology' he hardly had any thought of methodology. He was fully aware of the state of Dalit communities, and that forced him to enter into this process of doing theology from the Dalit perspective. He made the following statement about the need for Dalit theology in that essay:

> Here I do not propose the rejecting of the known expression of Indian Christian theology for its usefulness. All I am saying is that we have to work out another expression of Indian Christian theology which should be relevant to the living situation of the vast majority of people in their widely dissimilar regions. A positive response to this situation can be found in the emergence of 'Dalit theology' which will be based on the living experience of Dalits themselves.[2]

'Towards a Dalit Theology' is about the understanding of the need and purpose of Dalit Theology. This came from the Christian Dalit dilemma concerning their future but, at the same time, 'it is equally certain that it is the concern for the total Dalit struggle, of which the Christian Dalit situations are integral to the rationale for Dalit theology'. M.E. Prabhakar sums up the following three factors which led to the emergence of Dalit theology: Dalit theology has been conceived in the context of the struggle against casteism and the aspirations for social justice, both in the Church and society. The principles and practices of caste are rooted in the religious-philosophical –traditions of the dominant Hindu culture. The theory of *varna* (ritual ranking based on colour) provides the doctrinal basis for hierarchy and discrimination between *jatis* or castes (functional groups) and for the exclusion of certain 'impure' castes as untouchables and outcastes. The critique of this system of inequality has to be theological. The insensitivity of the Church and Indian Christian Theology to Dalit concerns and the deeper dimensions of their struggle and aspirations for fuller humanity, despite the majority of Christians being of Dalit origin, make it imperative for the formulation of a Christian Dalit theology with a universal appeal.

These observations, derived from the contents of essays and articles, represent the earliest contributors of the first generation of Dalit theologians (both Dalit and non-Dalit). Though they were not directly concerned about the methodological issues, yet they have given enough information about the ways they formed their thoughts about Dalit theology. Now, based upon their ways, the present generation of theologians can give concrete shape and form to a methodology of doing theology from the Dalit perspective.

It is imperative to look at the present state of Dalit theology, particularly how it stands in the first decade of the 21st century; the content of this work has so far concentrated on the last quarter of the 20th century. At that early period of Dalit theology and its development, there was the commitment of the individual Dalit thinkers and activists. At the same time their efforts were supported by other organisations, which included the programme on 'Caste-Class studies' of the Christian Institute for the Study of Religion and Society, Gurukul Lutheran Theological College, Chennai, and the Christian Dalit Liberation Movement.Dalit theology grew to its present form through a process of doing theology from the Dalit perspective.

By the end of the second decade at the end of the 20th century, this process came to a standstill. But at that time the majority of the early Dalit thinkers, activists and supporting institutions were either weakened or, for a variety of reasons, had abandoned the process. One reason behind this situation was the absence of clear-cut direction and guidelines.

The process of Dalit theology had not discovered for itself any straightforward methodology. The true priority for the first generation of Dalit theologians was to achieve the goal of realising full humanity. But even to reach that goal they needed systematic thinking and organisation,namely the issue of 'constructing' or 'reconstructing' the scope and methodology of Dalit theology to enable the process of liberation for the Dalits.As Dalit theology entered the 21st century more and more Dalit theologians (Dalits and Non-Dalits) became aware of this gap or weakness in the process of doing Dalit theology.A major thrust during this first decade of the 21st century has been to make clear some of the basic methodological issues and scope which will give direction in the future to Dalit theologians, especially the new generations, which will ensure continuity for the process of Dalit Theology.

This observation of the need of a suitable methodology was called for to ensure that the works of the marginalised people 'might see the light of day'. The presence of the marginalised Dalits has a special significance in the context of global trends. Indicative of theologians' commitment to justice is a need to understand power relations in the complex world of new economic realities. This part of the study adds to strengthening the ongoing studies of Dalits and their heritage which bring insights for Dalit theology to reconstruct its scope and method.Basically, Dalitism means Dalit ideology based on the Dalit world view which in turn is based on Dalit Religion i.e. whatever happens in and through their life context. The term 'Dalits' refers to that 'great mass of common people' who, though unsophisticated, have powerful liberative traditions reflected in their faith expression. These traditions may differ from more classical forms of religion. While they have an oral tradition, theologians are keen to draw out deliberately liberative aspects from their artistic expression of shared values and goals in life.

However weak Dalits may be, there is a certain ambivalence in doing a study about the phenomenon of Dalits. Yet it is my hope that this study will provide an opening to study the 'shared values' of human communities while providing a theology of social transformation for the marginalised. One has to realise that this has its own limitations because it is not a study from an anthropological perspective but from that of a theologian. It is theological perspectives that will help in the study of the Indian Dalit scenario.

Given the pluralism characterising human existence and the socio-political and religio-cultural traditions, theology will be plural and will call for a plurality of methods. What follows are some tentative reflections and suggestions for one possible theological method. If theology, for example, is addressed to all people, we will certainly need a corresponding change in methodological orientation. The methodologies of today cannot be the same as when metaphysical categories dominated theology. At the global level we could notice a shift in methodology when theology moved from metaphysical categories to more historical ones. Today, the need of the hour is for contextual categories, derived both from sociological experiences and from the religio-cultural realm.

The question of methodology is a common issue in the various disciplines of the humanities and science. Theology could comfort itself with the thought that the methodological flux is not peculiar to it, but has become a common problem of all disciplines. In particular, the study would like to point out that theology has in the past had strong metaphysical moorings. No wonder then that the dissolution of metaphysics is today seen as coinciding with the 'dissolution' of Christianity in the

West – be it through the interpretation of secularism or through the advent of postmodernity. Be that as it may, the point here is to underline that theology may take a dangerous and fundamentalist turn if it wants to still be confined within the metaphysical realm. In other words, there should be an epistemological vigilance over the realm of theology. The truths of its assertions need to be sensitive to the epistemological question and process of acquiring, critically developing and organising knowledge. If so, theology will be able to share with the sciences similar epistemological concerns.Crucial to the question for all sciences in grappling with methodology is the epistemological issue of objectivity. Objectivity is a question which has been common to any form of knowledge, and the question is posed much more sharply with regard to humanities. Theology also shares with other organised forms of knowledge the traditional question of the validity of its knowledge which is commonly supposed to be to the extent to which it is objective.

Dalit theology needs to become more and more empirical. The proposal of the study of empirical data is different from what was known as positivist theology, meaning thereby the attempt to spell out passages and texts from Scripture and tradition with reference to any particular theme.Empirical theology is the theological investigation and pursuit that begins from socio political facts and data. This is something very important because in this way every single issue theologians are treating will have a concrete social location. For, in India, the Dalits have taught about the earthliness of human existence and the importance of paying attention to concrete realities related to survival. One just cannot build a theological castle without taking into account the facts and figures about poverty, oppression, and the experience of rejections which the various segments of people undergo.Vague descriptions or rhetoric on the same cannot furnish an adequate and reasonable basis for the beginning of theology.

If theology is being done in a particular community or group, the empirical data pertaining to them and their condition will need to be studied and recorded in detail. The first stage of methodology requires that, while dealing with any theological treatise or theme, the researcher would ask,what is the corresponding empirical data to do with that treatise or issue?. The data needs to be collected and studied in depth and thoroughly. This is also part and parcel of the theological process. It is a fact that most often theological discourse makes too general and sweeping statements about empirical realities in order to be able to quickly ascend to ahistorical plane.And if there is any effort to relate to these realities, theological discourses often content themselves with making impressionistic and anecdotal statements.

A critical analysis is subjective writing because it expresses the writer's opinion or evaluation of a text. Analysis means to break down and study the parts. Writing a critical paper requires two steps: critical reading and critical writing.The collection of empirical data will be followed by critical interpretation. This should happen in three stages. These three stages could be also viewed as three different streams of interpretation which meet and merge.

Generally, this is the research program undertaken by a variety of social theorists that are strongly influenced by critical theory. Critical theory of society, in turn, can be characterised as a blend of practical philosophy and explanatory social science, sharing and radically reforming the intentions of both. Practical philosophy is concerned with the specifics of ethical and political life (praxis) and the actions that must be undertaken to achieve the good life; explanatory social science produces scientific knowledge of the general causes of social action.Depending on the theological question or the issue, one or other critical approaches or techniques in Humanities need to be drawn into the picture. In so doing, the tools and methods specific to that particular discipline need to be followed. Often, the help of more than one science may be required to interpret the data.It is important that the collaboration of sciences is part and parcel of the theologising process itself. One could look at the process analytically from two angles.

Religious scriptures have a unique place since they are the documents of faith. The process of knowledge does not end with the operation of reasonwhich, in any case, cannot give us the truth·but only function as a regulatory and ordering principle. In interpreting Christian scriptures, all the tools will be employed which have been developed to study and understand the Bible, its background and its universal message. Similarly, the Christian traditions will also be explored to study how a particular issue or theme has been treated in different historical contexts. The presupposition here is that the Bible and Christian traditions are meant to serve for the flourishing of life in all its expressions. Also presupposed is that these resources are oriented to effect change and transformation at all levels. Since theology has to have constant reference to the empirical data and its analysis, it will be helpful in studying the particular traditions to note also how particular beliefs and doctrines affected society and with what consequences. In other words, the social effects of Christian doctrines are important for relating them to the particular theological questions or issues we may be dealing with today in our contexts.

Brahminical Hinduism took over the organised or existing forms of support, destroying the cordiality and mutual-inter-relatedness that provided to Dalit communities grace for the fallen and help for the helpless by providing space for the weaker ones. The Dalits' way of life helped sensitise them to their fellow-humans and their context. On the other hand, organised religion became institutional and made it difficult to articulate concerns for the context or sensitivity to the needs of the people. This was because all belief and practices were defined and non-negotiable. In Dalit religions, women had an important and mystical role to play. They were at times prophetic in these traditions. The subordinate role of women from the Judeo-Christian tradition calls the theologians to reconsider the role of women in the life of the Church and society, for gender equalities were greater in Dalit religion and tradition.

Much has been spoken and written about the first foundations, namely, the Dalit context or Dalit experience as a whole. Another insight Dalit theologians gained was that the existing Dalit theologies were not able to deal satisfactorily with the Dalit issuethat is the judgement of Dalit communities. New theologies like Liberation theology have given rise to a new starting point for theology.And these new sprouts do give helpful tools for developing a theological method for Dalit theology, for as with Liberation theology it is understood that the pain and pathos experienced by the Dalits has to be the starting point of a new Dalit theology. Experience here is twofold. One is the painful and conscious awareness of what it is to be a Dalit in Indian society. The daily experience of discrimination in social gatherings, in areas of work, difficulties with table fellowship, obstacles created for inter-caste marriages, bans on entering sacred places like templesetc., are among the typical experiences. And it is admitted by all that the Dalit women suffer most in this respect.

The second kind of experience is what one encounters when organised efforts are made to free society from caste practice. Direct physical assault, burning down of homes and villages, open sexual molestation, denial of civic and health facilities, are among the many ways of resistance to any liberative effort. There are also other, subtle and sophisticated, ways like buying off promising leaders and domesticating them, co-opting their cause in order to stifle the movement among the awakened and similar strategies employed in order to blunt and dissipate Dalit movements.These experiences should raise theological questions, which should be pursued at different levels. With such question in the past, the theological tools for such questions usually came from philosophy, but in the case of Dalit theological analysis and for Dalit theological research the tools will have to come from the social sciences.

Since the production, organisation and distribution of various forms of knowledge are themselves very much linked to external factors and motivations, it is also important to be critical in employing the sciences for the interpretation of data. Often an uncritical approach allows social sciences to become supporters of the status quo. Since within the same discipline there could be very different approaches, one needs to choose the kind of approach that is geared to change and transformation. That would tally with one of the basic presuppositions of any genuine theology, namely that all theology is directed to change – personal, collective and societal, etc. The theological enterprise needs to guard itself against the danger of social sciences becoming new forms of absolutism, a temptation to which theology itself has been exposed.

In order to pursue these questions that are raised by contemporary experience one has to seek the assistance of the social sciences. The history of Caste in India shows that in the evolution of the system, economic issues played a major role. Sociology is another discipline whose assistance is required for clearer understanding of the empirical social realities. Anthropology also is needed. In other words, the tools of the social sciences have to be systematically used in order to secure clarity about the issues under consideration and to avoid generalities. Since there exists close linkage between the economic activities and concerns of a given community, the role of economics in the creation and maintenance of caste needs to be explored, researched and highlighted.

The presence of social science in theology at the point when it is important to have a deeper understanding of the concrete world of human beings does not imply an undue submission of theological reflection to secular thought. Hence

Dalit theology must take into account the contribution of the social sciences, while always appealing to its own sources. This point is fundamental, for whatever the context in which theological reflection takes place, Dalit theology now must take a new route, and in order to do so, it will have to appeal to its own forms.

Culture would take us beyond the social sciences since the concept deals with the whole complex reality of the life of a particular community. Emerging Dalit Theology has to be in dialogue with the cultures of the times. Close study of the constitutive elements of a culture, positive and negative, has to be part of research in Dalit Theology. Beliefs, values, customs, traditions and institutions of a particular society need to be closely observed and data collected, analysed and interpreted. For such interpretation the tools of social sciences as well as the normativeness of the Bible are required.

Theology itself needs to be balanced by the social sciences and humanities. One needs only to study the views of an influential thinker with regard to theology to see that it is so overarching that it can not only do away with other sciences, but even replace them. But in fact, the consciousness of the socio-economic conditions in which theological discourse are produced calls for a critique of the ideological elements, as well as the very language of these discourses themselves.Working hand in hand with Dalits of all traditions is a major requirement. Such solidarity on the journey presupposes solidarity in perception. Here there are problems. For belief systems across religions vary. For example, Christian understanding of God, revelation, and scripture etc., collide with the sources of other religions.

However, a sound theology of religions will be of great help to press forward towards the goal of Dalit liberation. Acceptance of diversity is central to solidarity. Some of the guidelines governing inter-religious dialogue can be helpful in cultivating mental dispositions that will promote solidarity, and yet at the same time affirm diversity and particularity in belief systems, practices, rituals and other aspects of religion.

A major irony of the Indian situation is that these discourses about Indian Dalit Theology have to be in the language of the onetime colonial rulers. We know that language is closely associated with culture. Theological articulation should be in the language of the very people in whom, with whom and for whom theological reflection is undertaken. But the problem here is whose language? For an aspect of the brokenness of the Dalits is that much of their life is under the influence of the dominant groups. Language also suffers the same fate. In many cases, the language of the particular group has either disappeared, or is not recognised by the dominant class or the State. This requires a close, critical research approach. For the identity of a person or of a community is linked with the language and culture of the individual or the group.

Dalit theology is a project of Dalit Christians aimed at overcoming their situation of 'Dalitness'.It is an attempt by Dalit Christians done on behalf of, for and by the Dalit community at large. But this Dalit Christian theology has certain limitations. That is to say, Dalits, who are not Christians, are also involved in doing theology or life-reflections. Life-reflections by the non-Christians Dalits are in the form of ideology. One may argue by saying that it is also theology, a theology which reflects on human experiences of suffering and misery and uses human words, though the exercise is not distinctively Christian. This then raises the issue of the dividing line between theology and ideology. In reality, the dividing line between theology and ideology wears thin and becomes obscure. When ideology is involved it identifies sources of domination and power located within the religio-cultural heritage. Therefore, the question raised here in this study is: Can we speak of Dalitism, including both Dalit Theology and Dalit Ideology? And in order for Dalit liberation to become an endeavour for establishing a coherent dynamic thought, action reflection process, is there a need to adopt this ideology-theology continuum?

Given the importance of the term 'ideology' in the theoretical framework of this part of the chapter, let me take a brief look at how other scholars have used it, and in turn how I use it.The literature on ideology expanded exponentially over the past several decades.Almost all those who write on it begin by stating how difficult, if not impossible, it is to define. Ferruccio Rossi-Landinbegins by giving eleven headings under which we can understand ideology[3] and Terry Eagleton outdoes him by presenting sixteen possible meanings.[4]Ideology is the most elusive concept in the whole of social science for it asks about the bases and validity of our most fundamental ideas. As such it is an essentially contested concept, that is, a concept about the very definition (and therefore application) of which there is acute controversy.With significant exceptions, the word ideology comes trailing pejorative connotation. Ideology is someone else's thought, seldom our own. That our thought might be ideological is a suggestion that we almost instinctively reject lest the foundations of our most cherished conceptions turn out to be composed of more shifting sand than we would like. Therefore, the history of the concept of ideology is the history of various attempts to find a firm Archimedean point outside the sphere of ideological discourse, an immovable spot from which to observe the levers of ideology at work.[5]

Unlike many other similarly controversial terms (democracy, say, or liberty), ideology is less than 200 years old. It is the product of the social, political and intellectual upheavals that accompanied the Industrial Revolution: the spread of democratic ideals, the politics of mass movements, and the idea that, since we have made the world, we can also remake it.Ideologies were the products of an increasingly pluralist society and were associated with rival groups whose sectional interests they served.

Like so many other enticing things, the word ideology is

of French origin. But although directly a product of the French Enlightenment, the notion obviously has its roots in the general philosophical questions about meaning and direction with which the breakdown of the medieval world view confronted Western European intellectuals. These questions were encouraged by the impact of Protestantism with its insistence on the individual, on liberty of conscience, and on the transformative power of the word rather than the reassuring presence of ritual. More direct precursors, however, of the original discussants of ideology, were thinkers such as Francis Bacon and Thomas Hobbes.Baconian Theory of Idols lies at the origin of modern social science.It strongly influenced both the English empirical tradition in Hobbes and Locke and the French Enlightenment which eventually produced the concept of ideology.[6]

The Enlightenment thinkers were the intellectual precursors of the French Revolution of 1789; and it was in the immediate aftermath of the French Revolution that the term ideology was first coined. Its originator, in 1797 was Antoine Destiutt de Tracy, one of a group of philosophers whom the revolutionary Convention had put in charge of the newly founded Institute deFrance specifically to spread the ideas of the Enlightenment. In his *Element d' Ideologie*, written between 1801 and 1815, de Tracy proposed a new science of ideas, an idea-logy, which would be the ground of all other sciences. Rejecting the concept of innate ideas, de Tracy explained how all our ideas are based on philosophical sensations.[7] A rational investigation of the origin of ideas, free from religious or metaphysical prejudice, would be the foundation of a just and happy society. For the investigation of the individual ideas would show their common origin in universal human needs and desires. Those needs would form the framework of laws regulating society on a natural basis and promoting the harmonious fulfilment of the relevant desires, for the natural and the social coincided. And this coincidence would be laid bare by the rational assessment of the origin of ideas, by ideology.

Thus, in its origin, the notion of ideology was positive and progressive. In the eyes of Napoléon, however, it quickly became pejorative. As his government evolved towards an empire supported by established religion, criticism from the liberal and republican ideologues(as they came to be called) became inevitable.[8]This oscillation between a positive and a negative connotation will be characteristic of the whole history of the concept of ideology.From a critical linguistic perspective, the term normally describes the ways in which what we say and think interacts with society. An ideology therefore derives from the taken-for-granted assumptions, beliefs and value-systems which are shared collectively by social groups. And when an ideology is the ideology of a particularly powerful social group, it is said to be dominant. Thus, dominant ideologies are mediated through powerful political and social institutions. Our perception of these institutions, moreover, will be shaped in part by the specific practices of the social groups who comprise them.Dominant ideologies operate as a mechanism for maintaining asymmetrical power relations in society.[9]

Much writing on ideology has been frankly hostile. Many others contrast their own reasoned pragmatism with what they characterize as the unreasoning rigidity of ideology. In an oft-quoted formula of Clifford Geertz the dominant attitude toward ideology is, 'I have a social philosophy, you have political opinions, he has an ideology'.[10], As a single example of this hostility on the part of one of the leading lights of critical theory, Michael Foucault has said that ideology is not a very useful category because 'it always stands in virtual opposition to something else which is supposed to count as truth'.[11]So in this study how am I using ideology? By it I mean a mode of interpreting reality based upon a systematic, idealistic quest for order. It is systematic in that it seeks to provide a set perspective from which a wide array of data can be brought together and harmonized within a single intellectual framework. An ideology often posits a number of binary oppositions:

> Ideologies like to draw rigid boundaries between what is acceptable and what is not, between self and non-self, truth and falsity, sense and nonsense, reason and madness, central and marginal, surface and depth.[12]

This systematic and unitary nature of the formulations means that it is taken as authoritative by its adherents. This authority may be locatable, such as the faith and life of the Dalit community. When ideology is based upon a transcendent reality or truth to the extent that such a truth is treated as sacred, means that the ideology takes on a distinctly religious cast.An ideology is presented as a timeless, universal truth, and its proponents resist the notion that it can ever change or needs to be changed. Changes that do occur are interpreted as simply restatements of earlier formulations or clearer perceptions of the truth.

An ideology is not separate from the society and culture in which its adherents live. It is, in the words of Clifford Geertz, a 'cultural system'.[13] It is part and parcel of society, even if the adherents attempt to renounce and withdraw from that society. An ideology is expressed in the language, actions, and symbols of the culture in which it is embedded. It shapes that culture, and in turn is shaped by it. For all that an ideology makes empirical claims, and to a large extent consists of literal, nonfigurative statements, it is not simply a rational, consciously understood intellectual framework. An ideology has affective, symbolic, mythic, and experiential elements to it. An ideology may present itself as systematic, unified, and rational and certainly appears so in contrast to less well articulated or unarticulated realms of value. Paul Ricoeur has argued that ideology even mediates between the interior world of thought, imaginations and emotions and the exterior world of social relations. The mechanisms of that mediation operate as symbols, and so are open to the ambiguities and multiple interpretations that are inherent in symbols.[14]

What this rough characterisation of ideology does not address directly is the relationship between ideology and power.For the most part, ideology has been seen either as an apologetic method of legitimating and rationalising the existing power structure, or as the programmatic agenda of those who are out of power but want to effect a total transformation of the power structure. Some have attempted to develop a more inclusive definition, but still one that ties ideology intimately to power relations,as in David McLellan's conclusion that ideology is best viewed as ' an aspect of every system of sign and symbols in so far as they are implicated in an asymmetrical distribution of power and resources'. McLellan's rhetoricaladdition to this statement – 'and of which system is this not the case' – indicates clearly that most scholars of ideology view power as ubiquitous.[15]By contrasting so exclusively on the relationship between ideology and power, scholars have obscured some of the ways in which ideology can operate within culture as a fundamental mode of organising reality. There is much to be gained by seeing ideology as a drive to impose intellectual order upon the world.

My use of ideology is similar to that of one of the great twentieth-century theorists on Indian culture, Louis Dumont, but differs from his in some key respects. His definition of ideology is relatively straightforward. 'The word 'ideology' commonly designates a more or less social set of ideas and values'.[16] He recognises that ideology does not make up the whole of Indian society: 'Ideology is not everything. Any concrete, localised, whole, when actually observed, is found to be decisively oriented by its ideology, and also to extend far by it… [I]n every concrete whole we find the formal principle at work, but we also find something else, a raw material which it orders and logically encompasses but which it does not explain, at least not immediately and for us'.[17]He further stresses that the sources to which we go to study ideology and these other principles are not the same: 'The distinction between the ideological (or conscious) aspects and the others is required methodologically in virtue of the fact that these are not both known in the same manner'.[18]

Here I differ from Dumont, however, in a key assumption. For Dumont, an ideology is always hierarchically superior to a non ideological realm of value. The ideology 'orders and logically encompasses'[19] these other realms. He states this quite clearly: 'Methodologically, the initial postulate is that the ideology is central with respect to the social reality as a whole'.[20] But in this he mistakes relative ease of perception and interpretation with logical and cultural priority. It is easier to see and interpret an ideology, because the ideologues themselves must be attentive to other voices in order to perceive the role of other values within a culture. There are times when the life affirming ideology appears clearly at the centre of Dalit culture, and takes precedence over all other values, but there are also times when it recedes into the background and wellbeing comes to the fore. There are some surface similarities between my usage of ideology and realm value, and the recent distinction made by William Sax between 'explicit formulations' and the 'implicit categories' and 'habitual practices' – the world view. But what Sax calls explicit formulations, which he says 'may be anything from simple statements to complex metaphysical systems', cover a wider range of articulations than an ideology.[21] Many of these explicit formulations lack the pragmatic critique, found in an ideology, of the implicit worldview assumptions, nor do they involve the totalising, conversion-oriented, and argumentative thrust of an ideolog

Further, many of them lack ideologues, which is essential for the very existence of an ideology.How the Dalit's life affirming ideology functions in relation to the Dalit culture as a whole should be explored further. But a word of caution should be voiced. Scholarship on ideology has shown that in many ways it is a universal or near-universal cultural activity. Even though the word was not coined until the very end of the eighteenth century in the context of revolutionary France, and much of its context derives from Marxist and post-Marxist thought, it is possible to speak of ideologies in earlier times and in other places. What is lacking in these other contexts is the concept of ideology itself. We can speak of the Dalit's ideology and ideologues of life. But this is not the same as to speak of an ideology and ideologues in nineteenth or twentieth century Europe or North America.

There is a tendency to separate ideology from theology.Likewise, many often think that ideology is closely related to politics, whereas in reality theology is concerned with religion. Since there are a number of theologies, God is understood in various ways. Out of a number of understandings, one of the most comprehensive definitions of Christian theology is that it should not start from a body of Church doctrines, lest it become insensitive to the situation around it, and the context from which it speaks. Theology's starting point cannot be an idea such as revelation, reason, nature, or Church doctrine; its point of departure rather must be specific to context reality and to the hopes and fears of people.

Theology ought to place humanity at the centre since they represent the image of God. God became incarnate in flesh and blood through Jesus Christ who identified Himself with humanity. From God's being we derive our being. In our being we manifest God's being. These two statements complement each other. They were dialectical and inherently linked with one another. Any system, ideology, theology or phenomenon that relegates or reduces human beings to the sub-human, from person to non-person, from the centre to the periphery, should be condemned. Any attempt by any force to minimise human worth and human dignity ought to be challenged.

Human beings *per se* occupy a unique position before God. They are the subjects and ends of God's creation. Therefore, 'Theology's goal... is to make clear God's identification with the disenfranchised, who have no one to speak for them, and to bring about those reforms necessary to ensure their full participation in society'.[22] The logical extension of this statement is that theology, ideology or liberation ought to enhance personhood i.e., the total entity of human beings. Theology and liberation should be complementary to each other.Previously oppression operates within a particular ideological and theological framework, now I see it in a more positive light. The philosophy, values and interests of casteism do not correspond to a vast majority of Dalits who live in India as a marginalised community. A counter-ideology and theology should break through the veil of oppressive social structure.

Caste oppression is partial, narrow, and above all exclusive and divisive, pervading all spheres of Dalit existence.The counter ideology to Dalit oppression is an ideology of life anchored in the central values of justice, equality, and the human dignity of all. The Ideology of Life incorporates all sections of people, emphasising the operation of liberation, justice, equality and fraternity as basic elements for a meaningful existence. The Ideology of Life is committed to translating the hopes and aspirations of people so that the marginalised and the segregated can be brought to the centre. It addresses the existential problems of those who lead a sub-human existence. Therefore, the ideology of Life's core ingredient is existence. Existence and life go together. Since the existence of a vast majority of Dalits is lived in a precarious, frightening, unthinkable and sub-human level, the Ideology of Life must articulate comprehensively the living conditions of those situated within a real historical epoch.

Thus,the Ideology of Life permeates all existence especially all those who have been denied life in all its fullness. It visualises a just, human, sustainable and inclusive community and thus transcends the exclusive, inhuman and divisive vision of oppression. The Ideology of Life translates the dreams of the victims of caste oppression, marginalisation, untouchability and exclusion and transcends the brutal realities of life.Dalit oppression is struggling with the impetus of ideological-theological thinking in its desire for preserving and furthering its domination. Hence, whatever may be the ideology or theology, it ought to seek and pursue the well-being and wholeness of life for all people. If the core of this underlying principle is negated, then by all means, it should be condemned and rejected.

A theology of resistance is not born in classrooms or in study material of particular disciplines. On the contrary, it is born out of the actual and concrete experiences of communities that struggle to build a world order which is humane, egalitarian and inclusive. Their vision of building a better world where everyone can lead a life of dignity and equality is being realised in their context. A theology of resistance emanates from a community of faith, a community that appreciates the Nazareth vision and prophetic tradition in a context which unmasks inequality and naked division among peoples. Resistance to the forces that negate life becomes the focus of one's faith articulation and theologising.

A theology of resistance is grounded in a desire to redeem the oppressed communities. It is embedded in particular philosophical, ideological and theological moorings. It is a theology of the present. Its primary focus is to translate the hopes and aspirations of the victims of the demonic forces of oppression and marginalisation. It identifies itself against the forces that work towards the exclusion and peripherisation of people at large. However,we must be careful here not to reify the existence of resistance, too easily pointing to an undeletable stratum in human beings that always continue to resist. On the contrary, analyses or descriptions of resistance seem to point to something quite different: the contingency of resistance, its frailty, and the possibility and actuality of its being at times obliterated. The fragility of resistance leads me to consider an element of specific histories of oppression that is often mentioned but rarely explained: the paucity of resistance.[23]

An Ideology of Life and a Theology of Resistance impinge upon one another and thus link theory and practice, faith and the transformation of social structures. The ideology-theology arrangement is a pragmatic and viable framework for the present via-a-vis translating the needs of humanity and its primary focus of determining problems addressed and answers given.

While the Dalits' quest for liberation is comprehensive, it is also specific. It is comprehensive in the sense that the liberation Dalits seek includes socio-economic and socio-political empowerment. It is specific in the sense that Dalit liberation is a process of socio-cultural emancipation, which both precedes and leads their socio-economic and socio-political empowerment. The question of specificity is more important for Dalit liberation because it is easier to theologise with such universal categories as the 'poor,' the 'oppressed,' etc. In this case, the 'poor' and the 'oppressed' remain faceless. It is only when a theology takes specificity seriously that 'identities' are established and 'no people' become 'My people, 'God's people' (Hosea's nomenclature). This is to say that in the Indian context, the Dalits are the poor and the oppressed, the faceless, the invisible and marginalised people.Their reality and struggle are the 'signs of the times,' where God is at work. A theology worth its name and which seeks to be relevant cannot ignore the Dalits' quest for liberation. In the Indian context, it is the Dalits whose identity is at stake and hence 'identity' should become a theological category. Dalit theology, like any other Third World theologies, is basically a theology of identity and, in that way, it is a true 'indigenous theology.'

To sum up, Dalit liberation should become a self-discovery of the Indian Church. Christ in India today is everywhere, but supremely in the suffering Dalit, the *Paraya*, the historical Jesus. The major task of the Indian Church as well as of Indian Christian theologians is to struggle for Dalit liberation. Dalit theology's first and foremost task is to empower the inner person of the Dalits and to strive for empowerment at all levels and in all spheres. In the final count, all strivings should lead to an inclusive humanism which affirms the identity and humanity of the Dalits within the human community.

Endnotes

1. A.P. Nirmal, *A Reader in Dalit Theology*, p. 26.
2. J. Massey, 'Ingredients for a Dalit Theology', 1994, p. 59.
3. R-L. Ferrucio, *Marxism and Ideology,* translated by Roger Griffin, Clarendon, Oxford, 1990.
4. T. Eagleton, *Literary Theory: An Introduction*, Minneapolis, University of Minnesota Press, 1980.
5. M. David, *Ideology*, Buckingham, OUP, 1987, p. 1.
6. Ibid., p. 3.
7. Ibid, p. 4.
8. Ibid, pp. 4-5.
9. S. Paul, *Language,Ideology and Point of View*, London, Routledge, 1993, p. 6.
10. G. Clifford, *The Interpretations of Culture*, New York, Basic Books, 1973, p. 194.
11. M. Foucault, 'Truth and Power', in *Power/Knowledge*, edited and translated by C. Gordon et al, Pantheon Press, New York, 1980, p. 118.
12. E. Terry, *Literary Theory: An Introduction*, Minneapolis: University of Minneota, 1980, p. 133.
13. G. Clifford, p. 195.
14. R. Paul, 'Ideology and Ideology Critique', in B. Waldenfels et al. (eds), *Phenomenology and Marxism*, translated by J.C. Evans Jr., London, Routledge &Kegan Paul Press, 1984, pp. 134-164.

15. M. David, *Ideology*, Minneapolis, University of Minnesota Press, 1986, p. 83.
16. D. Louis, *Home Hierarchicus* (revised edition), translated by Mark Sainsbury et al., University of Chicago Press, Chicago, 1980, p. 343.
17. Ibid, pp. 37-38, 343.
18. Ibid, p. 343.
19. Ibid.
20. Ibid.
21. S.S. William, *Mountain Goddess: Gender and Politics in the Himalayan Pilgrimage*, New York, OUP,, 1991, p. 9.
22. L. Nicholas et al., *Dictionary of the Ecumenical Movement*, Geneva, WEEC Publications, 1991, p. 1004.
23. S.D. Welch, *Communities of Resistance and Solidarity*, Maryknoll, New York, Orbis Books, 1985, p. 39.

Conclusion

Dalit theology, which is taking shape in India, can be considered as one of the attempts to do a local theology which takes seriously the context of struggles of the people who are marginalized and oppressed, reflecting on their struggles for liberation from the structures which marginalize them. It is very much committed to the liberation and humanization of the Dalits, the most oppressed people of India. It is understood as the systematic reflection on the liberating and humanizing actions done by and on behalf of the oppressed, which becomes the mediation as well as the sacrament of God's saving action in history. Its concern is not mainly what would happen to the soul after death, but what happens to enable human beings to have human dignity and honour as anybody else.Dalit theology not only shows a relevant perspective for doing a local theology, but also questions the so-called neutral philosophical perspectives of theology. It exhibits its conflict with the elite perspective, which justifies the status quo that leads to exploitation and oppression.

Dalit theology is a 'theology from the underside of history'; that means, it is based on the discernment that theological reflection should be done from the perspective of those who are victims of domination and oppression. It is clearly an attempt to give voice to the voiceless of Indian society. That is why it provides a paradigm for assessing the signs of the times. The irruption of the poor and the oppressed is one of the greatest signs of the times. It is also the time of the irruption of God in history to establish his reign and righteousness. It is needless to say that no theology can be done today that ignores the signs of the time. Dalit theology is not a theology created by the intelligentsia, the affluent, the powerful, those on the top. It is a theology from the bottom, from the underside of history created by the victims, the poor and the oppressed.

It is not a theology spun out in a series of principles of timeless truths that are applied to the contemporary scene, but a theology springing out of poverty oppression, the heartrending conditions under which the great majority ofDalits live. Moreover, Dalit theology affirms the Biblical faith that the poor are today's suffering servants, today's 'crucified peoples'. Their suffering sheds light on and condemns the evil and injustices prevalent today in religion and society. Their struggle for a full human life and dignity announces the hope of a new world, the redeemed humanity. Despite the fact that Dalits are India's suffering servants and crucified people, their theology calls for an 'obligatory solidarity' with the poor of the whole world, a necessary task in doing theology today.

Dalit theology as a local theology differs very much from the missionary theology which is evangelistic in nature and aimed at the conversion of Dalits to Christianity. The teachings of the missionaries in India provided only a half salvation to the Christians. It was a half salvation, because no effort was taken to relate the teachings of Christian faith to the real life of the people. But Dalit theology seeks to help Dalits to live in solidarity with their fellow Dalits whatever the religious background. Since it assumes religious pluralism of our context, it not only helps the Christian Dalits but also shares a common ideology with other Dalits in their common struggle for liberation, justice and dignity.

Further, Dalit theology shows a radical discontinuity with the Indian Christian Theology of the Brahminical tradition. In this case Dalit theology is a counter theology in relation to other dominant theologies. The dominant theologies are considered to be normative and are therefore imposed upon the oppressed. As the Brahmanic theological tradition is the dominant one, it has been imposed upon Dalits who are the Christian majority.

The growing interest in Dalit theology has raised a number of questions. Is not Christian theology common for all Christians irrespective of caste, colour, and the different historical contexts in which Christians find themselves? Are we not in danger of creating divisions and encouraging polarizations, thereby endangering Christian unity by speaking about Dalit theology? Would we then accept non-Dalits in developing a non-Dalit theology? Although we cannot give a satisfactory answer to these questions, it is evident from the above discussions that Dalit theology is not meant to reject the known expressions or the usefulness of Indian Christian theologies. Rather, it is another expression of Indian Christian theology based on the lived experience of Dalits themselves, which has been neglected in earlier Indian Christian theology. It comes as a powerful voice from the Dalit people, in their language, and for the service of the people. As a contextual theology it seeks to confront situations of oppression perpetuated by the dominant religious traditions without neglecting the ecumenical concern for the one human community. As a matter of fact, an active commitment to peace and justice becomes an integral concern of this theological enterprise. It can also provide an opportunity for the non-Dalits to repent of their past participation, either directly or indirectly, in the unjust structures, practices and attitudes produced and nurtured by the caste system.

Dalit theology is part of the postcolonial struggle of different communities for their distinct identity and space. In a largely homogenizing trend influenced by two processes, namely globalization and Hinduisation, Dalits and Dalit Christians are still struggling for a Dalit identify of their own. Intra-Dalit conflicts and Dalit sub-groups still continue despite the striving for a common Dalit identity and solidarity. Therefore, the challenge for Dalit theology is to strike an ideal balance.

Hindutva revival/reform movements are trying to absorb Dalits into a monolithic Hindu fundamentalist culture. Their systematic propaganda concentrates on the message that Dalits had been truly part of the 'Hindu' religio-cultural structures. Several Hindu organizations are involved in re-conversion efforts to drive home this ideology. Although it is a clear historical distortion, Dalits are caught up in a dilemma whether to declare their solidarity with Hindus or with Dalits. This historic dilemma appears to have had its impact upon Dalit Christians and Dalit theological movement too. This may be the reason why this new strand of theology currently appears to be at a standstill.

The almost total dependence on Biblical thought for theological construction needs further reconsideration in the light of the historical experience of Dalits.Pre-existing/Christian egalitarian thoughts and struggle for equality and justice were evident in Dalit history and memory, but the early Dalits had their own ways of protest and resistance. This is ignored by Dalit theologians.Dalit theologians also need to widen the definition of 'texts', given the oral emphasis in Dalit Tradition. By probing into Dalit folklore and songs they are likely to unearth extra textual sources for doing Dalit theology. This could also help create new hermeneutical principles unique to the Dalit theological movements.

Ancestral worship and female deities appear prominently in Dalit myths and songs. Dalit theologians could explore how the pre-existing religio-cultural ideas might have shaped their journey into Christianity and how they deal with such questions in their everyday life. All these could function as a rich source of theologising and Dalit faith articulation in India.While pathos, suffering and pain have found a place in Dalit theology, the rich Dalit traditions of celebrating life in the context of communitarian values seem to have been completely forgotten by Dalit theologians with few exceptions. The rich cultures of the Dalit have many egalitarian ideas. This needs to be further explored by Dalit theologians.

The 'dialogue' and 'accommodation' that take shape at the popular level of both Hinduism and Christianity need systematic consideration by Dalit theology. It appears that in a silent way people at the village level are moulding meaningful 'systems' of interaction in a pluralistic socio-religious setting like that of India. If the reality of the religion of a people can be studied only through empirical enquiry into the meaning appropriated by them as persons and community of persons in their life situations,then Dalit theology needs to look carefully into the popular level of Hindu-Christian religious encounter. Recent studies reveal that religious boundaries at the level of belief systems and rituals are not so marked in the minds of people in villages. In the popular worship context, there is mutual sharing of practices, symbols and values without so much fuss.These marginalised spaces deserve systematic attention. The intention of this study is not to invent a new Dalit theology but to provide an alternative methodological framework to reconsider the scope and method of present Dalit theology to move towards a theology of Dalitism for which the Ideology of Life and theology of Resistance would provide a base for future direction.

Glossary

Adharma	:	Not right; what is unjust; evil; unrighteousness
Adhi	:	First, original
Adi-Dravida	:	First or Original Dravidians
Adi-Sudhra	:	First or original Sudhras
Advaita/Advaitic	:	Vedanta of non-dualism consolidated the Advaita Vedanta, an interpretation of the Vedic scriptures. Continuing the line of thought of some of the Upanishadic teachers, Adi Shankara expounded the doctrine of Advaita — a nondualistic reality.
Advaitin	:	One who follows the Vedanta of non-dualism
Ahamkara	:	Ego
Arya Samaj	:	Arya Samaj was founded on April 7th, 1875 at Bombay, India, by Maharishi Dayanand Saraswati.. The purpose was to move the Hindu Dharma away from all the fictitious beliefs, and go back to the teachings of Vedas. The goal of the Arya Samaj has always been, 'Make This World Noble.'
Atman	:	Soul, Being; Self; Supreme Being
Avatar/Avatara	:	Incarnation

Avyakat	:	Ignorance
Bhagvad Gita	:	A Teaching of Lord Krishna to Arjuna the charioteer in Mahabarata Epic
Bhakti	:	Devotion
Bhakti marga	:	Way of liberation through devotion to a personal God
Brahmo Samaj	:	Is the Assembly of Believers, it is started by Raja Ram Mohan Roy as an institution
Brahman	:	The Absolute; The Supreme Being
Brahmins	:	Priest by caste division and duty
Chammbhars	:	Untouchable caste in Maharastra
Chaturvarna	:	Fourfold Colour Division
Chetty	:	Sub-caste within the Vaishyas/Vaisias: caste, involved in business and commerce
Chipko	:	Hug/Embrace
Chit	:	Word
Dalit Sena	:	Dalit Army
Darsan	:	Vision
Devadasi	:	Temple Prostitutes
Dharma	:	What is right; righteousness; law; merit; religious duty; duty of one's state of life; virtue.
Dhotis	:	Men's wear
Guna	:	Quality, attribute, constituent of reality
Harijan	:	'Children of God' (People of Scheduled Caste Origin)
Isvara	:	God
Izahavas	:	Untouchable caste in Kerala
Jajimani	:	Traditional caste relationship for division of labour and had provided some material security for them.

Jananamarga	:	Way of liberation through Wisdom
Janata	:	Ordinary People
Jati	:	An endogamous Caste Unit
Jatav	:	Backward caste in North India
Jeevanmukta	:	A person free from all impulses such as greed, anger, etc.
Karma	:	Willed activity; result of such an activity
Karmamarga	:	Way of liberation through duty
Karmasansara	:	One who involved in willed activity
Karmayoga	:	Devotion through duty
Koinonia	:	Fellowship
Kshatriyas	:	Business Community (Caste based)
Lokasamgraha	:	Worldly life (One of the stages of Hindu way of life)
Lokayata/Charuvaka	:	Pleasure seeking philosophy
Mahar	:	An untouchable community in Maharastra
Manusmiriti	:	The Code of Institutes of Manu; a collection of laws based on customs and precedent and teaching of the Vedas.
Marga	:	Way
Missio Dei	:	Mission of God
Mukkuvas	:	Untouchable caste from Kerala region
Nirguna Brahman	:	God without attributes
Niskama karma	:	Disinterested action; action without the desire for the results
Ochlos (Greek)	:	Ordinary people
Oikoumene (Greek)	:	Fellowship
Parangis	:	A Foreigner
Paravas	:	Fishing Community
Pariah (Tamil)	:	One of the castes within the Dalit community in particular, but generally

		untouchable castes are called as Pariah which is a derogatory term.
Pramanas	:	Supreme Commandments or Documents of faith
Purushatva	:	Personality
Saguan Brahman	:	God with attributes
Sahitya Movement	:	Literary Movement
Sakti	:	Power
Samaj	:	Assembly or society
Samsara	:	Family life
Sanatana Dharma	:	Religion based on Caste division and practise
Sastras/Shastras	:	Law codes; Vedic Law; testimony of the scriptures
Sat	:	Nothingness
Satchitananda	:	Ultimate Source (God), Will (Son) and Bliss (Holy Spirit)
Satva	:	Being; Existence; reality; goodness
Satyagraha	:	Literally "Truth force"; Gandhi's method of non-violent protest
Satyagrahi	:	One who follow the truth even in the most testing times
Satya Shodak Samaj	:	Truth Seeking Society
Shudra/Sudra	:	Servant; the fourth caste in the hierarchical order
Svadharma	:	Dharma appropriate to one's own station
Swaraj	:	Self governing/Independence
Swayam Sevak Dal	:	Self-Service Group (A political wing within Indian National Congress Party)
Vaishnavite	:	Devotees of Lord Vishu as (A stream within Hinduism)

Vaishyas/Vaisias	:	The third category within the four fold caste division, their caste duty is do business.
Varna	:	Broad categories into which Jatis were classified.
Varnashrama	:	Social order based on varnas (colour division)
Vedanta	:	Perennial philosophy, is based on the Vedas, the main scripture of the Hindus. It is not based on the life and teachings of any one particular saint or prophet. It is a federation of faiths and a commonwealth of spiritual concepts.
Vedas	:	Hindu Scriptures
Vishita Advaita	:	Qualified Non-Dualism; derived from vishishta (qualified) + advaita (non-duality). The general term vishistadvaita may refer to a variety of philosophies within Sanatana Dharma, but without qualifiers specifically refers to a school of Vedanta philosophy expounded by Ramanujar.
Vykat	:	Knowledge
Yukti	:	Mind/Imagination

Abbreviations

CCA	:	Christian Conference of Asia
CCPD	:	Churches' Participation in Development
CDLM	:	Chrisltian Dalit Liberation Movement
CELAM	:	Conference of the Latin American Bishops
CISRS	:	Christian Isntitue for the Study of Religion and Society
CISS	:	Christian Isntitue of Sikh Studies
CPI	:	Communist Party of India
CPI (M)	:	Communist Party of India (Marxist)
DCLM	:	Dalit Christian Liberation Movement
DLET	:	Dalit Liberation Education Trust
EATWOT	:	The Ecumenical Assocaiton of the Third World Theologians
GLTC&RI	:	Gurukul Lutheran Theological College & Research Institue
IMC	:	International Missionary Council
INC	:	Indian National Congress
ISPCK	:	Indian Society for the Propagation of Christian Knowledge
NCCI	:	National Council of Churches in Inida
SCM	:	Students Christian Movement
SPCK	:	Society for The Propagation of Christian

		Knowledge
TTS	:	Tamilnadu Theologicl Seminary
UNICEF	:	United Nations International Children's Education Fund
UTC	:	United Theological College
WCC	:	World Council of Churches
WCSRC	:	William Carey Study & Research Centre

Bibliography

Abbasayulu, Y. B. (1978) *Scheduled Caste Elite*. Hyderabad: Centre for Harijan Studies, OsmaniaUniversity.

Abbasayulu, Y. B. (1979). *Sociology of Depressed Groups*.Hyderabad: Centre for Harijan Studies, OsmaniaUniversity.

Abraham, K. C. (1990) *Third World Theologies: Commonalities and Divergences*. Maryknoll: Orbis.

Agarwal, Partap C. and Ashraf, M. Siddiq. (1976) *Equality through Privilege: A Study of Special Privileges of Scheduled Castes in Haryana.* New Delhi: Shri Ram Centre for Industrial Relations and Human Resources.

Aggarwal, L. B. (1934). *The Harijans in Rebellion*.Bombay: Taraporewala and Sons.

Agrawal, S. P., and Aggarwal, J. C. (1991).*Educational and Social Uplift of Backward Classes: At What Cost and How? Mandal Commission and After. Part I.* New Delhi: Concept Publishing Co.

Ahir, D.C. (1991) *The Legacy of Dr. Ambedkar*. Delhi: B.R. Publishing Corporation.

Ainapur, L. S. (1986). *Dynamics of Caste Relations in Rural India.* Jaipur: Rawat Publications.

Aiyappan, A. (1965). *Social Revolution in a KeralaVillage: A Study in Cultural Change*. Bombay: Asia Publishing House.

Aleaz, K.P. (1997) *An Indian Jesus from Sankara's Thought.* Calcutta: Punthi Pustak.

Amalorpavadass, D. S. (ed.) (1981) *The Indian Church in the Struggle for a New Society.*Bangalore: National Biblical Catechetical and Liturgical Centre.

Ambedkar, B. R. (1925) *What Congress and Gandhi Have Done to the Untouchables.* Bombay: Thacker & Co.

Ambedkar, B. R. (1943) *Mr. Gandhi and the Emancipation of the Untouchables.*Bombay: Thacker & Co.

Ambedkar, B. R. (1946) *Who Were the Sudras? How They Came To Be The Fourth Varna in Indo-Aryan Socie*ty. Bombay: Thacker and Co.

Ambedkar, B. R. (1948). *The Untouchables: Who Were They and Why They Became Untouchables.*New Delhi: Amrit Book Co.

Ambedkar, B.R. (1948) The Untouchables. Bombay: Bheem Patrika Publications.

Ambedkar, B. R. (1957). *The Buddha and His Dhamma.*Bombay: SiddharthCollege Publications.

Ambedkar, B. R. (1990). *Annihilation of Caste: An Undelivered Speech.* Edited by Mulk Raj Anand.New Delhi: Arnold Publishers.

Anand, J. H. (1995) Dalit Literature is the Literature of Protest.In Bhagwan Das and James Massey (eds.),*Dalit Solidarity.*Delhi: ISPCK. pp. 177–184.

Anand, Mulk Raj; and Zelliot, Eleanor. (eds.) (1992). *An Anthology of Dalit Literature.* New Delhi: Gyan Publishing House.

Anant, S. S. (1979) 'Changing Caste Hindu Attitudes towards Harijans: A Follow Up After Four Years,' in G. R. Gupta (ed.),*Main Currents in Indian Sociology – III: Cohesion and Conflict in Modern India.*New Delhi: Vikas.

Anderson, Gerald. (ed.)(1976) *Asian Voices in Christian Theology.*Maryknoll, New York: Orbis Books.

Arulaja, M. R. (1996) *Jesus the Dalit: Liberation Theology by*

*Victims of Untouchability, an Indian Version of Apartheid.*Hyderabad: Volunteer Centre.

Aruldoss, T. (1998) *Dalit Theology*. Sivakasi: Alfa Technic Prints.

Assmann, Hugo. (1975) *A Practical Theology of Liberation*, London: Search Press Ltd.

Athyal, J. John & Jesudas (ed.) (1995)*Religion, State and Communalism: A Post-Ayodhya Reflection.* Hong Kong: CCA.

Ayrookuzhiel, A. M. Abraham. (ed.) (1990) *The Dalit Desiyata: The Kerala Experience in Development and Class Struggle.* Delhi: ISPCK.

Azariah, M.*The Un-Christian Side of the IndianChurch: The Plight of the Untouchable Converts.*Bangalore: Dalit Sahitya Academy, 1985.

Azariah, M. (1989) *Mission in Christ's Way in India Today.*Madras: The Christian Literature Society.

Azariah, M. (2000) *A Pastor Search For Dalit Theology*. Delhi: ISPCK.

Bailey, F. G. (1957) *Caste and the Economic Frontier: A Village in Highland Orissa*. Manchester: University of Manchester.

Bailey, F. G. (1960) *Tribe, Caste and the Nation*. Bombay: OxfordUniversity Press.

Bailey, F. G. (1963) *Politics and Social Change in Orissa.* Berkeley: University of California Press.

Bauckham, Richard. (1995) *The Theology of Jurgen Moltmann.* Edinburgh: T&T Clark.

Berwa, Laxmi N. (2000) *Asian Dalit Solidarity*. New Delhi: ISPCK.

Beteille, Andre. (ed.) (1969) *Caste: Old and New*. Bombay: Asia Publishing House.

Beteille, Andre. (1972). *Inequality and Social Change*. Delhi: OxfordUniversity Press.

Bhagwat, Vidyut. (1995) Dalit Women in India: Issues and Perspectives – Some Critical Reflections, in P. G.Jogdand (ed.),*Dalit Women in India: Issues and Perspectives.*New Delhi& Pune: Gyan Publishing House, in collaboration with University of Poona.

Bhatt, Anil. (1970) Caste and Political Mobilisation in Gujarat District.In Rajni Kothari (ed.),*Caste in Indian Politics.*Delhi: Orient Longman.

Bhatt, Anil. (1975) *Caste, Class and Politics: An Empirical Profile of Social Stratification in Modern India.* Delhi: Manohar Book Service.

Blunt, E. A. H. (1931) Caste System of Northern India. London: OxfordUniversity Press.

Boel, J. (1975) *Christian Mission in India: A Sociological Analysis.* Amsterdam: Academische Pers.

Bonhoeffer, Dietrich. (1959) Creation and Fall, Temptation. New York: MacMillan Publishing Company.

Bonhoeffer, Dietrich. (1972)*Letters and Papers from Prison*, (ed.) Eberhard Bethge, New York: Macmillan Publishing Coedited by Eberhard Bethge / Translated by Reginald H. Fuller, Macmillan 1953

Bono, Jose Miguez. (1980)*Doing Theology in a Revolutionary Situation.* Philadelphia: Fortress.

Bosch, D.J. (1980) *Witness to the World.* London.The Christian Mission in Theological Perspective.Atlanta: John Knox Press.

Bosch, D.J. (1991) *Transforming Mission: Paradigm Shifts in Theology of Mission.* New York: Maryknoll.

Bose, Aurobindo *(1984) The Bhagavad Gita*, Delhi: Orient Paperbacks. (Reprint, Delhi: OrientPaperbacks.

Bose, N. K. (1969) *The Scheduled Castes and Tribes and Their Present Conditions.* B. C. Mazumdar Memorial Lectures. Calcutta: University of Calcutta.

Bose, Pradip Kumar. (1985) Social Mobility and Caste Violence: A Study of the Gujarat Riots.In I. P. Desai (ed.),*Caste, Caste Conflict and Reservations. Centre for Social Studies*. Delhi: Adjanta Publications.

Boyd, Robin. H. S.(1969)*An Introduction to Indian Christian Theology*.Madras: Christian Literature Society.

Breman, Jan. (1974) Mobilisation of Landless Labourers: Halpatis of South Gujarat.*EPW*, vol. 9, no. 6–8, Feb.

Brewer, Rose M. (1993) Theorizing Race, Class and Gender: The New Scholarship of Black Feminist Intellectuals and Black Labour Women. InStalie M James and Abena P.A. Buisa (eds.),*Theologizing Black Feminism*. London: Routledge.

Buren, Paul M. van. (1963) *The Secular Meaning of the Gospel*. New York: MacMillan Publishing Company.

Carvalho, Marcello Pinto. (1978) Die Stimme des Volkes Gottes in *Information*, December.

Census of India 1911.Calcutta, India, Published Superintendent Government Printing, 1912

Census of India 1961–1991, Published by Census Commissioner for India, New Delhi.

Census of India 1991.1993:11Published by Census Commissioner for India, New Delhi.

Chandran, J. Russell. (1997) Rev. A. P. Nirmal: A Tribute. *NCCI Review*, January.

Chardin, Pierre Theilhard de.(1956) *Man's Place in Nature*.New York: Harper & Row.

Chatterjee, Partha. (1994) Caste and Subaltern Consciousness.In Ranajit Guha (ed.),*Subaltern Studies VI: Writings on South Asian History and Society*.Delhi: Oxford University Press. pp. 169–209.

Chatterjee, Saral K.(1994) 'Why Dalit Theology?'In James Massey (ed.),*Indigenous People: Dalits, Dalit Issues in Today's Theological Debate*, Delhi: ISPCK.

Chethimattam, John B., C.M.I.(1981) Problems of an Indian Christian Theology: A Critique of Indian Theologizing. in M. Amaladoss, T. K. John, and G. Gispert-Sauch. (ed.) *Theologizing in India.*Edited by Bangalore: Theological Publications in India, pp. 195–207.

Clarke, Sathianathan. (1998) *Dalits and Christianity: Subaltern Religion and Liberation Theology in India.* Delhi: OxfordUniversity Press.

Cobb, John B. Jr. (1980) *Process Theology as Political Theology*, Philadelphia: The Westminster Press.

Cohan, B. N. (1955) The Changing Status of a Depressed Class.In McKim Marriott (ed.),*Village India: Studies in the Little Community*. Chicago: The University of Chicago Press.

Commissioner for Scheduled Caste and Scheduled Tribes.1978–9.*Report of the Commissioner for Scheduled Caste and Scheduled Tribes.*New Delhi: Government of India.

Cone, James. (1986) *A Black Theology of Liberation.*Maryknoll, New York: Orbis Books.

Conn, Harvey M.(1979) Theologies of Liberation: An Overview.InS.N. Gundry and A.F.Johnson (eds.),*Tensions in Contemporary Theology.*Chicago: Moody Press.

Costa, Orlando. (1974) *The Church and Its Mission: A Shattering Critique from the Third World,* Coverdale: Tyndale House Publishers.

Cox, Oliver C. (1948) Caste, Class and Race. New York: Modern Reader.

Cox, Harvey. (1965) *TheSecularCity*. New York: MacMillan Publishing Company.

Dalton, Dennis. (1993)*Mahatma Gandhi: Non Violent Power*. New York: Columbia University Press.

Dangle, Arjun. (ed.) (1992) *No Room for the New Sun.*New Delhi: Orient Longman.

Dangle, Arjun. (ed.) (1992) *Poisoned Bread: Translations from Modern Marathi Dalit Literature*. New Delhi: Orient Longman.

Das, Bagwan and James Massey (eds.) (1995) *Dalit Solidarity*.Delhi: ISPCK.

Das, Bhagwan. (1995) Socio-Economic Problems of Dalits.In Bhagwan Das and James Massey (eds.),*Dalit Solidarity*.Delhi: ISPCK.

Desai, A.R. (1982) *Social Background of Indian Nationalism*. Bombay: Popular Prakasm.

Deshpande, Vasant. (1978) *Towards Social Integration: Problems of Adjustment of SC Elites*. Pune: Shubhada-Saraswat.

Devasahayam, V. (1992) *Outside the Camp: Bible Studies in Dalit Perspective*. Chennai: Gurukul Lutheran Theological College & Institute.

Devasahayam, V. (ed.) (1992) Dalits & Women: Quest for Humanity. Chennai: Gurukul Lutheran Theological College and Research Institute, 1992.

Devasahayam, V. (1997) *Doing Dalit Theology in Biblical Key*. Delhi& Chennai: ISPCK/Gurukul Lutheran Theological College & Institute.

Devasahayam, v. (ed.) (1997)*Frontiers of Dalit Theology*.Delhi& Chennai: ISPCK &Gurukul Lutheran Theological College & Institute.

Dewan, R. P. (1979*) How to Erase Untouchability*.New Delhi: R. P Bookwala.

Dhasal, Namdeo. (1974)*Itihasachi Chakra Ulti Firvu Naka Nahitarjal*. Pamphlet (in Marati) Bombay: Namdeo Dhasal.

Dietrich, Gabriele.& Bas Wielenga.(1998)*Towards Understanding Indian Society*.Tiruvalla: Christava Sahitya Samithi.

Dietrich, Gabriele. (1992)*Reflections on the Women's Movement in India: Religion, Ecology, Development*. New Delhi; Horizon India Books.

Dillenberger, John. (1969) *Contours of Faith-Changing Forms of Christian Thought.*Nashville and New York: Abingdon Press.

Director's Report. (1989) Dalit Theology Project.*in The Biennium of CISRS and Joint programmes 1988–1989*. Bangalore.

Draper, Theodore. (1979) *The Rediscovery of Black Nationalism.* New York: Kegan Paul Ltd.

Dube, S. C. (1955) *Indian Village.*Ithaca, NY: CornellUniversity Press.

Dumont, Louis. (1970) *Homo Hierarchicus: The Caste System and Its Implications*. London: Paladin, Granada Pub. Ltd.

Dumont, Louis. (1980) *Home Hierarchicus*, Mark Sainsbury et.al,. (Trans) Chicago: University of Chicago Press (Revised Edition)

Eagleson (ed.) (1975) *Declaration of the 80 in Christian and Socialism: Documentation of the Christians for Socialism Movement in Latin America*. New York: Orbis.

Eagleton, Terry. (1980) *Literary Theory: An Introduction*, Minneapolis: University of Minnesota Press.

Egbert, de Viries. (1961) *Man in Rapid Social Change.*London: SCM Press.

Emmett, P. B. et. al., n.d.The Malas and Madigas.Religious Life of India Series.Calcutta: Association Press.

Engineer, Asghar Ali. (ed.) (1991) *Mandal Commission Controversy.*Delhi: Ajanta Publications.

Enrique, Dussel. (1979)*History and the Theology of Liberation.*New York: Orbis Books.

Epstein, T. S. (1973) *South India: Yesterday, Today and Tomorrow.* London: Macmillan Press.

Evanston to New Delhi 1954–1961. (1961) Report of the Central Committee to the Third Assembly of the WCCs, Geneva:WCC.

Fernandes,W. (1981). *Caste and Conversion Movements in India*.Delhi: Indian Social Institute.

Fey, Harold E. (ed.) (1970) *The Ecumenical Advance*. Philadelphia: The Westminster Press.

Fischer, Louis. (ed.) (1983) *The Essential Gandhi: An Anthology*.New York: Vintage Books.

Fisherman, A. T. (1941) *Cultural Change and Underprivileged: A Study of Madigas in South India*. Madras: Under Christian Guidance.

Flannery, Austin P. (ed.) (1984) *Documents of Vatican II*. Grand Rapids: W.B.Eerdmans.

Forrester, Duncan. (1977). The Depressed Classes and Conversions to Christianity, 1860–1960. In G.A. Oddie (ed.),*Religion in South Asia*.New Delhi: Manohar Publications.

Forrester, Duncan. (1980) *Caste and Christianity: Attitudes and Policies on Caste of Anglo-Saxon Protestant Missions in India*. London, Dublin: Curzon Press Ltd.

Francis, Broderick. (ed.) (1971) *The Black protest Thought in Twentieth Century*. New York: Routledge.

Freeman, James M. (1979) *Untouchable: An Indian Life History*. CA: StanfordUniversity Press.

Fromm, Erich. (1961) *Marx's Concept of Man*. New York: Ungar.

Foucault, Michael (1980), 'Truth and Power' in *Power/Knowledge* (ed. & Trans.) Colin Gordon et.al, New York: Pantheon Press.

Fuchs, S. (1951) *The Children of Hari: A Study of the Nihar Balahis in Madhya Pradesh*. Ahmedabad:

Fuchs, S. (1981) *At the Bottom of Indian Society*.New Delhi: Munshiram Manoharlal Pub. Pvt. Ltd.

Galanter, Marc. (1984) *Competing Inequalities: Law and the Backward Classes in India*. CA: University of California Press.

Gandhi, M. K. (1954) *For Workers against Untouchability*. Ahmedabad: Navjivan Publishing House.

Gandhi, M.K.(1982) *The Collected Works of Mahatma Gandhi*. Vol.39. New Delhi:Ministry of Information and Broadcasting, Government of India.

Ganesan, L. (1991) Relevance of Reservation. Madras: Valentina Publications.

Gangadharan, K. K. (1970) *Sociology of Revivalism: A Study of Indianisation, Sanskritisation and Golwalkarism*. New Delhi: Kalmakar Prakashan.

Geertz, Clifford (1973) *The Interpretations of Culture*, Basic Books, New York.

Ghadially, Rehana.(ed.) (1988) *Women in Indian Society: A Reader*. Delhi: Sage Publications.

Ghurye, G. S. (1950) *Caste and Class in India*. Bombay: Popular Books.

Ghurye, G. S. (1961) *Caste, Class and Occupation*. Bombay: Popular Prakashan.

Glen, M. and Johnson, S. B. (1979) Social Mobility among Untouchables.In G. R. Gupta (ed.),*Main Currents in Indian Sociology – III: Cohesion and Conflict in Modern India*. New Delhi: Vikas.

Gnanadason, Aruna. (1990) Dalit Women – The Dalit of the Dalit.In Arvind P. Nirmal (ed.),*Towards A Common Dalit Ideology*. Madras: Gurukul Lutheran Theological College and Research Institute, pp. 109–120.

Gorhe, Neelam. (1995) Social Development and Dalit Women.In P. G. Jogdand (ed.),*Dalit Women in India: Issues and Perspectives*.New Delhi: Gyan Pub. House in collaboration with University of Poona, Pune. pp. 8–17.

Gough, Kathleen. (1955) The Social Structure of a TanjoreVillage. In Mckim Marriot (ed.),*Village India*.Chicago: University of Chicago Press.

Gough, Kathleen. (1973) Harijans in Thanjavur.In Kathleen Gough and Hari P. Sharma (ed.),*Imperialism and Revolution in South Asia*.New York: Monthly Review Press.

Government of India 1997, Crime in India 1995, National Crime Records Bureau, Ministry of Home Affairs, Delhi.

Government of India.(1957). Report of the Advisory Committee on the Revision of the Lists of Scheduled Castes and Scheduled Tribes.

Government of India.(1969) Report of the Committee on Untouchability, Economic and Educational Development of the Scheduled Castes and Connected Documents (Elayaperumal Report).

Goyal, Bhagat Ram.(1981) *Educating Harijans*. Haryana: Academic Press.

Gupta, S. K. (1985) *Scheduled Castes in Modern Indian Politics: Their Emergence as a Political Power.*New Delhi: Munshiram Manoharlal Publishers.

Gupta, Shanti S. (1991) *Varna, Castes and Scheduled Castes: A Documentation in Historical Perspective with a Classified Index to Scholarly Writings in Indian Journals (1890–1990).*New Delhi: Concept Pub Co.

Gurukal, Rajan. (1994) The Formation of Caste Society in Kerala. in K. L. Sharms (ed.),*Caste and Class in India*. New Delhi: Rawat Publications.

Gutiérrez, Gustavo. (1979) *A Theology of Liberation.*London: SCM Press.

Hamilton, Kenneth. (1977) Liberation Theology: An Overview. *in* Carl E.Armerding (ed.), *Evangelicals & Liberation.* Grand Rapids, MI: Baker Book House.

Hamilton, William. (1966) *The New Essence of Christianity*. New York: Association Press.

Hardgrave, Robert L. Jr. (1965) The Dravidian Movement. Bombay: Popular Book Depot.

Hardgrave, Robert L. Jr. (1969) *The Nadars ofTamilnad.* Bombay: OxfordUniversity Press.

Hardgrave, Robert L. Jr. (1979) *Essays in the Political Society of South India.*New Delhi: Usha Publication.

Harper, Edward B. (1968) Social Consequences of an 'Unsuccessful' Low Caste Movement.In James Silverberg (ed.),*Social Mobility in the Caste System in India.*The Hague: Mouton Publishers.

Henninger, F, n.d. The Bhangis.Calcutta: Religious Life of India Series.

Hocart, A. M. (1950) *Caste.* London: Mathew and Co.

Hoefer,Herbert E. (ed.) (1979) *The Debate on Mission – Issues from the Indian context.*Madras: Gurukul publication.

Hoekendijk, J.C.(1966) *The Church Inside Out.* London. Translated by Isaac C. Rotenberg, Philadelphia: The Westminster Press.

Hopkins, Dwight L. (2004) Sermon delivered at the Reformation Sunday worship. Chennai: Gurukul Lutheran Theological College.

Hugo, Assmann. (1975) *Practical Theology ofLiberation.*London: Search Press limited.

Hutton, J. H. (1946) *Caste in India: Its Nature, Function and Origins.* 3rd Edition.London: CambridgeUniversity Press.

India – Eighth Five Year Plan 1992:419. Publications Division, Ministry of Information and Broadcasting, New Delhi.

Irschick, Eugene. (1969) *Politics and Social Conflict in South India.*Bombay: OxfordUniversity Press.

Isaacs, Harold R. (1965) *India's Ex-Untouchables.*Bombay: Asia Publishing House.

Jag Parvesh Chander (ed.) (1946–47) *Gita the Mother.* Lahore: Indian Publishing Works.

Jaiswal, S. (1977) Studies in the Social Structure of the Early

Tamils.In R. S. Sharma (ed.),*Indian Society: Historical Probings*. Second Edition.New Delhi.

Jeevaratanam, A. G. (1973) *Political Implications of Untouchability*.Hyderabad: Kondaveedu Press.

Jeyakumar, Samuel. (1999) *Dalit Consciousness and Christian Conversion: Historical Resources for A Contemporary Debate*. Oxford: Regnum International & Delhi: ISPCK.

Jha, D. N. (1977) Temples as Landed Magnates in Early Medieval South India (c. A.D. 700–1300). In R. S. Sharma (ed.),*Indian Society: Historical Probings*. Second Edition.New Delhi. pp. 202–216.

Jogdan, Prahlad G. (1991) *Dalit Movement in Maharashtra*. New Delhi: Kanak Publications.

Jogdand, Prahlad G. (ed.) (1995) *Dalit Women in India: Issues and Perspectives*.New Delhi: Gyan Publishing House in collaboration with University of Poona.

John, T. K. (ed.) (1991) *Bread and Breath: Essays in Honour of Samuel Rayan, S. J.*Delhi: Vidyajyoti.

Johnson, Glen and Bose, Sipra.(1978) Social Mobility among Untouchables.In G. R. Gupta (ed.),*Cohesion and Conflict in Modern India*.New Delhi: Vilas.

Joshi, Barbara R. (1982) *Democracy in Search of Equality: Untouchable Politics and Indian Social Change*.Delhi: Hindustan Publishing Co.

Joshi, Barbara R. (ed.) (1986) *Untouchable! Voices of the Dalit Liberation Movement*.London:Zed Books.

Juergensmeyer, Mark. (1979) *Religion as Social Vision: The Movement against Untouchability in 20th Century Punjab*. Berkeley: University of California Press.

Juergensmeyer, Mark. (1988) *Religion Rebels in the Punjab: The Social Vision of Untouchables*. Delhi: Ajanta Pub.

Kadetotad, N. Religion and Society among Harijans. Dharwar: Karnataka University.

Kakade, S. R. (1990) *Scheduled Castes and National Integration: A Study of Marathwada.*New Delhi: Radiant Pub.

Kallarackal, K. etal. (ed), (1983).Training Priest for Human Liberation.In *Human Liberation in the Indian Context.* Pune: Jana Deep Vidyapeeth, pp. 223–236.

Kamble, J. R. (1979) *Rise and Awakening of Depressed Classes in India.* New Delhi: National Publishers.

Kamble, N. D. (1981) *Atrocities on Scheduled Castes.*New Delhi: Ashish Publishing House.

Kamble, N. D. (1982) *The Scheduled Castes.* New Delhi: Ashish Publishing House.

Kamble, N. D. (1983) *Deprived Castes and their Struggle for Equality.* New Delhi: Ashish Publishing House.

Kananaikil, Jose. (1984) *Constitutional Provisions for the Scheduled Castes.*New Delhi: Indian Social Institute.

Karve, Irawati. (1961) *Hindu Society: An Interpretation.* Poona: Sangam Press.

Katppo, Marianne. (1976) *Compassionate and Free.*Geneva: WCC.

Kaul, Rekha. (1993) *Caste, Class and Education: Politics of the Capitation Fee Phenomenon in Karnataka.*New Delhi: Sage Publications.

Keer, Dhanjay. (1987)*Mahatma Jyoti Rao Phuley*, Bombay:Dhanjay Keer Prakashan.

Khan, Mumtaz Ali. (1980) *Scheduled Castes and their Status in India.* New Delhi: UppalPublishing House.

Khan, Mumtaz Ali.(1994) *Identity Formation and Self Identity among Harijan Elite.*New Delhi: Uppal Publishing House.

Khan, Mumtaz Ali. (1994) *Reservation for Scheduled Castes: Gaps between Policy and Implementation.* New Delhi: Uppal Publishing House.

Khan, Mumtaz Ali.(1995) *Human Rights and the Dalits.*New Delhi: Uppal Publishing House.

Khare, R. S. (1984) *The Untouchable as Himself: Ideology, Identity and Pragmatism Among the Lucknow Chamars.* London: Cambridge University Press.

Killen, R. Allan. (1977) *The Theology of the Third World,*Jackson, MS: Reformed Theological Seminary.

Kofi Buenor Hadjor (1993) *Penguin Dictionary of the Third World Terms.*London: Penguin Books.

Kosambi, D.D. (1956) *Myth and Reality: Studies in the Formation of Indian Culture.* Bombay: Popular Prakashan.

Kosambi, D.D. (1975) *Introduction to the Study of Indian History.* Bombay: Popular Prakashan.

Kshirsagar, R. K. (1994) Dalit Movement in India and Its Leaders (1857–1956). New Delhi: MD Pub. Pvt. Ltd.

Kulke, H. (1976) Kshyatriyaization and Social Change: A Study in Orissan Setting.in S. D. Pillai (ed.),*Aspects of Changing India: Studies in Honour of G. S. Ghurye.* Bombay. pp. 398–409.

Kumar, Dharma. (1965) *Land and Caste in South India: Agricultural Labour in Madras Presidency During the Nineteenth Century.* London: Cambridge University Press.

Kumarappa, Bharatan. (1954) *The Revolt of Untouchability.*Ahmedabad: Navajivan Publishing House.

Kumari, Prasanna.(ed.) (1995)*Liberating Witness* (Dr. K. Rajaratnam's Platinum Jubilee Commemoration Volume I) Gurukul Theological College, Madras.

Kuruvilla, K. P. *Dalit Theology: An Indian Christian Attempt to Give Voice to the Voiceless.* Unpublished Paper.

Lakshmanna, C. (1973) *Caste Dynamics in Village India.* Bombay: Nachiketa Publications.

Lakshmanna, C. (1974) *The Study of Scheduled Caste and*

Scheduled Tribe High Students in Andhra Pradesh. ICSSR Report.

Lakshmanna, C. (1977) *Harijans and the Social Discrimination: A Study of Some Telangana Villages.* Hyderabad: Osmania University, Department of Sociology.

Lal, Sheo Kumar and Nahar, Umed Raj. (ed.) (1990).*Extent of Untouchability and Pattern of Discrimination.*New Delhi: Mittal Publications.

Lal, Shyam. (1981) *Caste and Political Mobilisation: The Bhangis.* Jaipur: Panchsheel Prakashan.

Lannoy, Richard. (1971) *TheSpeaking Tree.* London: OxfordUniversity Press.

Leach, E. R. (ed.) (1960) *Aspects of Caste in South India, Ceylon and North-West Pakistan.* London: Cambridge University Press.

Lernmoux, Penny. (1979) The Long Path to Puebla.*in* John Eagleson and Phillip Scharper (eds.),*Puebla and Beyond: Documentation and Commentary.* New York: Orbis Books.

Liddle, J., and Joshi, R. (1986) *Daughters of Independence: Gender, Caste, and Class in India.* NJ: Rutgers University Press.

Lischer, Richard. (1979)*Marx and Theilhard.* Maryknoll: Orbis Books.

Lossky, et al.(1991) *Dictionary of the Ecumenical Movement.*Geneva: WEEC Publications.

Lukas, Vischer. (1970)The Ecumenical Movements and the Roman Catholic Church.*in* Fey Harold (ed.),*The Ecumenical Advance.* London: SPCK.

Lynch, Owen M. (1969) *The Politics of Untouchability: Social Mobility and Social Change in a City of India.* New York: Columbia University Press.

Macquarrié, John. (1967) *God and Secularity.*Philadelphia: The Westminster Press.

Mahadevan, T.M.P. and G.V. Saroja (eds.) (1981) *Contemporary Indian Philosophy*.New Delhi: Sterling Publishers.

Mahar, Michael J. (ed.) (1972) *The Untouchables in Contemporary India*. Tucson, Arizona: University of Arizona Press.

Majumdar, D. N. (1958) *Caste and Communication in an Indian Village*.Bombay: Asia Publishing House.

Maliekal, John. (1980) *Caste in India Today*.Bangalore: CSA Publication.

Mallik, Suneila. (1979) *Social Integration of the Scheduled Castes*.New Delhi: Abhinav.

Mann, K. (1987) *Tribal Women in a Changing Society*.Delhi: Mittal Publications.

Marriott, Mckim. (ed.) (1955) *Village India: Studies in the Little Community*. Chicago: The University of Chicago Press.

Marriott, Mckim. (ed.) (1965) *Caste Ranking and Community in Five Religious of India and Pakistan*.Poona: Deccan College.

Mascaro, Juan.Tr. (1982) *The Bhagavad Gita*. Harmondsworth: Penguin.

Massey,James. (ed.) (1993) *Contextual Theological Education*.Delhi: ISPCK.

Massey, James (ed.) (1994) *Indigenous People: Dalits –Dalit Issues in Today's Theological Debate*.Delhi: ISPCK.

Massey, James (1995) Dalits in India: Religion as a Source of Bondage or Liberation with Special Reference to Christians, Delhi: Manohar Publications.

Massey, James. (1996)*Roots of Dalit History, Christianity, Theology and Spirituality*.Delhi: ISPCK.

Massey, James.(1997) *Down Trodden: The Struggle of India's Dalits for Identity, Solidarity and Liberation*. Geneva: WCC Publications.

Mathew, Joseph. (1986) *Ideology, Protest and Social Mobility: Case Study of Mahars and Pulayas*. New Delhi: Inter India Publications.

Mathew, P. D. (1983) The Law on Abolition of Untouchability: Theory and Practice. in J. Kananaikil (ed.),*Scheduled Castes and Their Struggle Against Inequality*. New Delhi: Indian Social Institute.

Maw, Martin. (1990) *Visions of India*.London: Vertag Perer Lang.

Mbiti, John. (ed.) (1977) *Confessing Christ in Different Cultures*. Report of a colloquium held at the Ecumenical Institute, Bossey, 2–8 July, 1977.Geneva: Ecumenical Institute.

McLellan, David (1986) *Ideology*, Minneapolis: University of Minnesota Press.

Meyer, Mark J. (1982) *Religion as Social Vision: The Movement against Untouchability in 20th Century in Punjab*. Berkeley: University of California Press.

Ministry of Education and Social welfare (1972) The *Indian Council of Historical Research: Aim and Objects*. New Delhi: Govt of India.

Minz, Nirmal. (1990) Dalit-Tribal: A Search For Common Ideology.In Arvind P. Nirmal (ed.),*Towards a Common Dalit Ideology*.Madras: Gurukul Lutheran Theological College and Research Institute.

Mitter, Sara S. (1991) *Dharma's Daughters: Contemporary Indian Women and Hindu Culture*. NJ: Rutgers University Press.

Moffatt, Michael. 1979. An Untouchable Community in South India: Structure and Consensus. NJ: Princeton University Press.

Mohan, P.E. (1993) *Scheduled Castes: History of Elevation, Tamil Nadu, 1900–1955*. Madras: New Era Publication.

Mookenthottam, Anthony. (1980) *Towards a Theology in the Indian Context*.Bangalore: Asian Trading Corporation.

Moreau, Scott, A. (ed.) (2000), Evangelical Dictionary of World Missions. Grand Rapids: Baker Books.

Mukherjee, Prabhati. (1988) *Beyond the Four Varnas*. Shimla: Indian Institute of Advanced Studies.

Murthy, B. S. (1969) *The Glimmer in Darkness*. Secunderabad: Lakshmi & Co.

Murthy, B. S. (1971) *Depressed and Oppressed – For Ever in Agony*. New Delhi.

Murugkar, Lata. (1991) *Dalit Panther Movement in Maharashtra: A Sociological Appraisal.*Bombay: Popular Prakashan.

Myrdal, Gunnar. (1994) *An American Dilemma: The Negro Problems and Modern Democracy*. New York: Harper Brothers.

Nagaraj, D. R. (1993) *The Flaming Feet: A Study of the Dalit Movement*. Bangalore: South Forum Press.

Naidu, A. Nagaraja. (1994) Caste and Land in Colonial South India.in K. L. Sharma (ed.), Caste and Class in India. New Delhi: Rawat Publications.

Narasimhan,V.K. (1967) *Kamaraj: A Study*. Bombay: Manaktala & Sons.

Narayanan, M. G. S.; and Veluthat, K. (1987) 'The Bhakti Movement in South India,' in D. N. Jha (ed.),*Feudal Social Formations in Early India.*Delhi. pp. 348–75.

Nataraj, V. K. (1990) Backward Classes and Minorities in Karnataka Politics.In Ramashray Roy and Richard Sisson (eds.),*Diversity and Dominance in Indian Politics: Division, Deprivation and the Congress.* Vol. II. New Delhi: Sage Publications, pp. 170–186.

Nath, Trilok. (1987) *Politics of the Depressed Classes.*Delhi: Deputy Publications.

National Commission for SC and ST, Annual Report 1993–94, New Delhi.

Nichols, Alan. (ed.) (1989) *The Whole Gospel for The Whole World: Story of Lausanne II Congress on World Evangelization, Manila 1989, Lausanne Committee for World Evangelization*. California: Regal Books.

Nirmal, Arvind, P. (1988) A Dialogue with Dalit Literature. In M.E. Prabhakar (ed.), Towards a Dalit Theology. Delhi: ISPCK.

Nirmal, Arvind P. (ed.) (1990) *Towards A Common Dalit Ideology*. Madras: Gurukul Lutheran Theological College and Research Institute.

Nirmal, Arvind. (1990) Heuristic Explorations. Madras: Christian Literature Society.

Nirmal, Arvind P. and Devasahayam, V. (eds.) (1991) *Dr.B.R.Ambedkar: A Centenary Tribute*. Madras: Gurukul Lutheran Theological College & Research Institute.

Nirmal, Arvind, P. (ed.) (1991) *A Reader in Dalit Theology*.Madras: Gurukul Lutheran Theological College & Research Institute.

Nirmal, Arvind, P. (1991) (ed.) *Towards a Common Dalit Ideology*.Madras: Gurukul Lutheran Thelogical College & Research Institute.

Nirmal, Arvind P. (1994) Toward a Christian Dalit Theology in R.S. Sugirtharajah (ed.) Frontiers in Asian Christian Theology: Emerging Trends. Maryknoll: Orbis.

Nye, Robert. (1973) Conflict among Harijans. NY: Springer Publications.

Oddie, G.A.(ed.) (1991) *Religion in South Asia: Religious Conversion and Revival Movement in South Asia in Medieval and Modern Times*. New Delhi: Manohar.

O'Malley, L. S. S. (1974) *Indian Caste Customs*.Delhi: Vikas Publishing House.

Omprakash, S. (1989) *Development of the Weaker Section: Problems, Policies and Issues*.New Delhi: Uppal Publishing House.

Omvedt, Gail. (1976) *Cultural Revolt in a Colonial Society: The Non-Brahmin Movement in Western India – 1873 to 1930.* Bombay: Scientific Socialist Education Trust.

Omvedt, Gail. (1978) Class Struggle or Caste War.*Frontier*, Calcutta. vol. 2, no. 8–11, Sept. 30, pp. 30–40.

Omvedt, Gail. (1982) *Land, Caste and Politics in Indian States.*Delhi: Authors Guild Publications.

Omvedt, Gail. (1991) *Theories of Violence.*New Delhi: Kali for Women.

Omvedt, Gail. (1994)*Dalits and the Democratic Revolution: Dr. Ambedkar and the Dalit Movement in Colonial India.* New Delhi: Sage Publications India Pvt. Ltd.

Omvedt, Gail. (1994) *Dalits and the Democratic Revolution: Dr. Ambedkar and the Dalit Movement in Colonial India.* New Delhi: Sage.

Omvedt, Gail. (1995) *Dalit Visions.Tracts for the Times no 8.*New Delhi: Orient Longman Ltd.

Omvedt, Gail. (1995) *Dalit Visions: The Anti-Caste Movement and the Construction of an Indian Identity.* New Hyderabad: Orient Longman Ltd.

Omvedt, Gail. (1995) Dalit Women and Communalism.In P. G. Jogdand (ed.),*Dalit Women in India: Issues and Perspectives.* New Delhi: Gyan Publishing House in collaboration with University of Poona, Pune,pp. 135–145.

Oommen, T.K. (1990) *Protest and Change: Studies in Social Movements.* New Delhi: Sage Publications.

Painadath, Sebastian. (1999) The Understanding of Christ in the Indian Renaissance. *Jeevadhara*, XXIX (No 171, May), 165–187.

Pandey, Gyan. (1983) Rallying Round the Cow: Sectarian Strife in the Bhojpuri Region, c. 1888–1917.In Ranajit Guha (ed.),*Subaltern StudiesII.*Delhi: Oxford University Press.

Pandit, M.P. (1977) *Light from the Gita*. Pondicherry: Dipti Publications.

Panikkar, Raymond. (1964) *The Unknown Christ of Hinduism*. London: Darton, Longman & Todd.

Pannenberg, Wolfhart. (1970) *Basic Questions in Theology*. Vol. 1 &11. Philadelphia: Fortress.

Paranjpe, A. C. (1970) *Caste, Prejudice and the Individual*. New Delhi: Lalvani Publishing House.

Parmaji, S. (1985) *Caste Reservations and Performance*. Warangal: Mamata Publications.

Parratt, John.(1996) *A Guide to Doing Theology*. London: SPCK.

Parvathamma, C. (1973) Ambedkar and After: The Position and Future of Indian SC Masses. *Eastern Anthropology*, vol. 26.

Parvathamma, C. (1984) *Scheduled Castes and Scheduled Tribes: A Socio-Economic Survey*. New Delhi: Ashish Publishing House.

Parvathamma, C. (1986) *New Horizons and Scheduled Castes*. New Delhi: Ashish Publishing House.

Parvathamma, C. (1989) *Scheduled Castes at the Cross Roads*. New Delhi: Ashish Publishing House.

Patmury, Joseph (ed.) (1996) *Doing Theology with the Poetic Traditions of India: Focus on Dalit and Tribal Poems*.Bangalore: PTCA/SATHRI.

Patnaik, Nitayananda. (1969) *Caste and Social Change: An Anthropological Study of Three Orissa Villages*.Hyderabad: National Institute of Community Development.

Patwardhan, Sunanda. (1973) *Change Among India's Harijans: Maharashtra a Case Study*.New Delhi: Orient Longmans.

Pelikan, Jaroslav. (1971) *Historical Theology – Continuity and Change in Christian Doctrine*.London: Hutchinson.

Penny, Lernmoux. (1979) The Long Path to Puebla. *in* Eagleson.

John and Scharper, Phillip (eds.) *Puebla and Beyond: Documentation and Commentary*. New York: Orbis Books.

Pillai, S. D. (1976) The Dravidian Milieu.In S. D. Pillai (ed.),*Aspects of Changing India: Studies in Honour of G. S. Ghurye*. Bombay. pp. 129–35.

Prabhakar, M.E. (1986) Struggles and Hopes of Christian Dalits in India: Perspectives for Ideology and Vision. Vellore.

Prabhakar, M.E. (ed.), (1987) Liberty to the Captives. Deenapur, Guntur, Andra Pradesh, India: Dalit Open University.

Prabhakar,M.E.(ed.), (1989) *Towards a Dalit Theology*. Delhi: ISPCK.

Prabhakar, M.E. (1989) The Search for a Dalit Theology in M.E. Prabhakar (ed.) Towards a Dalit Theology. Delhi: ISPCK.

Prabhakar, M.E. (1994) The Search for a Dalit Theology. In James Massey (ed.), Indigenous People: Dalits, Dalit issues in Today's Theological Debate. Delhi: ISPCK.

Prabhakar, M. E. (1995) Dalit Education and Youth. In Bhagwan Das and James Massey (eds.),*Dalit Solidarity*.Delhi: ISPCK. pp. 94–124.

Prabhavathi, M. (1995) Dalit Women in Contemporary Indian Situation.In P. G. Jogdand (ed.),*Dalit Women in India: Issues and Perspectives*.New Delhi: Gyan Publishing House, in collaboration with University of Poona, Pune. pp. 82–92.

Prabhu, P. N. (1955). *Report of the Seminar on Casteism and Removal of Untouchability*.Bombay: Indian Conference of Social Work.

Prasad, D. Manohar Chandra. (1994) *Dalit Christian Consciousness*.Bangalore: Rachana Publications.

Prasad, D. Manohar Chandra. (1996) *Broken God, Broken People: The Plight of Dalit Christians*.Bangalore: Rachana Publications.

Programme for Scheduled Castes. (1994) *Dalit Organizations: A Directory. Second Edition*. New Delhi: Indian Social Institute.

Punalekar, S. P. (1995) On Dalitism and Gender.In P. G. Jogdand (ed.),*Dalit Women in India: Issues and Perspectives.* New Delhi: Gyan Publishing House in collaboration with University of Poona, Pune, pp. 8–17.

Purandare, C. K. (1995) 'People of India': Some Prima Facie Inferences With Reference to Scheduled Castes and Scheduled Tribes.In P. G.Jogdand (ed.),*Dalit Women in India: Issues and Perspectives.* New Delhi: Gyan Publishing House, in collaboration with University of Poona, Pune, pp. 37–81.

Puthanangady, Paul (ed.) (1986) *Towards an Indian Theology of Liberation.*Bangalore: Indian Theological Association and National Biblical Catechetical and Liturgical Centre.

Raj, Antony. (1992) *Children of a Lesser God.* Madurai: DCLM Publications.

Raj, V. Manuel.(1990) *A Santal Theology of Liberation.*New Delhi: Uppal Publishing House.

Rajaratnam, K. (2004) *Sent Into the World*! (Keynote Address delivered at the Assembly of the Kerala Council of Churches, Kottayam, 25 May.

Rajshekar, V. T. (1987) Christians and Dalit Liberation. Bangalore: Dalit Sahitya Academy.

Rajshekar, V. T. (1994) *Brahminism: Father of Fascism, Racism, Nazism.* Bangalore: Dalit

Rajasekaran, V. C. (1995) Reflections on Indian Christian Theology. Madras: CLS.Sahitya Academy.

Ram, Jagivan. (1980) *Caste Challenge in India.* New Delhi: Vision Books.

Ram, Nandu. (1995) *Beyond Ambedkar: Essays on Dalits in India.* New Delhi: Har-Anand Publications.

Rao, Katti Padma. (1995) *Caste and Alternative Culture*.Chennai: Gurukul Lutheran Theological College and Research Institute.

Rao, M.S.A. (1979) *Social Movement and Social transformation*. Delhi: Macmillan Company.

Rao, Hanumantha G. (1977) *Caste and Poverty: A Case Study of Scheduled Castes in a Delta Village*. Mulikipuram: Savithri Publication.

Rao, Hemlata and Babu, M. Devendra. (1994). *Scheduled Castes and Tribes: Socio-Economic Upliftment Programmes*.New Delhi: Ashish Publishing House.

Rao, M. S. A. (1978) *Social Movement and Social Transformation: A Study of Backward Class Movement*.New Delhi: Macmillan Press.

Rao, M.S.A. (1981) *Social Movements and Social transformation*. New Delhi: Manohar Anand Publications.

Rao, M.S.A. (1984) *Social Movements in India*. Vol 2, New Delhi: Manohar Anand Publications.

Rathnaiah, K. (1991) *Social Change among the Malas: An Ex-Untouchable Caste in South India*. New Delhi: Discovery Publishing House.

Rayappa, P. Hanumantha and Grover, Deepak. (1980) *Employment Planning for the Rural Poor: The Case of Scheduled Castes and Scheduled Tribes*. New Delhi: Sterling Press.

Rege, Sharmila. (1995) Caste and Gender: The Violence against Women in India.In P. G. Jogdand (ed.),*Dalit Women in India: Issues and Perspectives*. New Delhi: Gyan Publishing House, in collaboration with University of Poona, Pune, pp. 18–36.

Report of the Central Committee to the Third Assembly of the WCC (1961) *Evanston to New Delhi 1954–1961*, Geneva: WCC.

Report of the Ministry of Human Resource Development 1995, New Delhi.

Robb, Peter. (1993) *Dalit Movements and the Meanings of Labour in India*. New Delhi: Oxford University Press.

Robinson, Gnana. (ed.), (1998) *Religious of the Marginalised: Towards a Phenomenology and the Methodology of Study*. UTC, Bangalore&Delhi: ISPCK.

Rossi-Lundi, Ferrucio.(1990) *Marxism and Ideology*. Translated by Roger Griffin Oxford: Clarendon, Press.

Rudolph, Lloyd and Sussanne Rudolph (1967) *TheModernity of Tradition*. Chicago: University of Chicago Press.

Ryerson, Charles A. (1988) *Regionalism and Religion The Tamil Renaissance and Popular Hinduism*. Madras: CLS.

Sachchidananda. (1976) *The Harijan Elite: A Study of their Status, Networks, Mobility and Role in Social Transformation*. Haryana: Thompson Press.

Sachchidananda and Sinha, R. P. (1989) Education and the Disadvantaged: A Study of Scheduled Castes and Tribes. New Delhi: Uppal Publishing House.

Samartha, Stanley J.(1974) *The Hindu Response to Unbound Christ*. Madras: CLS.

Samartha, Stanley J.(1987)*The Search for a New Hermeneutic in Asian Theology*.Madras: The Christian Literature Society.

Sanjana, J.E. (1946) *Caste and Outcaste*. Bombay: Thancker &Co.

Sarkar, J. (1984) *Caste, Occupation and Change*. Delhi: B. R. Publishing Co.

Sax, William. S.(1991) *Mountain Goddess: Gender and Politics in the Himalayan Pilgrimage*, New York: OUP.

Searle-Chatterjee, Mary; and Sharma, Ursula. (1994) *Contextualising Caste: Post-Dumontian Approaches*. Oxford: Blackwell Publishers/Sociological Review.

Sergio Torres, John Eagleson (1976) Theology in the Americas, New York: Orbis Book.

Shah, Ghanshyam. (ed.), (2000) *Dalits and the State*. New Delhi: Concept Publish Company.

Shah, Ghanshyam. (1975) *Politics of Scheduled Castes and Scheduled Tribes*. Bombay: Vora and Co. Pvt. Ltd.

Shah, Ghanshyam; and Chaturvedi, H. R. (1985) Caste in Contemporary India. In Centre for Social Studies (ed.),*Caste, Caste Conflict and Reservations*.Delhi: Ajanta Publications.

Shankar, Jogan. (1990) *Devadasi Cult: A Sociological Analysis*. New Delhi: Ashish Publishing House.

Sharma, B. D. (1994) *Dalits Betrayed*. New Delhi: Har-Anand Publications.

Sharma, G. S. (1975) *Legislation and Cases of Untouchability and Scheduled Castes in India*. Bombay: Allied Publishers.

Sharma, K. L. (1974) *The Changing Rural Stratification System*. New Delhi: Orient Longman.

Sharma, K. L. (1986) *Caste, Class and Social Movements*. Jaipur: Rawat Publications.

Sharma, K. L. (1994) *Caste and Class in India*. New Delhi: Rawat Publications.

Sharma, Rama. (1995) *Bhangi: Scavenger in Indian Society – Marginality, Identity and Politicization of the Community*. New Delhi: M D Publications Pvt. Ltd

Shetty, V. T. Rajshekar. (1978) *Dalit Movement in Karnataka*. Madras: Christian Literature Society.

Silverberg, James. (ed.), (1968) *Social Mobility in the Caste System in India*. The Hague: Mouton Publishers.

Simpson, Paul. Language, Ideology and point of view, London: Published by Routledge: 1993.

Singh, K. K. (1967) *Patterns of Caste Tensions*. Bombay: Asia Publishing House.

Sivendra Prakash-Murray Rogers (1971) Hindu-Christian

Dialogue Postponed *in Dialogue between Men of Living Faiths*. Geneva, WCC Publications.

Smith, B.L. (ed.), (1978) *Religion and Legitimation of Power in South Asia.*Leiden: E.J. Brill.

Smith, D.E. (ed.), (1966 &1969) *South Asian Politics and Religion.* Princeton: Princeton University Press.

Srinivas, M. N. (1962) *Caste in Modern India and Other Essays.* Bombay: Asia Publishing House.

Srinivas, M. N. (1966) *Social Change in Modern India.* New Delhi: Allied Publishers.

Srivastava, S.N. (1980) *Harijans in Indian Society: A Cultural Study of the Status of Harijans and Other Backward Classes from the Earliest Times to the Present Day.* Lucknow, U.P.: The Upper India Publishing House Pvt. Ltd.

Staffner, Hans, S.J. (1985) *The Significance of Jesus Christ in Asia.*Anand, Gujarat, India: Gujarat Sahitya Prakash.

Stevenson, Margaret S. (1930) *Without the Pale: The Life Story of An Outcaste.* Calcutta: Association Press (Y.M.C.A.)

Stott, John. (1975) *Christian Mission in the Modern World.* London: Falcon.

Sudarisanam, A. (ed.), (1938) *Rethinking Christianity.* Madras: CLS.

Sugirtharajah, R. S. and Cecil Hargreaves (eds.) (1993) Readings in Indian Christian Theology. Volume 1. London: SPCK.

Sugirtharajah, R. S. (ed.), (1994) *Frontiers in Asian Christian Theology: Emerging Trends.*Maryknoll: Orbis.

Suh, Nam Dong. (1976)*Theology at a Turning Point.*Seoul: Korea Theological Study Institute.

Sumithra, Sunand. (1990) *Christian Theology from an Indian Perspective.*Bangalore: Theological Book Trust.

Tagore, Rabindranath. (1918) *Gitanjali*, Delhi, New York Macmillan.

Thangaraj, M. Thomas. (1994)*The Crucified Guru: An Experiment in Cross-Cultural Christology*.Nashville: Abingdon.

The Complete Works of Swami Vivekananda, Advaita Ashrama, Calcutta, Vols I-VIIII, 7th Edition, 1985.

The Confession of 1967, The Constitution of the United Presbyterian Church in the USA. 9.07.

The New Delhi Report, The Third Assembly of the World Council of Churches 1961, New York: Association Press, 1962.

The New Lexicon Webster's Dictionary of the English Language Lexicon Publication, New York: 1988.

Theology and Social Ethics, Study Encounter, Vol II, No. 2, 1966, 26–33.

Thomas, M.M. Renewal in Mission, NCCI, p. 220, The NCCI Consultation in the 1960s on 'Renewal in Mission').

Thomas, M.M. (1962) *The New Delhi Report, The Third Assembly of the World Council of Churches 1961*. New York: Association Press.

Thomas, M. M. (1969) The Acknowledged Christ of the Indian Renaissance. Madras: CISRS/CLS.

Thomas, M.M. (1971) *Salvation and Humanization*. Madras: CLS.

Thomas, M.M. (1975) *Man and the Universe of Faiths*. Madras: CLS.

Thomas, M.M. (1976) *The Secular Ideologies of India and the Secular Meaning of Christ*. Madras: CLS.

Thomas, M.M. (1981) *Religion and Revolt of the Oppressed.* Delhi: ISPCK.

Thomas, M. M. (1987) Risking Christ for Christ's Sake. Geneva: WCC.

Thomas, M. M. (1990) My Ecumenical Journey. Trivandrum: Ecumenical Publishing Centre Private Limited.

Thomas, M. M. and P. T. Thomas. (1992)Towards an Indian Christian Theology: Life and Thought of Some Pioneers. Tiruvalla: The New Day Publications.

Zelliot, Eleanor. (1996) *From Untouchable to Dalit: Essays on the Ambedkar Movement*. Delhi: Manohar.

Unpublished Papers

Abraham, Dr. K. C. (2002) Address Delivered at the Platinum Jubilee if Gurukul, 25th November.

Appavoo, Parattai J. Theophilus. (2004)*A Dalit's Reflection on Technology* (Address delivered at the Sixteenth Convocation of the Academy of Ecumenical Indian Theology and Church Administration, Chennai, 20 August. Unpublished)

Bhawat, Vidyut; and Rege, Sharmila. (1993) *Towards a Gender-Sensitive Sociology*. Un published paper presented University Grants Commission (UGC) National Seminar, March.

Blise, Richard H. (2003) *The New Missiology: A Call to Freedom* (Paper presented at the 'Consultation on Contemporary Reflections on Global Oppressed Communities: A Multi-Faith Approach'.) Chennai: Gurukul, February 23–26.

Chandran,J.R. (1981) *AnUnderstanding of Christian Responsibilities in Development/Liberation*, Unpublished manuscript.

Clarke, Sathianathan. (1998) *Subaltern Culture as Resource for people's Liberation: A critical Inquiry into Dalit Culture Theory*, Unpublished paper presented by at the Carey Society Valedictory Address, Bangalore: UTC.

Clarke, Sathianathan. (2003) *Theory of Atonement: An Indian Cross-Cultural theology of the Cross*. Unpublished paper presented at the CTI-UTC Study project on 'Interrogating Mission', Bangalore: UTC, January 16–19.

Clarke, Sathianathan.(2003) *Theory of Atonement: An Indian Cross-Cultural Theology of the Cross (*Unpublished Paper presented at the CTI-UTC Study Project on 'Interrogating Mission'), UTC, Bangalore.

Hopkins L. Dwlight, Sermon delivered (University of Chicago Divinity School) at the Reformation Sunday Worship Service, Gurukul, Chennai on 31st October, 2004.

Kuruvilla, K.P. *Dalit Theology: An Indian Christian Attempt to Give Voice to the Voiceless.* Unpublished paper.

Manchala, Deenabandhu. *Re-visioning Ecclesia in the light of the Dalit Experience* (Unpublished doctoral thesis)

Melanchthon, Monica. (2001) *A Dalit Women's Perspective.* Unpublished Paper presented at Gurukul Lutheran Theological College & Research Centre, Chennai.

Muthumary, J.(1999)*Dalit Women in India.* Unpublished Paper.

Oommen, George. (1993). *The Struggle of Pulaya Christians for Social Improvement*, Unpublished PhD thesis. Sydney: University of Sydney.

Prabhakar, M.E.(1985) *The Struggle of the least of my Brothers and Sisters.* Unpublished paper at the first National Conference New Delhi March 25–27.

Robinson, S. (1997) *Early Protestant Missionaries in India.* Unpublished paper, presented at a colloquium on Indian Missions at held Southern Asia Christian College, Madras.

Sousa, Desmond de.*What Happened to the Church of the Poor?*

Thambusamy, Samuel. *The Significance of Ambedkar for Theologising in India.*

Zachariah, Aleyamma. (1982) *Social Action in the Gita, According to Sri Aurobindo Ghosh.* Unpublished PhD Thesis. Mysore: University of Mysore.

Journals& News Papers

Abraham, K.C. (1996) Re-interpretation of Christian Tradition in Contemporary India. *Jeevadhara* 26/151, 35–44. And also in *Asia Journal of Theology* 9/2 (1995) 263–74.

Aleaz, K. P.(1994) The Convergence of Dalit and Advaitic Theologies: An Exploration.*Indian Journal of Theology* 36/1, 97–108.

Aleaz, K. P. (1994) Gospel and Culture: Some Indian Reflections. *Indian Journal of Theology* 36/2, 54–70

Alexander, K. C. (1968). Changing Status of Pulaya Harijans of Kerala. *EPW*, July, Special Number, pp. 1071–75.

Amaladoss, M. (1994) An Emerging Indian Theology: Some Exploratory Reflections.*VJTR* 58/8–9, 473–84, 559–72.

Anon. (1986). Scheduled Castes and Marginalization. *Social Action*, vol. 36, no. 2, pp. 137–94.

Arockiadoss, P.(1994) Ambedkar's Theological Significance. *VJTR* 58/8, 508–11.

Arulsamy, S.(1985) Liberation Theology in India.*Indian Theological Studies* 22/3, 266–88.

Ayrookuzhiel, Abraham. (1978) Religion, Spirituality and Aspirations of the People. *Religion and Society*, XXV (1 Mar), 20–9.

Azariah, M. (1978) Injustice and Discrimination against Christians of Scheduled Caste Origin.in *Madras Diocesan News and Notes*, August, 29–37.

Azariah, M. (1979) Biblical Basis for Church's Concern for the Christians of Scheduled Caste Origin.*South India Churchman*, February, 4–5.

Azariah, M. (1986)The Church's Concern for 'Dalit' Christians.*National Christian Council Review* 106/9, 546–55 (reprinted from *South Indian Churchman*).

Balasuriya, Tissa.(1992) Issues in the Relationship between the Contextual and Universal Dimensions of Christian Theology. *Bangalore Theological Forum* 24/3–4, 24–38.

Barik, R. (1985) Caste System and Economic Backwardness of Orissa.*Social Science Probings*, vol. 2, no. 2, pp. 254–62.

Basu, S. K. (1968) Agrarian Problems of Scheduled Castes and Tribes of West Bengal. *Bulletin of Cultural Research Institute*, Vol. 7, nos. 1–2.

Bernard, Jessie. (1965) The Future of the Backward Classes: The Competing Demands of Status and Power Perspectives. *Supplement to the Indian Journal of Public Administration,* vol. 11, no. 1, pp. 1–39.

Berremen, Gerald D. (1962) Caste in India and the United States. *American Journal of Sociology*, vol. 10, pp. 386–394.

Bhattacharya, Amit. (1982–83) Tanning and Leather Workers in the Providence of Bengal.*The Quarterly Review of Historical Studies*, vol. xxii, no. 2.

Bhattacharya, S and Almeida, Fleur. (1986) The Caste System and Discrimination in Historical Perspective.*New Frontiers in Education*, vol. 16, no. 2, pp. 25–32.

Boyd, R.H.S. (1973) The Shape of Indian Christian Theology.*Indian Journal of Theology* 22/4, 15–20.

Breman, Jan. (1974) Mobilisation of Landless Labourers: Halpatis of South Gujarat. *EPW*, vol. 9, no. 6–8, Feb.

Carvalho, Marcello Pinto. (1978) Die Stimme des Volkes Gottes in *Information*, December.

Chanana, Karuna. (1993) Accessing Higher Education: The Dilemma of Schooling Women, Minorities, Scheduled Castes and Scheduled Tribes in Contemporary India. *Higher Education,* vol. 26, no. 1, pp. 69–92.

Chandran,J. Russell. (1997) Rev. A. P. Nirmal: A Tribute. *NCCI Review*, January.

Change of Perspective within the CISRS. *Religion and Society,* XI (1&2 Mar–June, 1993), 77–8.

Chatterjee, Saral K.(1993) Emerging Perspectives of the Network. *Religion and Society*, XI (1 & 2 Mar–June), 10–12.

Chauhan, B. R. (1969) Scheduled Castes and Scheduled Tribes. *EPW*, January, pp. 257–63.

Choudhury, K. (1990) Reservation: A Systematic Compulsion.*Mainstream*, vol. 28, no. 19, pp. 23–25.

Clarke, Sathianathan.(1986) Re-doing Indian Theology: Reflections from a Rural Parish. *Bangalore Theological Forum* 18/2–3, 125–36.

Cohen, S. P. (1969) The Untouchable Solider: Centre, Politics and the Indian Army. *Journal of Asian Studies*, vol. 18, no. 3, pp. 453–68.

Cohn, Bernard S. (1958) Changing Tradition of a Low Caste. *Journal of American Folklore*, vol. 21, July.

Cohn, Bernard S. (1961) Chamar Family in a NorthIndianVillage: A Structural Contingent. *Economic Weekly*, vol. 13, nos. 27, 28 and 29, pp. 1051–55.

Cohn, Bernard S. (1962) Review of M. Marriott, 'Caste Ranking and Community Structure in Five Regions of India and Pakistan'.*Journal of the American Oriental Society*, vol 82: 425–430.

Das, Man Singh. (1976) A Cross-National Study of Inter-Caste Conflict in India and the United States. *International Journal of Contemporary Sociology*, vol. 13, nos. 3/4, pp. 261–77.

Das, Somen.(1988) A General Survey of Asian Christian Theology.*Bangalore Theological Forum* 20/4,1–23.

Desai, Haribhai G., and Uchat, D.A. (1981) Self-concept of Harijan Students and Attitudes of Other Students towards Them.*Indian Educational Review*, vol. 16, no. 3, pp. 44–50.

D'Souza, Victor S. (1962) Changing Status of Scheduled Castes. *EPW*, vol. 16, no. 48.

D'Souza, Victor S. (1967) Caste and Class – A Reinterpretation. *Journal of Asian & African Studies*, vol. 2, no. 3–4.

Dunn, Dana. (1993) Gender Inequity in Education and Employment in the Scheduled Castes and Tribes of India.

In *Population Research and Policy Review*, vol. 12, no. 1, pp. 53–71.

Dushkin, Lelah. (1979) Backward Class Benefits and Social Class in India, 1920–1970. in*EPW*, April 7th.

Galanter, Marc. (1963) Law and Caste in Modern India. *Asian Review*, vol. 3, no. 2: 3544–59.

Glenn, Evelyn Nakano. (1992) Race and Gender Stratification.*Review of Racial Political Economic*, 38 (1) 35–36.

Gopal,Guru. (1985) Casteism in the South. *Mainstream*, vol. 23, no. 47, pp. 20–22.

Gough, Aberle E. K. (1959) Criteria of Caste Ranking in South India. *Men in India*, vol. 39, pp. 115–26.

Gupta, Dipankar. (1984) Continuous Hierarchies and Discrete Castes. *EPW,* vol. 19, nos. 46–47, 48. pp. 1955–58; 2003–2005; and 2049–53.

Gupta, Shiva K. (1980) Harijan Legislation: Their Alienation and Activism: A Case Study of Harijan Power. *Indian Journal of Political Science*, vol. 41, no. 3, pp. 457–70.

Harijan (14 April &5 May 1946)

Heredia, Rudi. (1986) Minority Rights and Reservation Policy: Towards Coherence and Consistence. *New Frontiers in Education*, vol. 16, no. 2, pp. 60–63.

Hindustan Times (28 April 1946)

Hoedemaker, Bert. (1995)The Legacy of J.C.Hoekendijk. *International Bulletin of Missionary Research*, 19, No.4.

Horsey, Anita. (1981) Conditions of Scheduled Castes and Tribes. *New Frontiers in Education*, vol. 11, no. 2, pp. 1–36.

International Herald Tribune, Tuesday 13, 1979.

International Review of Missions, 62 (1973) pp. 199–201.

Jathanna, O. V.(1986) Indian Christian Theology: Methodological Reflections. *Bangalore Theological Forum* 18/2–3, 59–74.

Jayagopal, R. (1986) Occupational Mobility amongSpecial Group of Scheduled Castes in Tamil Nadu: A Survey.*Indian Journal of Adult Education*, vol. 47, no. 1, pp. 8–12.

Jha, Hetukar. Lower Caste Peasants and Upper Caste Zamindars in Bihar (1921–1925): An Analysis of Sanskritization and Contradiction between the Two Groups. In *The Indian Economic and Social History Review*, vol. xiv, no. 4.

John C. B. Webster, Book Review (Dalit Consciousness..., Dharma Deepika (January 2000), p. 76.

John, T. K. (1986) Some Major Concerns of Christian Dalits. *National Christian Council Review* 106/9, 534–45.

Jones, Charles E. The Political Representation of the Black Panther Party. *Journal of Black Studies*, 18(4) June: 38–45, 416–41.

Joseph, Ipe. (1992) Editorial: The Dalit Struggle. *National Christian Council Review* 112/8, 495–502.

Joshi, Barbara. R. (1987) Recent Developments of Inter-Regional Mobilization of Dalit Protest in India. *South Asia Bulletin*, vol. 7.

Justice, 14 September 1927.

Kamila, Banu Behari. (1985) A Study of Attitude of Students towards School of Harijans and Tribal Welfare Department High School of Orissa.*Journal of Education and Psychology*, vol. 43, vol. 3–4, pp. 187–92.

Kananaikil, Jose. (1986) Scheduled Caste Converts in Search of Justice. *National Christian Council Review* 106/9, 556–63.

Kannibaran, V., and Kannibaran, K. (1991) Caste and Gender: Understanding Dynamics of Power and Violence. *EPW*, Sept. 14.

Karlekar, M. (1982) Some Perspectives on the Employment of Scheduled Castes Women.*Social Action,* vol. 32, pp. 292–302.

Khurana, G. (1979) Education Facilities for Scheduled Castes. *Education Quarterly*, vol. 31, nos. 3 and 4, pp. 31–35.

Kriesberg, Louis. (1968) Abolition of Untouchability in Andhra Pradesh. *Social Welfare*, vol. 15, no. 2.

Kurien, C. T. (1982) Economic Conditions of Scheduled Castes. *Yojana,* vol. 26, no. 19, 13–17.

Larbeer, P. Mohan.(1990) The Spirit of Truth and Dalit Literature. *National Christian Council Review* 110/10, 640–51.

Lynch, Owen M. (1970) Political Mobilisation and Ethnicity Among Adi-Dravidas in a Bombay Slum. *EPW*, vol 9, no. 39, 1657–68.

Mahar, Pauline M. (1960) Changing Religious Practices of an Untouchable Caste. *Economic Development and Culture Change*, vol. 7, no. 3, pp. 279–87.

Manickam, Sundaraj. (1987)Origin and History of the Christian Dalits in Kerala and Tamilnadu.*Religion and Society*, XXXIV (no 3, Sep), 21–24.

Mankidy, Aruna. (1979) Inter-generational Mobility among the Scheduled Castes. *Social Change*, vol. 9, nos. 1–2:10–17.

Marriott, Mckim. (1959) Interactional and Attributional Theories of Caste Ranking. *Man in India*, vol. 39, no. 2, pp. 92–107.

Marulasiddaish, H.M. (1971) Caste, Consolidation, Social Mobility and Ambivalence: A Case Study of Caste Hostels in Mysore State. *Indian Journal of Social Work*, vol. 31, no. 4, pp. 391–399.

Massey, James. (1992) The Role of Partner Churches in the Whole Dalit Issue. *National Christian Council Review* 112/8, 503–512.

Mayer, Adrian C. (1956) Some Hierarchical Aspects of Caste. *South Western Journal of Anthropology*, vol. 12, no. 2, pp. 144–45.

McMullen, C. (1977) The Self-Image of the Christian in the Punjab. *Bulletin of the Christian Institute of Sikh Studies*, January, 21.

Mehta, Pratap Bhanu. (2004) Affirmation without Reservation. *Economic and Political Weekly*, July 3, 2951.

Mehta, Pratap Bhanu. (2004) Affirmation without Reservation. *Economic and Political weekly*, July 3.

Meillassoux, Claude. (1973) Are There Castes in India? *Economy and Society*, vol. 2.

Michael, S. M. (1996) The Cultural Context of the Rise of Hindutva and Dalits Forces, *Vidyajyoti* 60/5, 294–310.

Mishra, Ajay M., et al. (1983) A Study of Attitude Towards Learning of Science Among Scheduled Caste Students.*Journal of Education and Psychology*, vol. 43, no. 3, pp. 112–116.

Mishra, N. (1978) Studies on the Scheduled Castes in Bihar.*Journal of Social Research*, vol. 21, no. 2:47–70.

Moffatt, Michael. (1975) Untouchables and the Caste System: A Tamil Case Study.

Contributions to Indian Sociology, New Series, vol. 9, no. 1.

Mohanty, Manoranjan. (1984) Social Roots of Backwardness in Orissa: A Study of Class, Caste and Power. in *Social Science Probings*, vol. 1, no. 2, June, pp. 184–228.

Mohanty, Manoranjan. (1985) Arguing with Bailey by Proxy. in *Social Science Probings*, vol. 2, no. 2, June, pp. 263–67.

Moltmann, Jurgen. (1975) Evangelism and Liberation, *Christian Thought*, April, 105–120.

Moltmann, Jurgen. (1975) The Hope in the Midst of the Struggle of Minjung, *Christian Thought,* April, 125–135.

Monga, Veena. (1967) Social Mobility among the Potters: Report of a Caste Conference. *EPW,* vol. 2:1047–1055.

Naidu, A. Nagaraja. (1985) Harijans in Semi-feudal Set-up: A Case Study of Karamchedu. *Social Science Probings*, vol. 2, no. 4, pp. 450–58.

Nair, Janaki. (1986) Fighting for Backwardness: Venkataswammy Commission Report and After *EPW,* vol. XXI, no. 42, pp. 1837–38.

Narayana, C. (1974) Emerging Elite in Scheduled Castes. *Secular Democracy*, vol. 7, no. 9.

Narayanan, R. (1978) False Concern for the Harijans. *Mainstream,* vol. 16, no. 24.

Nargolkar, V. S. (1969) Removal of Untouchability: Goals and Attainments. *Indian Journal of Social Work*, v30, n3.

Nirmal, Arvind. P. (1988) A Synopsis of Syllabus for a Course in Dalit Theology. *NCCR*, CVIII (Jan), 88–9.

Omvedt, Gail. (1978) Class Struggle or Caste War. *Frontier*, Calcutta. vol. 2, no. 8–11, Sept. 30, pp. 30–40.

Oommen, George.(2000) The Emerging Dalit Theology: A Historical Appraisal. *Indian Church History Review*, Vol. XXXIV, Number 1, June, 19–37.

Oommen, T. K. (1968) Strategy for Social Change: A Study of Untouchability. *EPW*, June 22, pp. 933–36.

Oommen, T. K. (1970) The Concept of Dominant Caste: Some Queries. *Contribution* to *Indian Sociology*, vol. 4, December, pp. 73–83.

Oommen, T. K. (1980) Sources of Deprivation and Styles of Protest: The Case of Dalits in India.*Contributions to Indian Sociology*, New Series, vol. 18, no. 1, January-June.

Painadath, Sebastian. (1999) The Understanding of Christ in the Indian Renaissance. *Jeevadhara*,XXIX (No 171, May), 165–187.

Pandey, Gyan. (1983) Rallying Round the Cow: Sectarian Strife in the Bhojpuri Region, c. 1888–1917.In Ranajit Guha (ed.),*Subaltern StudiesII.*Delhi: OxfordUniversity Press.

Pandya, B. V. (1959)Trends and Patterns of Indebtedness Among Harijans. *Journal of the Cultural Research Society,* vol. 21, pp. 99–115.

Pannenberg, Wolfhart. (1970)*Basic Questions in Theology*. Vol. 1 &11. Philadelphia: Fortress.

Parratt, John.(1994) Recent Writing on Dalit Theology: A Bibliographical Essay. *International Review of Mission* 83, 329–37.

Parvathamma, C. (1968) The Case for the Indian Untouchable. *United Asia*, vol. 20, no. 5, pp. 279–86.

Parvathamma, C. (1973) Ambedkar and After: The Position and Future of Indian SC Masses. *Eastern Anthropology*, vol. 26.

Patankar, B. and Gail Omvedt (1978) Kanjhawala.*Frontier*, December 2.

Pathy, Jaganath. (1982) Politics of Reservation in India: Case Study of Political Agitation in Bihar and Gujarat. *Philosophy and Social Action*, vol. 8, no. 2.

Pathy, Suguna. (1985) The Untouchables – Protectors Fail.*State and Society*, vol. 5, no. 3,July-Sept., pp. 37–44.

Patil, Sharad. (1989) Mobilizing Scheduled Castes and Scheduled Tribes. *EPW*, col. 24, no. 35–36, pp. 2002–06.

Patwardhan, Sunanda. (1968) Social Mobility and Conversion of Mahars. *Sociological Bulletin*, vol. 17, no. 2: 187–202.

Pimpley, Prakash N. (1976) Politization among the Scheduled Castes Students of Punjab. *Social Action*, vol. 30, no. 2, pp. 138–61.

Pinto, Ambrose. (1992) Caste Conflict in Karnataka.*EPW* July 11, Vol. XXVII no. 28.

Pinto, Ambrose. (1997) Dalits and Globalisation.*Integral Liberation*, September 1997, 153–54.

Pinto, Carvalho. Marcello. (1978) Die Stimme des Volkes Gottes.*Information,* December.

Pinto, Carvalho.Marcello (1979) Latin Bishops Expected to Keep to Centre. *International Herald Tribune*, Tuesday 13.

Potter, Social Questions – The Responsible Society.*Ecumenical Perspectives Ecumenical Review*, pp xii–xiii.

Prabhakar, M.E.Beginning and Growth of Dalit Studies in the CISRS and its Joint Programmes.*Religion and Society,*XI (1 & 2 March–June), 117.

Prasad, Pradhan H. (1978) Caste and Class in Bihar. *EPW*, annual number, February. Prasuna, N.G. (1997)

Premi, Kusum K. (1976) Scheduled Castes and Educational Opportunities.*The Indian Journal of Social Work,* vol. 37, no. 3.

Premi, Kusum K. (1984) Education Equality and Economic Opportunities: A Comparative Study of Scheduled Castes and Non-Scheduled Castes.*Journal of Higher Education,* vol. 9, no. 3, pp. 363–72.

Pullapilly, C. K. (1976) The Izhavas of Kerala and Their Historic Struggle for Acceptance in the Hindu Society.*Journal of Asian and African Studies*, vol. 2, nos. 1 & 2, pp. 24–46.

Punalekar, S. P. (1975) Harijans of Eastern U.P. Region: A Profile on Marginality. *The North-Eastern Research Bulletin*, vol. 6, pp. 30–40.

Puri, Balraj. (1971) Caste and Class and Party Polarisation. *EPW*, 6 (27):1317–18.

Pury, de Pascal (1954) WCC, CCPD, 1962.*Ecumenical Studies leaflet*, 3, Geneva: WCC.

Raj, Antony. (1992) The Dalit Christian Reality in Tamilnadu.*Jeevadhara* 22/128 95–111.

Ramaswamy, Uma. (1984) Preference and Progress: The Scheduled Castes. *EPW*, vol. 19, pp.1214—17.

Ramaswamy, Uma. (1986) Protection and Inequality among Backward Groups. *EPW*, vol. 31, no. 9:399–403.

Ramu, G. N. (1968) Untouchability in Rural Areas.*Indian Journal of Social Work*, vol. 25, no. 2.

Rao, N. V. Kameswara and Raju, M. V. T. (1975) Malas and Madigas: An Ethnographic Study of Two Scheduled Castes of Telangana. Journal of Social Research, vol. 18, no. 2, pp. 59–68.

Rasquinha, Dionysius. S.J. (2002). A Critical Reflection on the Meaning of Dalit Christian Theology. *VJTR*, April, 251–69.

Ravindranatha, M.N. (1981) Educational Problems of Scheduled Castes.*Educational Review*, vol. 87, no. 4, pp. 69–74.

Rayan, Samuel. (1978) The Churches and Justice to Christians of Scheduled Caste Origin. *Word & Worship*, XI (no.6, July), 227–39.

Rayan, Samuel. (1992)People's Theology.*Jeevadhara* 22/129, 175–202.

Reddy, Subha N. (1950) Community Conflict Among the Depressed Castes of Andhra. *Man in India*, vol. 30, no. 4, pp. 1–12.

Saberwal, Satish. (1972) The Reserved Constituency: Candidates and Consequences. *EPW* 7(2):71–80.

Sachchidananda and Iyer, Gopal G. (1969) Caste Tension in India.*Eastern Anthropologist* 22(3):327–48.

Sachchidananda. (1974) Emergent of Scheduled Castes Elite in Bihar. *Religion and Society* 21(3):55–61.

Sahay, K. N. (1975) Eradication of Untouchability and the Caste System.*Journal of Social Research*, vol. 18, no. 2, pp. 1–8.

Sharma, Satya P. (1983) A Materialistic Thesis on the Origin and Continuity of the Caste System in South Asia: A Review Article. *Eastern Anthropologist*, vol. 36, no. 1, pp. 55–77.

Sharma, Ursula M. (1976) Status Striving and Striving to Abolish Status: The Arya Samaj and the Low Castes.*Social Action*, vol. 26, July-September.

Shelke, Christopher. (1994) Dalit Theology: Emergence and Emergency, in *Neue Zeitschrift fur Missionwissenchaft*Vol. 41.

Shelke, Christober. (1994) Dalit Theology: Emergence and Emergency.*Neue Zeitschrift fur Missionwissenschaft*, 50/ 4, 257

Singh, Yogendra. (1968) Caste and Class: Some Aspects of Continuity and Change. *Sociological Bulletin*, vol. 17, no. 2, pp. 165–86.

Sinha, Arun. (1977) *Class War, Not 'Atrocities' Against Harijans.* EPW, vol. 12, no. 50, pp. 2037–40.

Srinivas, M. N. (1959) The Caste of the Potter and the Priest.*Man in India*, vol. 39, no. 3, pp 109–209.

Sugirtharajah, R. S. and Cecil Hargreaves (eds.) (1993) *Readings in Indian Christian Theology.*Volume 1.London: SPCK.

The Hindu (Chennai Edition), 15 October 2004.

The Hindu (Chennai Edition), 9 November 2004.

The Hindu, Madras, 9 April 1921.

The New Delhi Report, The Third Assembly of the World Council of Churches 1961, New York: Association Press, 1962.

Theological Thought (Spring 1979): 116.

Theology and Social Ethics, Study Encounter, Vol II, No. 2, 1966.

Thiyagarajan, A.P. (1981) A Study of the Scheduled Caste Students in Some Secondary Schools of Tamil Nadu. *Indian Education*, vol. 11, no. 5, pp. 22–26.

Washington, Booker T.(1915) Inferior and Superior Races. *North American Reviews*, April.201 (Apr. 1915), 538–42.

Webster John,C. (1975) The Gospel for the Punjab. *Bulletin of the Christian Institute of Sikh Studies*, July, 14.

Wilfred, Felix. (1988) The Liberation Process in India and the Church's Participation. *Indian Theological Studies* 25/4, 301–33.

Zechariah, Mathai. (1986) Editorial: The Emerging Dalit Theology. *National Christian Council Review* 106/9, 531–33.